Screen Writings

Screen Writings

Scripts and Texts by Independent Filmmakers

Scott MacDonald

UNIVERSITY OF CALIFORNIA PRESS

BERKELEY / LOS ANGELES / LONDON

University of California Press
Berkeley and Los Angeles, California

University of California Press
London, England

Library of Congress Cataloging-in-Publication Data

Screen writings : scripts and texts by independent filmmakers /
[edited] by Scott MacDonald.
p. cm.
Includes bibliographical references.
ISBN 0-520-08024-6 (cloth : alk. paper). — ISBN 0-520-08025-4
(pbk. : alk. paper)
1. Motion picture plays—History and criticism. 2. Experimental
films—History and criticism. 3. Narration (Rhetoric). 4. Motion
picture authorship. I. MacDonald, Scott, 1942– .
PN1995.S4188   1995   791.43'75—dc20   92-30429   CIP

Printed in the United States of America

The paper used in this publication meets the minimum requirements of American
National Standard for Information Sciences—Permanence of Paper for Printed Library
Materials, ANSI Z39.48-1984 ⊗

This book is a print-on-demand volume. It is manufactured using toner in place of ink.
Type and images may be less sharp than the same material seen in traditionally
printed University of California Press editions.

The publisher gratefully acknowledges the contribution provided by the General
Endowment Fund of the Associates of the University of California Press.

To Ernest Callenbach, Martha Gever, David Trend—
editors who were fun to work with

Contents

Acknowledgments

I am deeply grateful to the filmmakers whose work is included here, for making their writings available to me, despite my inability to offer them financial compensation. Thanks are due as well to Anthology Film Archives in New York, especially to Robert Haller and Jonas Mekas, to John Hanhardt at the Whitney Museum of American Art, to my typist Carol Fobes, and to Utica College of Syracuse University for support of this project in the form of several grants and a sabbatical leave.

Thanks to the following journals and individuals for permission to publish or reprint texts and scripts:

James Benning, for permission to publish "New York 1980"

Camera Obscura, for permission to reprint Trinh T. Minh-ha's "Reassemblage: Sketch of a Sound Track," no. 13/14 (1985): 104–111

Cinematograph, for permission to reprint the narration and visual texts for Naked Spaces— Living Is Round, vol. 3 (1988): 65–79; and the script for Sink or Swim, vol. 4 (1991): 116–129

Morgan Fisher, for permission to publish the text and narration for Standard Gauge

Ann Marie Fleming, for permission to publish the narration, the dialogue, and the text of You Take Care Now and the conversation from New Shoes

Su Friedrich, for permission to reprint "(Script) for a Film without Images" (originally published in the first, and only, issue of Film/Feminism, published in Spring 1984); the text from Gently Down the Stream (originally published in a limited edition book by Friedrich); and the script for Sink or Swim (originally published in Cinematograph)

The Hollis Frampton estate, for permission to publish "Notes on Zorns Lemma," to reprint the text of Poetic Justice (originally published as a book by the Visual Studies Workshop Press in 1973), and to publish the computer texts from Gloria!

William Greaves, for permission to publish "Symbiopsychotaxiplasm: Take One/Director's Early Notes Prior to Production in the Spring of 1968," a transcription of an excerpt of Symbiopsychotaxiplasm: Take One; and the program notes on the film originally written for the 1991 Brooklyn Museum Retrospective of Greaves's films

Millennium Film Journal, for permission to reprint the script for Ann Marie Fleming's You Take Care Now, no. 25 (Summer 1991): 10–13

Laura Mulvey and Peter Wollen, for permission to reprint the script of Riddles of the Sphinx, originally published in Screen

Yoko Ono, for permission to reprint "Film Script 3," "Film Script 5," "Omnibus Film," "Imaginary Film Series/A FILM OF SUPER-REALISM," originally published in Grapefruit (New York: Simon and Schuster, 1970); to reprint "The Walk to the Taj Mahal," "Mona Lisa & Her Smile," "Film Script 4," and "Thirteen Film Scores, London, 1968," previously published in This Is Not Here, a catalogue for a show at the Everson Museum in Syracuse, New York, in 1971; and to publish "Film No. 13 (Travelogue)"

Yvonne Rainer, for permission to publish the script of Privilege

Peter Rose, for permission to publish the scripts of "Introduction to Pleasures of the Text" and Secondary Currents

Michael Snow, for permission to publish the text of So Is This

Screen, for permission to reprint the script of Riddles of the Sphinx, vol. 18, no. 2 (Summer 1977): 61–77

Trinh T. Minh-ha, for permission to reprint "Reassemblage: Sketch of a Sound Track," originally published in Camera Obscura, and the script of Naked Spaces—Living Is Round, originally published in Cinematograph.

Introduction

During the first century of cinema's existence, text—in the form of titles, credits, intertitles, subtitles, rolling introductions, scenarios, and screenplays—has been nearly as inevitable a part of the commercial film experience as flexible roll film. And particular forms of text—specific ways of presenting titles or credits, specific types of scenarios and forms of dialogue—have been central conventions of each cinema-historical period. Even at the dawn of film history, film was dependent on written text in at least two general ways. First, the "playscript" and the "scenario" have always been central to the process of film production. Indeed, they had developed as forms *before* the advent of motion pictures.[1] Second, visual text, in the form of titles and intertitles, quickly became a standard part of film narrative. As the popular market for cinema developed during the first decades of this century, both kinds of cinematic text became increasingly conventional, and audiences developed expectations about the kinds of scenarios they would see enacted in the movie theater and about the ways in which visual text would function to frame and elaborate these scenarios.

Over the years, the very conventionality of the various cinematic uses of text has inspired a variety of creative responses by filmmakers working within the industry and by independent filmmakers who have critiqued industry conventions. Of course, the attempt to maintain or reinvigorate the commercial cinema audience with new, creative approaches to scenarios and screenplays has been central throughout industry history, but even in the less discussed area of visual text, commercial filmmakers have often been ingenious. As early as 1907, Edwin Porter (in *College Chums*) included a passage during which a young man and woman "discuss" the Other Woman on the phone by means of

---

1. See Patrick G. Loughney, "In the Beginning Was the Word: Six Pre-Griffith Motion Picture Scenarios," in *Early Cinema: Space, Frame, Narrative*, ed. Thomas Elsaesser, 211–219 (London: BFI, 1990).

Man and woman argue in Edwin Porter's *College Chums* (1907). Courtesy Charles Musser.

animated words that collide mid-screen when the conversation grows heated. Periodically throughout the teens and twenties, live-action directors (Keaton in *The General* (1926), for example) and animators (Sullivan and Messmer in the Felix the Cat cartoons) explored the potential of printed intertitles and other forms of visual text to energize the experience of silent cinema. Indeed, F. W. Murnau's well-known rebellion against intertitles in *The Last Laugh* (1924)—on the grounds that they were intrinsically unfilmic—was accomplished in part by the use of "more intrinsic" forms of text within the imagery.

Of course, the coming of sound dramatically changed the nature of the texts used in commercial films. Silent acting interspersed with printed intertitles was replaced by extended dialogue. The sound stage became a central focus of industry filmmaking. And the axiom of the industry that films begin with writing was powerfully reconfirmed. Hollywood became famous for trying to lure the most inventive American fiction writers and playwrights to the studios, and a cadre of

writers became and remained as inevitable a part of film studios as producers, directors, actors, and cinematographers.

No longer necessary for the development and clarification of narrative, visual text became less important. Sound did make possible the inventive singalong animations of the Fleischer brothers (and others), but in general, visual text became confined to conventionalized titles and credits. In the commercial industry, spoken text has maintained its cinematic priority over visual text throughout the sound era, though there has been some variation in the significance of titles and credits. As the power of the studio system weakened during the fifties and sixties and the TV audience cut into film revenues, directors felt increasingly free to use titles and credit sequences aggressively. Who can forget Saul Bass's credits for *Psycho* (1960)? Indeed, by the mid-sixties, many directors were expanding the visual drama of their opening credits by making them an integral part of introductory sequences.

Text has also been of considerable importance throughout the history of

First poetic text and first image of Manhattan in Charles Sheeler and Paul Strand's *Manhatta* (1921). Courtesy Jan-Christopher Horak.

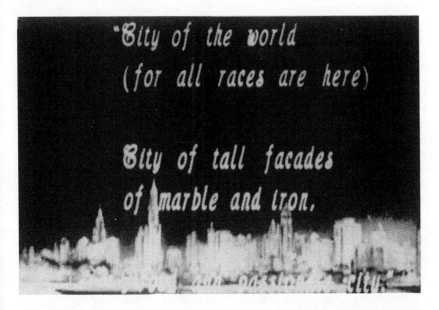

those forms of filmmaking which have functioned for makers and audiences as explicit or implicit critiques of commercial moviemaking. In the silent era, independent filmmakers often used visual texts as an element of new forms of film that can be seen as general responses to the growing conventionality of the industry, especially its dependence on narrative and on a limited range of narrative forms. In other instances, visual texts were used to subvert particular expectations created by specific industry conventions.

In 1921 Charles Sheeler and Paul Strand collaborated on *Manhatta*, which intercuts between images of Manhattan and poetic texts reminiscent of Sandburg and Whitman.[2] The goal was not storytelling, but a form of text/image cinepoetry. In *Anemic Cinema* (1926) Marcel Duchamp broke even more fully from industry convention and from the assumption that textual intertitles were a function of narrative development. He intercut between spiral designs that create optical illusions, and spirals of words so dense with puns that they "spiral" in on themselves.[3] For *Un Chien Andalou* ("An Andalusian Dog," 1929), Luis Buñuel and Salvador Dali devised texts that confronted specific audience expectations that had developed during the

first three decades of film history. The title of the film has no particular connection with any of the action. The film's introductory text, "Once upon a time," leads not to a fairy-tale narrative but to the grisly spectacle of Buñuel slicing a woman's eyeball in extreme close-up (the still-shocking image has often been understood as an attack on conventional ways of cinematic seeing). And the subsequent titles—"Eight Years Later," "Around Three in the Morning," "Sixteen Years Before," and "In the Spring"—have no relationship at all to the activities they appear to introduce, except to elaborate the filmmakers' defiance of conventional narrative means and of the conventional credibility of visual cinematic texts.[4]

The coming of sound created an expanded rift between the industry and those forms of filmmaking that had, during the twenties, become known as the Avant-Garde. Most independents did not have the financial resources to make synch sound films, and those critiques of the commercial cinema they were able to produce tended to fall back on silent-film methods. The implicit critique of Hollywood moviemaking in the Nykino group's (silent) *Pie in the Sky* (1934), for example, was accomplished in part by clever use of the lyrics of the song "Pie

---

2. *Manhatta* may be the earliest instance of what in recent years has become known as the "poetry-film." Jan-Christopher Horak discusses *Manhatta* in *Afterimage*, vol. 15, no. 4 (November 1987): 8–15. William C. Wees discusses the poetry-film in "Words and Images in the Poetry-Film," in *Words and Moving Images*, ed. William C. Wees and Michael Dorland, 105–113 (Montreal: Mediatext, 1984). One notable contributor to the "poetry-film," whose work is closely related to *Manhatta* is Rick Hancox, whose *Waterworx (A Clear Day and No Memories)* (1982) recycles the Wallace Stevens poem, "A Clear Day and No Memories." Other Hancox films include *LANDFALL* (1983) and *Beach Events* (1984).

3. The Duchamp puns are translated and discussed in "Marcel Duchamp's *Anemic Cinema*," by Katrina Martin, *Studio International*, no. 189 (January 1975): 53–60; and in "Image and Title in Avant-Garde Cinema," by P. Adams Sitney, *October*, no. 11 (Winter 1979): 97–112.

4. In the film, these texts are in French; I have used the standard translations. Other Avant-Garde filmmakers of the twenties and thirties who used visual text inventively include Man Ray (in *L'Etoile de mer*—"Starfish," 1928), Slavko Vorkapich (in *The Life and Death of 9413— A Hollywood Extra*, 1928), and Len Lye (in *Trade Tattoo*, 1937; and *Musical Poster No. 1*, 1939).

One of the spiral texts from Marcel Duchamp's *Anemic Cinema* (1926). The words create an almost-nonsense sentence—"Elude the bruises of the eskimos who have exquisite words"—in which the sound (and appearance) of the words play off each other in an amusing way. Courtesy Anthology Film Archives.

in the Sky" as silent intertitles.[5] By the sixties, what had been an economic limitation had become a "virtue": it was an axiom of many North American independent filmmakers that since synch sound was so central to the materialistic film industry, it should be avoided as aesthetically corrupt, even when economically feasible. When spoken text was part of independent films, in the form of narration or as lyrics of songs, its use tended to critique the conventional assumption that what we see on the screen and the words we hear on the soundtrack should be related in obvious ways that smooth the development of narrative action or, in documentaries, the predictable explorations of the subjects. The soundtracks and the visual imagery of films such as Willard Maas's *Geography of the Body* (1943), Sidney Peterson's *The Lead Shoes* (1949), Bruce Conner's *Cosmic Ray* (1963), and Hollis

Frampton's *nostalgia* (1971) are related in complex ways.

Post–World War II independent filmmakers maintained the tradition, begun in the twenties, of using visual texts as elements in a variety of new, unconventional cinematic forms. For *The Big "O"* (c. 1953), animator Carmen D'Avino used a stenciled *O* as the basic figure of an organic painting. In the "Poemfield" series (1966–67) Stan Vanderbeek made computer-generated texts the viewers' central focus. George Landow's *Film in Which There Appear to Be Sprocket Holes, Edge Lettering, Dirt Particles, Etc.* (1966), as the title suggests, foregrounds elements of film's material nature, including edge lettering along the celluloid strip. Bruce Baillie's *Tung* (1966) includes a visual poem as part of his lyrical evocation of the woman Tung. In Paul Sharits's *Word Movie/Fluxfilm* (1967), viewers listen to two speakers alternate

5. Nykino was a film production organization founded by Leo Hurwitz, Irving Lerner, and Ralph Steiner in 1934. See William Alexander, *Film on the Left: American Documentary Film from 1931 to 1942* (Princeton, N.J.: Princeton University Press, 1981), chapters 2 and 3.

O's in Carmen D'Avino's *The Big "O"* (c. 1953). Courtesy Carmen D'Avino.

Introduction 6

one-word-at-a-time readings of two distinct texts on the soundtrack, while Sharits presents approximately fifty words, one word per frame, in a graphic arrangement that causes the words to "optically-conceptually fuse into one 3 3/4-minute long word."[6] Joyce Wieland's *Sailboat* and *1933* (1967) use the words "sailboat" and "1933" as central formal elements. And for *White Calligraphy* (1967), Taka Iimura scratched Japanese characters from *The Kojiki,* Japan's oldest story, into the emulsion, frame by frame, so that when the film is projected, the characters are transformed into a graphic dance.

While these and other experiments threw the general predictability of commercial forms into relief, other filmmakers were maintaining the tradition of using visual text to critique particular dimensions of conventional cinema. In Bruce Conner's *A Movie* (1958), the title "A MOVIE" and the credit line "BY

BRUCE CONNER" become central motifs throughout the film, suggesting that *this* film is made by a single filmmaker, not a collaborator who must efface himself in conventional ways. Conner also uses the familiar "10-9-8-7-6-5-4-3-2" of Academy leader as a central formal element in *Cosmic Ray* (1961), rather than as an (accidental) introduction to the "real film" that follows. Beginning in the late fifties, Stan Brakhage began to scratch his titles directly into the emulsion, one frame at a time, and to sign his films "by Brakhage" in the same way. Brakhage's direct titles and credits were/are as polemical as the films they frame: they demonstrate that his films are the personal, hand-crafted creations of an individual (and individualistic) film artist, not products of corporate conformity. Other filmmakers used intertitles and/or superimposed texts for other kinds of critique. In Marie Menken's *Notebook* (1962) and in

6. This is Sharits's description: *Film Culture,* no. 65–66 (1975): 115. As the title indicates, *Word Movie/Fluxfilm* was part of the *Fluxfilm Program* assembled by George Maciunas in 1966 and available (in part) at the Film-makers' Cooperative in New York. The *Fluxfilm Program* includes other experiments with visual language, including George Brecht's *Entry-Exit* which focuses on the words "entry" and "exit" as, among other things, a movement into and out of the film experience.

Frame sequence of Stan Brakhage's scratched signature at the end of *Window Water Baby Moving* (1959). Courtesy Anthology Film Archives.

A text analyzes a fashion photograph in Anthony McCall and Andrew Tyndall's *Argument* (1978). Courtesy Anthony McCall.

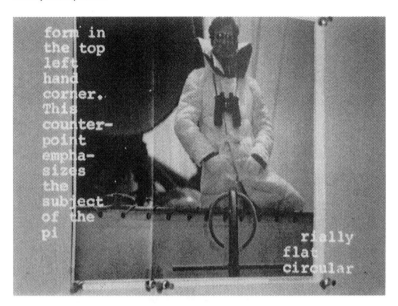

Jonas Mekas's diaries, beginning with *Walden* (1969), the filmmakers were committed to the use of film as a way of saving and honoring moments of simple, unpretentious beauty; both returned for inspiration to the beginnings of cinema (especially to the Lumières, whose films were seen as simple, unpretentious records of everyday life identified by simple titles), using intertitles to identify imagery—a method of commentary generally abandoned as old-fashioned once sound-on-film had transformed the industry.[7]

By the seventies and eighties, some filmmakers were dramatically extending the length and scope of films that relied largely or exclusively on printed texts. Hollis Frampton (in *Zorns Lemma*, 1970, and *Poetic Justice*, 1972), Robert Nelson (in *Bleu Shut*, 1970), Anthony McCall and Andrew Tyndall (in *Argument*, 1978), Patrick Clancy (in *Peliculas*, 1979), Bruce Elder (in *1857: Fool's Gold*, 1981, *Illuminated Texts*, 1982, and other films), Michael Snow (in *So Is This*, 1982), David Goldberg and Michael Oblowitz (in *The Is/Land*, 1982), Peter Rose (in *Secondary Currents*, 1983), James Benning (in *American Dreams*, 1983), and others centered films on visual texts as a means of exploring such issues as the development of the intellect, the distinction between reading a text in a book and in a movie theater, the potential of text to define and control a cinematic experience, and—in the case of McCall/Tyndall and Benning—to reveal central gender assumptions of American culture.[8] For Yvonne

7. To my knowledge, the original Lumière films did not have titles, but the Lumière prints in circulation by the fifties and sixties did; independent filmmakers discovering the pioneers of cinema apparently assumed that the way they saw the early films was basically the way original audiences saw them.

8. For a discussion of some films in which printed or written texts are a film's central imagery see my "Text As Image," *Afterimage*, vol. 13, no. 8 (March 1986): 9–20; and *Mot: dites, image*, a catalogue for a show of such films during October and November 1989, organized by the Museum of Modern Art at the Centre Georges Pompidou in Paris. The show and catalogue were largely the work of filmmaker Yann Beauvais, whose essay "Des mots encore des mots," is one of several included in the well-illustrated catalogue.

Patrick Clancy's *Peliculas* (1979) must be read as a scroll (a surreal narrative is handwritten along the filmstrip in various colors) *and* seen projected (clusters of frames regularly interrupt the handwriting). Courtesy Patrick Clancy.

Rainer, extensive use of visual text became an integral dimension of a critique of the conventional cinema's marketing of voyeuristic eroticism. By using text, along with photographs and a variety of forms of self-reflexive live-action imagery, to chronicle the lives of the characters in *Film About a Woman Who . . .* (1974), for example, Rainer was able to develop a narrative that allowed viewers to understand her women characters, without exploiting their physical presence in conventional, male-oriented ways.

The increasing interest among North American independent filmmakers in the cinematic possibilities of visual text was certainly not an isolated phenomenon. The same period saw a wide range of experiments with visual language by the group of French artists known as the Letterists (their explorations included film: John Isador Isou's *Treatise on Drivel and Eternity* (1951), for example); by the international movement of "concrete" or "visual" poets, like Emmett Williams, whose *THE VOYAGE* (1975) explores the literal and historical "seam" between reading a text and watching animated motion pictures; and by a wide range of visual artists who incorporated text into painting, sculpture, graphic design, and multimedia works. And of course, experiments in artistic circles paralleled, influenced, and were influenced by the worlds of magazine and television advertising and a wide range of phenomena in the culture at large.

The sixties and seventies also brought a variety of critiques—in the form of films and film-related writings—of the commercial cinema's dependence on conventional, melodramatic scenarios and screenplays. Some of these critiques confront the formal construction of industry screenplays and/or their particular relationships to the films that develop from them. Others confront the fundamental attitudes about gender, race, and class that are conventionally embedded in commercial scenarios and screenplays.

By 1964, Yoko Ono was critiquing the narrow range of industry narrative forms by writing mini film scripts that defied conventional presentation and cinematic logic. What could be less conventional, and less marketable, than a script that simply directs the reader to "ask audiences to cut the part of the image on the screen that they don't like. Supply scissors"! For Ono, film "scripts" did not need to be precise indications of what characters in a melodrama will say to one another; they could suggest entirely new approaches to filmmaking that anyone might appropriate. William Greaves's scenario for *Symbiopsychotaxiplasm: Take One* (1967) provided dialogue for his two central characters—a man and woman arguing—but during the shooting, this dialogue was performed by five different pairs of actors, some of whom spoke the lines, while others sang them. Greaves assumed that five separate films would result from this one scenario. In 1972, Hollis Frampton revenged himself on the conventional assumption that films must be based on written screenplays: his *Poetic Justice* provides poetic justice for the conventional filmgoer. Instead of filming dramatized action, Frampton filmed a 240-page *screenplay*, one page at a time; viewers must "shoot the movie" in their minds. A more particular kind of critique is evident in James Benning's scenario, "New York 1980" (the resulting film was called *Him and Me*, 1982), where the mysterious death that motivates all the action is the *last* information readers/viewers learn, not the first, as it would be in most conventional Hollywood narratives.

As synch sound equipment became increasingly available to independents in the late sixties and the seventies, new avenues for critique opened up. Filmmakers could now develop screenplays for films that demonstrated the limitations of conventional industry screenplays from positions generically much closer to the problematic industry product than had been possible before. Certainly, by the seventies, many filmmakers had come to see the now-"traditional" avant-garde resistance to synch sound as at best counterproductive: to refuse synch sound (and the necessity for carefully designed scenarios and screenplays) on the grounds that the choice of silence was in some sense "purer" than a "surrender" to sound was to consign independent filmmaking to the arty margins, to refuse opportunities for effectively confronting those very limitations of commercial film that had inspired generations of avant-garde filmmakers. To choose silence when sound was economically feasible came to seem an implicit maintenance of the status quo, rather than a meaningful critique of it. The seventies saw a wide range of new, independent sound films, made by independents working in 35mm (Chantal Akerman's *Jeanne Dielman . . .* , 1975, is a notable instance) and in 16mm (Charles Burnett's *Killer of Sheep*, 1977), by individuals or small crews using increasingly portable 16mm *cinéma-vérité* rigs (Ed Pincus's *Diaries*, 1976, for example) and by filmmakers using the new, inexpensive Super-8mm sound equipment that had become available (Beth and Scott B's *Black Box*, 1978, and *G-Men*, 1978).

In general, these independent filmmakers used their new access to sound technology to produce melodramatic narratives that confronted the industry's traditional failure to deal progressively with issues of gender, race, and class—gender most centrally, expecially in the seventies and eighties. Yvonne Rainer's features, from *Film About a Woman Who . . .* through *Privilege* (1990), are especially good examples, as are Laura Mulvey and Peter Wollen's *Riddles of the Sphinx*, and Su Friedrich's *Damned If You Don't* (1987) and *Sink or Swim* (1990). All these films

focus on aspects of women's experiences that have been marginalized or ignored by the commercial cinema and devise ways of depicting women without participating in those forms of cine-"voyeurism" so typical of conventional cinema. In other cases, filmmakers confronted the tradition of spoken narration in commercial film and in documentary by writing narrations to be spoken by women. Notable instances include Trinh T. Minh-ha's *Reassemblage* (1982) and *Naked Spaces—Living Is Round* (1985) and Ann Marie Fleming's *You Take Care Now* (1990). Trinh's early films also confront the tradition of the narrator who speaks in a conventional white, "educated" accent, by using multiple women narrators, each of whom speaks with a different, "nonmainstream" accent.

The function of this volume is to make accessible some of the most interesting and inventive texts and scripts independent filmmakers have written and/or filmed during the past twenty-five years. The particular texts and scripts included were chosen to accomplish a variety of goals. The most obvious is to facilitate the study of films and filmmakers of considerable reputation in those sectors of academe and the culture at large where the potential of using independent film as critique is recognized. While the majority of scripts and texts included here are of some reputation, I have also included a number of writings by lesser-known filmmakers (Ann Marie Fleming, for example), as well as lesser-known texts by more widely known filmmakers: Yoko Ono's mini film scripts, for instance, and Su Friedrich's "(Script) for a Film without Images."

My particular choices of scripts and texts and my organization of the selections are also meant to provide a sense of at least one trajectory through the recent history of independent filmmaking and a reminder of the many ways in which writing has functioned in relation to films that critique the mainstream cinema. The scripts and texts are arranged chronologically, according to the dates when they were written and/or appeared in films. The volume begins with the mini film scripts Ono wrote in 1964 and ends with the script of Yvonne Rainer's *Privilege*, which was completed in 1990. Of course, this arrangement distorts one's sense of this twenty-seven-year period, since the chronology of individual works does not account for the longevity of particular careers. As has been suggested, Rainer's contributions to the creative uses of cinematic text began twenty years before *Privilege*, and other filmmakers whose work is included in *Screen Writings* have continued to make contributions for years after they wrote the selection included here. The individual introductions to the particular filmmakers provide some sense of the historical terrain represented and a more thorough context for each of the films and filmmakers selected.

One particular historical issue implicit in *Screen Writings* is what was seen, at least for a time, as a rift in the history of avant-garde film between the early-seventies Anthology Film Archives project of defining "the essential cinema" and the widespread suspicion and rejection of this project, and especially its valorization of what P. Adams Sitney was to call "structural film"—on the part of filmmakers and commentators who came to see the Anthology selection committee as a group of old-fashioned, territorial males.[9] For some, my inclusion of "structural filmmakers" identified with "the essential cinema"—Frampton, Snow—in the same volume as Rainer, Mulvey/Wollen, Trinh, and Friedrich—filmmakers who represent a more progressive cinematic commitment to issues of gender and race—may seem strange. But the coexistence of these filmmakers in the same volume makes sense on at least two levels. First, the rift I've mentioned has less to do with particular filmmakers than with the cultural politics of defining which films are worth watching. Though there are differences between the work of Frampton and Snow and the work of Rainer, Mulvey/Wollen, Trinh, and Friedrich, there are also significant elements of continuity. Indeed, the formal inventiveness of Snow and Frampton was, according to Mulvey, a major influence on *Riddles of the Sphinx*, and Friedrich's use of the alphabet as her fundamental organizational principle in *Sink or Swim* can be understood as an implicit response to Frampton's use of the alphabet as the central organizational principle in *Zorns Lemma*.[10]

Second, whatever limitations one sees in the critical/curatorial project of the Anthology selection committee or in the more overtly political analyses of a later generation of commentators dedicated to expanded gender, racial, and class awareness, many of the filmmakers of recent decades who have been championed by

---

9. The selections and the thinking of the Anthology selection committee are set forth in *The Essential Cinema*, ed. P. Adams Sitney (New York: Anthology Film Archives and N.Y.U. Press, 1971). The members of the committee were James Broughton, Peter Kubelka, Ken Kelman, Jonas Mekas, and Sitney.

10. Mulvey discusses this influence in "Interview with Laura Mulvey: *Riddles of the Sphinx*," in *A Critical Cinema 2*, by Scott MacDonald (Berkeley, Los Angeles, Oxford: University of California Press, 1992). Friedrich indicates that the "allusion" to *Zorns Lemma* in *Sink or Swim* is, at best, unconscious, though she agrees that Frampton is an influence, in "Daddy Dearest: An Interview with Su Friedrich," by Scott MacDonald, *The Independent*, vol. 13, no. 10 (December 1990): 28.

In some cases, the interplay of these two "schools" of filmmaking is even more direct: Frampton left a space in his *Magellan* (1972–1980) for any one of Rainer's features—the only filmmaker he so honored; Rainer dedicated *The Man Who Envied Women* (1985) to Frampton—her only dedication of a film to a filmmaker.

one group or another share basic concerns about the film industry and the audience it has generated. Frampton's *Poetic Justice* (1972) is as much about the nature of the spectator's identification with camera and character as is Rainer's *Film About a Woman Who . . .* or Mulvey's influential essay "Visual Pleasure and Narrative Cinema."[11] Snow's *Wavelength* is as much an attack on conventional narrativity as is Trinh T. Minhha's *Reassemblage*. It is the assumption of this collection that one of the most interesting developments in the recent history of independent film has been the interplay of various avant-garde approaches by filmmakers mounting a sustained critique of the conventional cinema and the cultural practices it encodes and polemicizes. The texts and scripts collected here are indices of this interplay.

The other consideration that informed my selection and arrangement of scripts and texts was to represent, as fully as seemed practical, the wide range of ways texts composed in connection with particular films have functioned. In some instances—*Riddles of the Sphinx, Privilege*—I have merely reprinted scripts or texts from completed films, so that the relevant films can be studied by students, critics, historians, and theorists more precisely and in greater depth. In other cases, I have included scenarios that functioned as sketches for possible or actual films. Yoko Ono's mini scripts are conceptual designs for films, only a few of which have resulted in actual films. James Benning's "New York 1980" was later fleshed out and became the screenplay for *Him and Me*.

In still other instances, the texts included here have less direct, and less conventional, relationships to the films they represent. The Trinh T. Minh-ha se-

lections are the spoken and printed texts of *Reassemblage* and *Naked Spaces—Living Is Round*, but these texts are also meant to stand on their own as poetry. Friedrich's "(Script) for a Film without Images" is not a film script at all, but a film-inspired written narrative that, however, relates in a variety of ways to her films, especially to *The Ties That Bind* (1984) and *Sink or Swim*. Peter Rose's "Introduction to *Pleasures of the Text*" is a transcript of a performance piece that offers an amusing and insightful critique on academic writing about film and serves as the introduction to the evening-long performance experience of which the film *Secondary Currents* is a part. Frampton's "Notes on *Zorns Lemma*" provides the filmmaker's own analysis of many dimensions of his influential film, as they were recorded in a set of notes found in the Frampton files at Anthology Film Archives. And William Greaves's original notes for *Symbiopsychotaxiplasm: Take One* suggest a context for a remarkable, recently rediscovered experiment.

Finally, I believe I have selected scripts and texts that are readable and suggestive on their own, whether one is familiar with the films represented by the texts or not. In fact, several selections—Frampton's *Poetic Justice*, Friedrich's "(Script) for a Film without Images," several of Ono's mini scripts—were originally published as literary texts (in limited editions no longer widely available). Of course, no matter how engaging the reader finds the scripts and texts included here, this book should be understood as a means to an end: it is meant to function as a resource for those who have had or will have experiences with the films themselves. Should the readability, the insight, and the inventiveness of these texts and scripts entice new audiences to the films

---

11. "Visual Pleasure and Narrative Cinema" is widely anthologized and also available in Mulvey's *Visual and Other Pleasures* (Bloomington/Indianapolis: University of Indiana Press, 1989).

and filmmakers—and toward the large and vital history of alternative cinema of which this collection is at most a tiny index—the author will be delighted.

Anyone familiar with the productive world of independent cinema will know of other scripts and texts that can compete, in terms of historical interest, variety, and readability, with those I have included in *Screen Writings*. Clearly the collection focuses on North American filmmakers (the only exception is Mulvey/Wollen), and this brief introduction has not so far mentioned many filmmakers and/or films—from North America and elsewhere—that have explored the possibilities of visual text, including Robert Florey and Slavko Vorkapich (*The Life and Death of 9413—A Hollywood Extra*, 1928), James Sibley Watson and Melville F. Webber (*The Fall of the House of Usher*, 1929), Len Lye (*Trade Tattoo*, 1937; *Musical Poster No. 1*, 1939), Ian Hugo (*Jazz of Lights*, 1954), Maurice Lemaitre (*Le film est deja commence?*, 1951; *Films imaginaires*, 1985), Peter Watkins (*The War Game*, 1965; *The Journey*, 1987), Stan Brakhage (*23rd Psalm Branch*, 1967), Paul Sharits (*Razor Blades*, 1968), George Landow (*Remedial Reading Comprehension*, 1970), Joyce Wieland (*Rat Life and Diet in North America*, 1968; *Raison avant le passion*, 1969), Diana Barrie (*The Living or Dead Test*, 1979), Liz Rhodes (*Light Reading*, 1978), James Irwin (*The Big Red Awk*, 1984; *Let's Be Pals*, 1985), Robert Breer (*Bang!*, 1986), Greta Snider (*Blood Story*, 1990), Yann Beauvais (*Vo/Id*, 1985), Jennifer L. Burford (*Cortex*, 1988), and Michele Fleming (*Private Property*, 1992), to name just a few.[12] Indeed, the recent publication of *The Films of Yvonne Rainer*, Rainer's scripts up through *The Man Who Envied Women* (1985); of Phyllis Rauch Klotman, ed., *Screenplays of the African American Experience*; and of the script of Craig Baldwin's *Tribulation 99: Alien Anomalies Under America* is evidence of how many interesting scripts are available. *Screen Writings* is my first anthology of this particular kind. I hope readers will find it interesting and useful enough to suggest that further volumes are in order.

---

12. A more complete listing of non–North American films that explore visual text is included in Yann Beauvais's *Mot: dites, image* (see note 8).

Yoko Ono

Between 1964 and 1968 Yoko Ono wrote a series of mini scripts for films (sometimes she called them "scores"), conceptual designs that in a few instances she would later use as the basis for films of her own and that she has continued to feel can serve as a resource for other filmmakers. At the time when she was writing the film scripts, Ono was deeply involved in Fluxus, an art movement with roots in Dada and Duchamp, dedicated to the creative *idea* and to the instigation of new kinds of spectator-art relationships. Her first films were a result of her connection with Fluxus, not of the film scripts.[1] But during the late sixties she collaborated with John Lennon on three films based on mini scripts copyrighted in 1968, but presumably written earlier: *Rape* (1969) was a version of "Film No. 5 Rape (or Chase)"; *Fly* (1970) was a version of "Film No. 11 (Fly)" (a.k.a. "Film No. 13 Fly"); and *Up Your Legs Forever* (1970)

was based on the film script, "Film No. 12 Up Your Legs Forever" (a.k.a. "Film No. 12 (Esstacy)").[2] In one other instance, the sequence of film and film script is difficult to determine. By the time the film script "Film No. 4 Bottoms" was copyrighted as part of "Thirteen Film Scores" in 1968, two versions of the film described had already been made: *No. 4* (1966), which was included in *Fluxfilm Program*, coordinated by George Maciunas, and a feature version, *No. 4 (Bottoms)* (1966).

In *Rape*, a camera crew follows a woman through a London park, along streets, and finally into her apartment where she tries, unsuccessfully, to persuade the camera crew to leave. The filming was candid, though later enhanced with laboratory effects. While it is shorter than the version envisioned in "Film No. 5 Rape (or Chase)," the seventy-seven minutes of *Rape* are enough to

---

1. In 1963 Ono had contributed a sound track to Taka Iimura's *Love (Ai)*.

2. The misspelling of *ecstasy* has been retained at Ono's request, as evidence of the informality of her aesthetic at the time.

make the camera rape relentless and exhausting, and near the end, the film does achieve something of the dreamlike quality envisioned by Ono. The interest in flies evident in "Film No. 11 (Fly)" fueled several Ono projects, including designs for installation pieces, and a Museum of Modern Art show (documented by a catalogue designed and printed by Ono in 1971—after MoMA distanced itself from the show), as well as one of the most memorable Ono-Lennon collaborations, the film *Fly*. During thirty minutes, the camera follows a fly as it explores the nude body of a sleeping woman (the situation is reminiscent of Gulliver's trip to Brobdingnag, and of Willard Maas's *Geography of the Body*, 1943). Late in the film, more flies appear on the body, which by then looks like a corpse; at the end the camera pans to an open window and to the blue sky outside. On the sound track of the film Ono provides fly vocalizations and, near the end, a bit of music in reverse. *Up Your Legs Forever* is a seventy-minute series of vertical pans up the bare legs of men and women, from their feet to their thighs, accompanied by a sound track of comments and sounds made during the filming. *Up Your Legs Forever* is less impressive than the other two film adaptations of the film scripts, perhaps because it does not advance beyond Ono's remarkable, previous feature, *No. 4 (Bottoms)*, which focuses on buttocks, rather than legs. In *No. 4 (Bottoms)* and in the earlier *No. 4*, Ono's camera films one pair of naked, walking buttocks after another. In the feature version, a treadmill was built so that the framing of the buttocks could be controlled: Ono wanted each moving bottom to exactly fill the frame. A sound track made up of comments by participants and nonparticipants and of

excerpts from the media coverage of the shooting (including an interview with Ono) accompanies the visuals.

Regardless of the degree of success—by whatever measure—of the adaptations of the film scripts, Ono's central mission in composing the scripts was not completed by her making the films. In the 1971 Touchstone edition of *Grapefruit*, the "Film" section is introduced by this statement:

> These scores were printed and made available to whoever was interested at the time or thereafter in making their own version of the films, since these films, by their nature, became a reality only when they were repeated and realized by other film-makers.
>
> A dream you dream alone may be a dream, but a dream two people dream together is a reality.

And in a recent interview, Ono confirms the idea that the film scripts should be considered resources for filmmakers: "I think one of the reasons I'm not making more films is that I've done so many film scripts. I'd like to see one of them made by somebody else."[3] Readers are invited to consider Ono's mini film scripts as a resource for films of their own.

What follows is the most complete collection of the Ono film scripts I am able to locate. I have included only the pieces Ono specifically labeled as "film scripts" and "film scores." I have not included proposals for and descriptions of the various film installations conceived and in some cases built by Ono and Ono/Lennon. Jon Hendricks includes a detailed, annotated listing of the installations and all of Ono's Fluxus work in his *Fluxus Codex*.[4] In several instances, film

3. Scott MacDonald, "Interview with Yoko Ono," in "Yoko Ono: Ideas on Film," *Film Quarterly*, vol. 43, no. 1 (Fall 1989): 16.

4. (New York: Harry N Abrams, 1988), 415–426.

scripts were published (and apparently copyrighted) more than once, in slightly different versions. In 1971 Ono and Lennon had a retrospective at the Everson Museum in Syracuse, New York, called "This Is Not Here." The catalogue for that show reprinted *Six Film Scripts by Yoko Ono* (Tokyo, June 1964) and *Thirteen Film Scores* (London, 1968). I have used the "This Is Not Here" versions of those pieces, along with "Imaginary Film Series: Shi (From the cradle to the grave of Mr. So)," which includes "A FILM OF SUPER-REALISM"—as printed in *Grapefruit*—and "Film No. 13 (Travelogue)." In one instance, there are two entirely different versions of a script with nearly the same title: "The Walk to the Taj Mahal" and "Film No. 1 A Walk to Taj Mahal." Both versions are reprinted.

Mini Film Scripts

These mini scripts are reprinted exactly as they originally appeared. At Ono's request I have not even corrected spelling errors (she believes such errors reflect the informal Fluxus aesthetic of the time) or her sometimes unusual punctuation. I have made the typography of the titles consistent. —S.M.

These scores were printed and made available to whoever was interested at the time or thereafter in making their own versions of the films, since these films, by their nature, became a reality only when they were repeated and realized by other film-makers.

A dream you dream alone may be a dream, but a dream two people dream together is a reality.

THE WALK TO THE TAJ MAHAL
1) The blind man or the musician's version *(All black)*.
2) The deaf man or the painter's version. *(Walk* and *ride* of *places—Times Square, Ginza*, etc. by *cars, motorcycles)*.
3) The real picture—winter scene. *(Snow—*in other words, *all white)**

*(can make *summer, autumn, & spring* versions *by sunglare, skies* or *cottons, flowers, all white* anyway)

Music composed by Yoko Ono, performed by the audience. (1 version, *white flowers* all silently picked) (2 version, no given music—just the *title*).

Note: Any of the above versions may be shown independently.

MONA LISA & HER SMILE
Ask audience to stare at a figure *(any figure)* for a long time and then immediately turn their eyes to the screen and see the reflection.

FILM SCRIPT 3
Ask audience to cut the part of the image on the screen that they don't like. Supply scissors.

FILM SCRIPT 4
Ask audience to stare at the screen until it becomes black.

FILM SCRIPT 5
Ask audience the following:
1) not to look at Rock Hudson, but only Doris Day.

2) not to look at any round objects but only square and angled objects—if you look at a round object watch it until it becomes square and angled.

3) not to look at blue but only red—if blue comes out close eyes or do something so you do not see; if you saw it, then make believe that you have not seen it.

OMNIBUS FILM

1) Give a print of the same film to many directors.

2) Ask each one to re-edit the print without leaving out any material in such a way that it will be unnoticed that the print was re-edited.

3) Show all the versions together omnibus style.

IMAGINARY FILM SERIES: SHI
(From the cradle to the grave of Mr. So)

A slow film taken in the time space of 60 years, following a person who's born and died. From about the 30th year, it becomes a film of a couple, as the man gets married. It really becomes "a film of waiting" towards the end since the film obviously starts to have a senile quality in its camera work, while the man in the film looks still robust. It is amazing that the death came so suddenly over the man in a form of diarrhea. Highly incredible film which makes one think.—You never know when you die.

A FILM OF SUPER-REALISM

SHI (From the cradle to the grave of Mr. So)
Interview with the director, Mr. Toyama.

Tell me, Mr. Toyama, you are relatively unknown in the film world, do you think it had something to do with the fact that you were devoted to the making of this film "SHI" (this is no misprint—means "death" in Japanese) of super-realism, as they call now?

Yes, definitely.

How long did it take for you to make this film?

Sisty years.

Incredible.

Well, you can say that, I suppose. But it could have been longer if he hadn't died then. I was lucky.

Now people are saying that this film will create a new move in the film world. Do you think this will happen?

It all depends on how you can outlive the film.

Yes, yes, I heard that in the end you were getting rather impatient, that you didn't know if you could wait until the death scene takes place. You didn't, of course, use any means to speed up the ending or anything?

No, no, everything took place naturally.

What was the cause of death?

Diarrhea.

I understand that the film was backed by a Japanese Ketchup Company?

Yes, and that's why the whole thing has a pink tone to it. They wanted me to use a red theme that reminds you of ketchup, but I used pink instead. But I made sure that the blood would look like ketchup, and the ketchup like blook, showing that both substances were equally essential. The ketchup company liked that. Also, this gave a little surrealistic touch to the film, which, otherwise, would have been too realistic.

THIRTEEN FILM SCORES London, 1968

Film No.1   A WALK TO TAJ MAHAL
The film consists of snowfall only. The camera will make a walk movement of a person in the snow. The camera will move sometimes in a circle, sometimes zigzag, sometimes slow, but mostly will be at a normal speed. Then at the last point, it will go up to the sky. It should make the audience feel as though they are the ones who are walking in the snow and who go up into the sky.

This should take something like an hour for the total walk.

For the sound, ask the audience to hold bunches of white flowers and pick them slowly.

Film No.2   WATCH
Film a group of people watching you and listening to you. Film all their reactions. What are you doing?

Film No.3   TOILET THOUGHTS
Prepare 365 copies of a poster and paste them in bar toilets around the city. Leave them for a week and take pictures of all 365 copies. Leave them again for a month and take pictures of them. Go on until you are satisfied, or until the

The crew "camera raping" the woman (Eva Majlata) in Yoko Ono's *Rape* (1969). Courtesy Lenono Photo Archive.

posters disappear. Make a film by stringing all the pictures together.

Film No.4   BOTTOMS
String bottoms together in place of signatures for petition for peace.

Film No.5   RAPE (or CHASE)
Rape with camera. 1½ hr. colour. Synchronized sound.

A cameraman will chase a girl on a street with a camera persistently until he corners her in an alley, and, if possible, until she is in a falling position.

The cameraman will be taking a risk of offending the girl as the girl is somebody he picks up arbitrarily on the street, but there is a way to get around this.

Depending on the budget, the chase should be made with girls of different ages, etc. May chase boys and men as well.

As the film progresses, and as it goes towards the end, the chase and the running should become slower and slower like in a dream, using a highspeed camera.

The woman in Ono's *Rape* confronts the camera. Courtesy Lenono Photo Archive.

**Film No.6   A CONTEMPORARY SEXUAL MANUAL
(366 sexual positions)**
1½ hr. colour, separate soundtrack. Cast: a woman, a man and
a child.

The whole film takes place in a bedroom with a large double
bed in the center and a window at the foot of the bed.

The film is a family scene of a quiet couple and a four-year-old
daughter lying on the bed for the whole night. All they do is just
sleep, and the 366 sexual positions are all in the mind of the
audience.

The delicate change of positions made by the threesome has
a slow dance movement quality to it on one hand, and a
comfortable domestic nature (scratching each other, etc.) on
the other.

The contemporary sex, unlike what you see in blue films,
reflects the complexity of our society, and it is subtle and
multi-leveled. So in this film you never see an obvious position
as two people on top of each other, or actually making love in
any form. They very rarely exchange words with each other
and when they do, the sound is not synchronized so all you see
is their mouths moving. But there is definitely an air of peaceful
unity and coziness among the three.

There are occasional breaks that take place in the film:
going to the toilet, for instance (in which case, all you see is

one of them getting up and going out of the room and coming back).

The camera will start panning from under the bed, then the foot of the bed, gradually it goes up, and finally up over their heads until the window at the foot of the bed starts to cover the whole screen. This camera movement can be compared to the moon rising and then disappearing at the other end in the time space of 1½ hr.

The soundtrack in contract to the screen consists mainly of tragic conversations between a couple who are about to split, whimpering of a child, whispers, sighs and love groans. Also, a sound-tape from a Trafalgar Square soap-bubble happening comes in as if they are sounds in a dream of one of them, or of the three, while they sleep. At dawn, milkbottle rattling and bird sounds will come in, and the film will end with increasingly heavy bird sounds.

Film No. 7   TEA PARTY
1½ hr. Colour. Synchronized sound. Cast: a woman.

A woman is having a tea party in a room. We never see others except the woman. She says *You weren't listening, were you.* After that she says nothing for the whole film.

The film is basically about a room with many different time worlds in it. A clock is going fast like crazy. A sugar in a glass melts spasmodically. The woman's dress deteriorates very fast. A car passing in the street, which is reflected in the woman's eyes, goes ever so slowly. A chair melts away like something made out of dust, etc. In the end, the telephone is the only thing remaining in the room. Everything else disappears with its own time rhythm.

The woman will have to be a Japanese woman with very good breasts. The scene has a peculiar mixture of a Japanese tea ceremony and an English tea party.

Film No. 8   WOMAN
1½ hr. Colour. Separate sound track. Cast: one woman.

This is a film about pregnancy and delivery.

The pregnant woman is the only person in the entire film, which symbolizes the lonely venture of conception.

She is contemporary, very sensitive and intelligent. Her mentality in all phases of her thinking is equivalent to that of a man of high intelligence in our society.

The audience becomes intimate with her skin, her swell, her vomit, her walk, her smile, everything about her except her exterior circumstances, such as whether she is married, if she has a job, etc. That part of her background is completely obscure.

The whole film can be thought of as a solo dance movement of a pregnant woman: first very light and pretty—gradually the body protruding—heavy and slow, and finally the dramatic delivery and a complete stillness to follow, with an underlying suggestion of peace/death (atonement).

We also see a lot of the town, the skies the stars through her pregnant eyes.

In the soundtrack, we go into her mind. It consists mostly of delivery groans, swearing, also interviews of the woman done by imaginary reporters. Also, questions are asked by the imaginary reporter or the pregnant woman to the audience, such as: *Did you see that bottle on the shelf in the last scene? Was there a window in the last scene? Are you sure?*, etc. She first conceives of her experience as a cancer growing in her stomach, etc. She is committed. But why her and not the man? What is the relationship between her and the growth inside her? etc., etc.

Except for medical reports, no film-maker as yet has taken this subject for a film. Maybe it is because most film-makers are men, and they are sensitive to this subject. I have noticed that whenever a pregnant woman is shown in a photograph or a film, she is over-beautified and romanticized with careful camera work. I want to treat this film with sensitivity but not with unnecessary beautification.

I want all the girls in the world to see this film before they become pregnant. Some mothers, because they have been wrongly informed that pregnancy is the most gratifying thing for women, etc., start to hate the child after the initial shock of going through the unglamourous reality of pregnancy.

I want to eliminate such tragedy in the world.

Financially, this is a film that can be made with minimum cost. Though it takes time to make it (6 months) and today most film-makers would like to spend less time in making a film.

Film No.9   DON'T WORRY LOVE

½hr. to 45min.Col.Highspeed camera. Synchronized sound.

This is a love message we send from England to all over the world and to the future.

The idea was conceived from the fact that when a star blinks, we only perceive it 2000 years after it's actually blinked. And they say that the love we feel now is the love that's been conceived by somebody 2000 years ago, or that somebody in the corner of the world is sending love vibrations just to keep us in love, etc.

The film will be 20 seconds each shot of people smiling and saying *Don't worry love*, but because the shots are done highspeed, each smile will actually be synchronized to the highspeed motion so that what you actually hear would be a strange elongated version of *Don't worry love*.

I hope this film will make the whole world a shade happier and rosier, and that our smile will encourage people of 2000 years later, just as the blinking of stars. It is actually a film that would be most effective if it's seen in our great, great grandchildren's time.

We must get a galaxy of people with strong good vibrations to smile in this film—people who represent our age.

Film No.10   SKY

It is a film about waiting.

Four people all dressed up are on a top of the hill. They are watching the sky. And waiting, and waiting.

Some small talk between the four (all improvised).

Then one suggests that he would bring something and he goes off. Remaining three talk about the one who went off.

Then another one goes off. Remaining two talk about the two who went off.

Then the third one goes off. Remaining one moves around by himself. Then goes off.

The first one comes back with incense. The second and third ones come back too. But they can't find any matches between them to light the incense.

One goes off to get matches. Another one goes off to get something. The remaining one lies down to take a nap. (Notice that the fourth one never came back)

Matches are brought back. The second one brings back a guitar. He starts to play and three of them sing. Then they decide that the singing might scare the *thing* away, so they stop singing.

(constant looking up to the sky and horizon with a telescope)

Then one suggests that somebody should bring a big ladder. There is a discussion about who should bring the ladder. They draw straws and the one who got the shortest goes off.

Then he comes back and says he needs another one to help him bring it. So finally all three of them go together.

Then the three bring back a ladder—a huge ladder. Two hold the bottom and one goes up and looks at the sky with a huge telescope.

Still nothing.

Gradually, it gets dark and they use matches to see each others' faces. It gets cold and they make fire. Also, one person gets extremely cold, so the rest of them give him all their coats.

Finally, they see the fourth guy, who was away all this time, come back.

Have you guys seen it yet?   *No, not yet.*

They are still checking the sky. Suddenly one says
Look, look!   Everybody looks.

Did you see it?   *No.*   !!!!!!!!!!!!!!!!!!!!!!!

They put out the fire they made, which was getting low anyway. And they go off with the ladder, telescope and each other.

Film No.11   PASSING
See the sky from the bottom of a very deep well. A cloud passes through slowly from left to right and disappears.

Film No.12   UP YOUR LEGS FOREVER
The camera work of the film should constantly go up, up, up non-stop. Collect 367 pairs of legs and just go up the legs (from

Frame sequences from Yoko Ono's *No. 4 (Bottoms)* (1966) and *Up Your Legs Forever* (1970, made in collaboration with John Lennon). Courtesy Lenono Photo Archive.

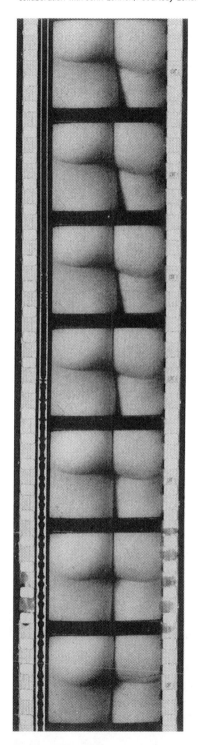 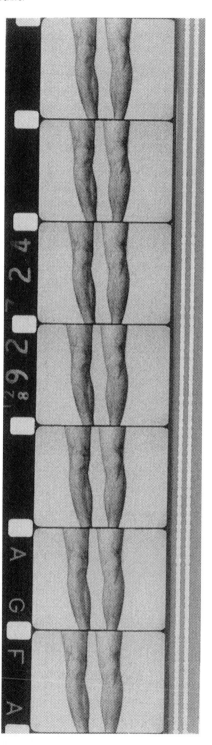

The fly explores the body in Yoko Ono's *Fly* (1970). Courtesy Lenono Photo Archive.

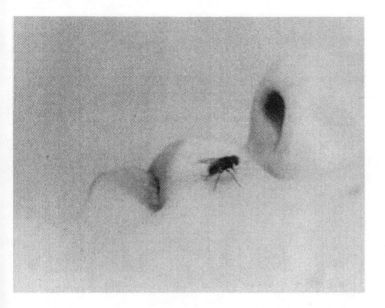

toes to the end of thighs) pair after pair and go on up until you run through the whole 367.

Film No.13   FLY

Let a fly walk on a woman's body from toe to head and fly out of the window.

Film No.13   (TRAVELOGUE)

Travelogue from a point of view of a person who could only see things in focus and close-ups. Show things in close-ups and in focus as the usual narration goes on about the things to discover and enjoy on your travel. For example, you introduce Tokyo and explain that what you see there are just knives—only because you focused in on a knife shop and *that* became Tokyo to you. On the screen, you don't see knives except a very large view of the blade or a tip of the blade without any background. You could explain how beautiful the Geisha girls are, but you only show strands of hair blowing in the wind in close-up. You talk about the mixed bath experience, and only show the steam. You talk about making love in the park and show two pieces of grass waving. You talk about the experience in a noodle shop and show a close-up of the noodles without the background so the heap of noodles would look like an abstract expressionist painting.

This travelogue can be made without leaving your apartment.

Make a travelogue of your home country that expresses your focus.

Make travelogues of different countries that express your focus.

Make a travelogue of an imaginary country.

William Greaves

When William Greaves's 1968 feature *Symbiopsychotaxiplasm: Take One* surfaced in 1991, it was a double-leveled surprise. It surprised those who assumed they were familiar with the major independent and experimental films of the sixties, and it surprised those who believed they understood Greaves's career, first, as a stage and film actor and a teacher of actors (in 1980 Greaves shared the Actors Studio's first Dusa Award with Marlon Brando, Robert De Niro, Jane Fonda, and others) and, subsequently, as a director and producer of documentary films: between 1952 and 1960 he worked on eighty films at the National Film Board of Canada; he then returned to the United States, where he has made dozens of documentaries (and several feature-length fiction films), including *The First World Festival of Negro Arts* (1966), *In the Company of Men* (1969), *Ali, the Fighter* (1971), *From These Roots* (1974), *Booker T. Washington: The Life and the Legacy* (1982), *Frederick Douglass: An American Life* (1984), *That's*

Black Entertainment (1985), and *Ida B. Wells: A Passion for Justice* (1989), to name a few. Neither Greaves's distinguished career in acting nor his prolific career as documentarian seemed to account for *Symbiopsychotaxiplasm: Take One*—and yet, as fully as any film he has made, his feature-length critique of the filmmaking process combines his interest in acting and in actors with his need to document and interpret real events.

Symbiopsychotaxiplasm: Take One was conceived as merely one part of a multipartite project ("take one" of a series of "takes") that would involve a crew filming various man-woman couples interpreting a basic scenario Greaves had devised: a painful argument in which the woman complains about the abortions her lover has pressured her to have and claims that he has been having homosexual affairs, and the man temporizes and denies.[1] Greaves was interested in the argument as, at least in part, a metaphor for the social and political struggles of the

---

1. Greaves discusses *Symbiopsychotaxiplasm: Take One* at some length in "Sunday in the Park with Bill," by Scott MacDonald, *The Independent*, vol. 15, no. 4 (May 1992): 24–29.

sixties and as a catalyst for an extended exploration of the filmmaking process itself. He arranged the shoot so that multiple cameras would be running simultaneously: while sometimes the focus would be on the actors playing their roles, at other times, the camerapeople would focus on Greaves in conference with the actors, on the various camerapeople and sound people at work, and on the larger social context that surrounded the shoot in Central Park. And Greaves had decided in advance that he would act the part of a director who is not entirely clear about where the process he has set in motion is going, and that he would, subtly but relentlessly, frustrate crew and cast until they were in a state of rebellion. For Greaves, in other words, the *Symbiopsychotaxiplasm* project was to be a metaphor for the sociopolitical experience of the sixties, a paean to rebellion against oppression—in this case, the oppression of the conventional, hierarchical power structure of director/actors/crew that had developed during the history of commercial cinema.

While the rebellion was slower and less violent than Greaves might have anticipated, it did occur. Part way through the shoot, the crew met secretly to discuss the project and filmed their discussion (they presented Greaves with the results at the conclusion of the shoot), and, ironically, when one of the actresses (Patricia Ree Gilbert) did storm away from Greaves in frustration, the crew, apparently no longer fully engaged in the process, failed to record the subsequent discussion between Gilbert and Greaves. By the conclusion of the shoot, Greaves had adequate material for at least five "takes," but no money to finance the completion of several features. In fact, it was not until 1971 that a seventy-seven-minute, 35mm blowup of *Take One* (with special split-screen effects Greaves had devised) could be struck—and even once he had a film in hand, Greaves couldn't

find a distributor willing to work with it. For all practical purposes, *Symbiopsychotaxiplasm: Take One* disappeared until 1991, when it began to resurface at museums and festivals (in the United States, the Brooklyn Museum led the way with a Greaves retrospective).

As an actor and acting teacher, Greaves has spent a good portion of his life interpreting a wide variety of scripts for both stage and screen, and in his work as documentarian he has used various types of visual text and scripted narration. Nevertheless, even for Greaves, *Symbiopsychotaxiplasm: Take One* was an unusual amalgam of the actors' interpretations of his original scenario and the spontaneous comments of cast and crew during the shooting and, from time to time, of onlookers: a group of teens watching the process, a mounted policeman wondering if Greaves has the necessary permits, and most notably a funny, eloquent, homeless alcoholic who drifts into the filming at the conclusion of *Take One*.

For *Screen Writings*, Greaves has kindly given me permission to publish the notes he made as he worked on the *Symbiopsychotaxiplasm* project, as well as an excerpt from *Take One* that begins with the passage of dialogue between Alice and Freddy that leads to Patricia Ree Gilbert's announcement to Greaves of her frustration with how the shoot is going. The excerpt includes a brief exchange with Greaves before they walk away from the cameras and mikes and then continues with a segment of the crew's secret discussion, with Gilbert and Fellows repeating their scene, with the crew in another discussion of the project (this time outdoors with Greaves), and, finally, with the homeless man's opening comment. Following the excerpt from the film are the program notes Greaves wrote for the Brooklyn Museum retrospective in 1991. The notes explain the meaning and implications of the title and describe some of the film's theoretical background.

Symbiopsychotaxiplasm: Take One
Director's Early Notes Prior to and during Production in the
Spring of 1968

The film must be simplicity itself. It should be made effortlessly, no pain no strain, no forcing symbolism, etc. All of that must be inherent in the chemical makeup of the SYMBIOPSYCHOTAXIPLASM operation. And yet the film is a series of analogies, metaphors, similes. Things standing for other things, a microcosm of the world, a fragment of the Godhead which is made up of other Godhead fragments.

It is a free-fall in space. We simply don't know where we will land with this creative undertaking. It is a study of the creative process in action. Also, the film is Jazz! It is improvisation. It is an exploration into the future of cinema art.

The film is about fire! Life Fire which is all around us. The task of our cameras is to spot and film the fire until like water hoses, they put the fire out (in a similar way, the electron microscope destroys the character of the atom it is observing!). The film is free association. The camera dashes from fire to fire.

A personal note: Refuse to give a total explanation of the film! First of all it is impossible anyway, due to its complexity. Give only as much of an explanation as will satisfy the performers and film crew. To give more will kill the truth and spontaneity of everyone.

Rumors of unrest and revolution in the crew should develop, should lead to encounters with the director.

The film is rebellion! Rebellion against traditional cinema form. The hippies on the crew are for love and rebellion, in contradistinction to the screen test characters, Alice and Freddy, who are suburbanites, caught in a life of conformity.

Part of the strength, along with the excitement and challenge of this project, is its basic conflict, which is that of identification . . . identification of the actor with the part, the characters with each other, the actors with the director, the crew with the script, with the actors, with the director etc.

What is the psychoanalytical significance of this piece? Is it a dream that has the facade of truth or truth with the facade of a dream? Is it chaos masquerading as order or order simulating chaos? The piece, i.e., this film, must be susceptible to analysis, and yet it must be as unfathomable as the cosmos.

A personal note to (myself): RE: The actors, Patricia Ree Gilbert &
Don Fellows. Call Don about the work he did at the Actors Studio, the
private moment, where he sang and played a guitar; try to get him to use
that level of vulnerability on the set!

   Shoot a scene where they do a line reading. Have them improvise
and "put clothes on" the dialogue which is naked . . . the kind of
"clothing" civilized people use to cover their psyches. Then let the
dialogue as written explode.

Other Thoughts:
   Influences, concepts and aesthetics for the film
   — Jazz
   — J. L. Moreno's psychodrama theory
   — Eisenstein film theory
   — 2nd Law of Thermodynamics
   — Arthur Bentley's "An Inquiry into Inquiries"
   — Heisenberg Theory of Uncertainty
   — Aurobindo on mysticism
   — Strasberg on acting
   — Stanislavsky on theatre and acting

   Possible Casts
   Andre Plamondon & Susan Anspach
   Bud Powell & Michel Arthur
   Patricia Ree Gilbert & Don Fellows
   Louise Archambault & Leslie Redford
   Manuel Melamed & Fay Lloyd
   Frank Baker & Audrey Heningham

A personal note to the director
   Tomorrow morning psychodrama, tomorrow afternoon.

   Let's get shots of tramps and drunks leading up to Victor.

   Is Victor the climax for the film?

   Order 30 rolls of film.

   Let's have crew meeting Friday afternoon to determine what we will
shoot on Saturday.

Random thoughts of the director in the editing room

What I have tried to make of this film:

1. A <u>conventional</u> theatrical short inside a major <u>unconventional</u>
   feature film
2. A <u>conventional</u> screen test inside a major <u>unconventional</u>
   feature film

This film will tell itself. This film is about us, about the cast,
crew and onlookers, about us all as part of nature, and nature has its
<u>own</u> story to tell. Our problem, or rather my problem, is to get out of
nature's way and let nature tell her story. That's what a good director
is—a person who gets his ego <u>out of</u> his own way, he is at best a
collaborator and servant of nature . . . but who, paradoxically,
<u>firmly</u> controls the conditions of spontaneity, theatricality and
drama on the set.

Transcript of Excerpt from *Symbiopsychotaxiplasm: Take One*

I have transcribed the following sequence as carefully as possible from a seventy-minute VHS version of the film, taped in 1991. At times during the film the actors—Patricia Ree Gilbert and Don Fellows—are filmed in close-up, so that their interchange fills the screen. In other instances, two images of the same conversation, filmed from different angles, are seen simultaneously within the frame. In still other instances, we see both actors and the crew (and director) at work. When the actors are in their roles, I identify them by their characters' names—Alice and Freddy—but when they speak about their roles or about each other, I designate them Gilbert and Fellows. In the scenes where the crew members meet to discuss the film, several people are often speaking simultaneously, with the camera moving informally from face to face. I've tried to give some sense of these overlapping conversations. From time to time, I have eliminated a distracting vocal mannerism from the transcription, though in other instances—and especially during the crew's secret meeting—I have included vocal awkwardnesses to accurately represent the viewer's experience.

The passage transcribed is continuous and occurs near the end of Symbiopsychotaxiplasm: Take One. As of 1992, however, the film remains in process: Greaves plans to revise it again, to include footage left out of earlier versions.—s.m.

Exterior Central Park. Gilbert and Fellows have just walked away across a bridge to get ready to continue their scene. Throughout the following exchange they are seen in medium shot in two separate, rectangular images within the frame, filmed with a hand-held camera from slightly different angles and distances.

Fellows: Are you rolling?

Greaves (off-camera): Yeah.

Freddy: Alice! C'mon, can't you wait . . . wait a minute, wait a minute . . .

Alice: Just leave me alone, OK? Just leave me alone!

Freddy: Well now, the least you can do is have the courtesy to tell me what's bugging you. All right? Come on.

Alice: Jesus Christ. I thought once we got married, you know, you'd change and . . . [laughs] . . .

Freddy: [mimics her laugh] You know, I really don't have any idea what you're talking about, Miss Balls.

Alice: Listen, you skinny little faggot, I am fed up, I am absolutely fed up with this shit. Half the time we go out, wherever we're going . . .

Freddy: No, no . . .

Alice: . . . you're trying to get with somebody, or on somebody—I don't know what you boys do . . .

Freddy: Give me . . . give me an example, then, all right?

Alice: You sure as hell don't do anything with me.

Freddy: No? [laughs] I what! I just want to hear it again . . .

Alice: You heard it, you heard it, you heard it, you heard it . . .

Freddy: And who stops me!

Alice: I never stop you!

Freddy: I can't even get started! You stop every . . .

Alice: That's your problem. You go see the head shrinker.

Freddy (Don Fellows) and Alice (Patricia Ree Gilbert) argue in Greaves's *Symbiopsychotaxiplasm: Take One*. Courtesy William Greaves.

Freddy: I have, haven't I?

Alice: Mmmm, three sessions . . .

Freddy: Oh no, more than that. More than you know about.

Alice: Five sessions.

Freddy: More than you know about, and all I can say is it's about time you started because you need it. Just remember, the person who says the other one is sick is always the sickest of all, baby.

Alice: Huh! You're the fag.

Freddy: I am not.

Alice: The fuck you're not!

Freddy: I'm not. That's something you keep hanging me with and I am not . . .

Alice: The hell you're not!

Freddy: I am not. You can't give me an example.

Alice: I just did!

Freddy: You said something about today. I have no idea what you are talking about.

Alice: I also talked about the first year we were married, about Chuck, Tim . . .

Freddy: I'm talking about today. Talk about today. All right, you've already talked about that . . .

Alice: Oh, oh, oh, oh, oh . . . we already talked about that. That's over with. Yesterday you were a fag, today you're not, tomorrow you're just going to fuck the little robins, or chipmunks here in the park. How about that, huh? Why don't you try a mosquito next?

Freddy: You are really sick. You are really sick.

Midway through Alice's next speech, the right-hand image-within-the-image expands and fills the frame.

Alice: You're damn right, I'm sick, I am sick of you.

Long shot of crew filming actors on bridge

Freddy: You have got to believe me . . .

Greaves: Let's kind of stop . . .

Gilbert: See, I mean this is . . .

Greaves: Now . . . now, take . . .

Gilbert: No, no, no, no, no!

Greaves: Take it easy, take it easy, take it easy . . .

Gilbert (raising her voice): Why should I take it easy! Why!

Greaves: It's going very well.

Gilbert (yelling back at Greaves as she walks away, across the bridge): It's not and you know it!

Fellows (talking quietly to a member of the crew): No, I think she's upset cause I think she was building towards the big climactic shooting or . . .

Crew Person (man, off-camera, talking quietly to viewer): Pat has just slightly flipped out. Unfortunately, both cameras ran out. They're changing magazines. Bill is on; I'm going to stay with him till I run out.

We hear crew member Maria Zeheri begin the following speech as we watch Greaves walk across the bridge following Gilbert. Then the film cuts to an interior scene of the crew meeting in the equipment room to discuss the progress of the shoot. The camera pans from one speaker to another; sometimes voices are heard off-screen; sometimes several crew members speak at once.

Maria Zeheri: Well, I was saying that in a way we are criticizing that he doesn't know at times what he's doing, but I think this is what he wants. This is what he's looking for. It's a certain experiment according to the synopsis or the idea of the film. It's a conflict between him and the actors in a way that he is doing a test screen or he's doing just one dialogue. Now he is experimenting [with] the different ways of directing this same dialogue . . .

Jonathan Gordon: But why film it?

Crew Person (off-screen): No, no, no, no . . .

Maria Zeheri: Well, because the only way he is, because the only way he is . . .

Clive Davidson: We're saying that giving them lines, you give them the lines and then each one acts it out differently. In that case, you shouldn't do that. You should give them a story and then <u>they</u> bring out the lines, something else would come out of it. Actuality is not the problem here. So what if they're running up a hill or sitting on a bench? It can be anywhere, it can be on the moon.

Jonathan Gordon: If he wanted to do this, he could do it on a stage or he could just simply do it. He's actually making a film of this, you know. It's not merely an experiment, it's an experiment that's culminating in a film. And a film not designed for Bill to keep in his basement; it's a film that's designed to play; it's a film that's designed to reveal something, to be a work of art . . .

Maria Zeheri: He first of all can do a lot of work with all this footage in the editing room, according to how the film is edited. Because it's a type of film that you can edit in three hundred different ways. Did you read the concept of it?

Jonathan Gordon: No, I didn't read the concept of it, and I don't know whether we ought to bring the concept in because Bill hasn't mentioned it . . .

Bob Rosen (off-screen): I read the concept, and the concept doesn't help you at all, not one bit . . .

Terry Filgate: The point is I don't see where there's a beginning, or a middle, or an end. I don't mean in a sort of conventional story fashion, but everything we shoot is the same: rather, let's be frank, indifferent actors. Stage actors, not film actors, which is to say it would be great on Sony videotape and you could do a critique, but I don't see where there's any build in the film at all . . .

Stevan Larner: Well, now you're getting down to the nitty-gritty . . .

Bob Rosen (off-screen): Every situation is new . . .

Stevan Larner: Not really much is happening, if you ask me . . .

Nicky Kaplan: I think there is, I think there's . . . excuse me . . .

Bob Rosen: OK, tell me, what is happening?

Nicky Kaplan: I've got to unload myself . . . I think . . . it seems to me . . . not having read Bill's concept, it seems to me that there's some exploration of the levels of reality and the supra-levels of reality. OK, so this is another level of reality that we're establishing here and it may be the biggest put-on of all time . . .

Bob Rosen: Recognizing the reality or nonreality, trying to establish that, is useless. For all anybody knows, Bill is standing right outside the door, and he's directing this whole scene. All right, it could be. Nobody knows. Maybe we're all acting, all right? Maybe we're all acting. You know? I'm acting. And that's it. Bill could have stood outside of the door and told me, "Now, Rosen, when you get in there, tell them about this when you get to a certain point." Nobody out there [in the viewing audience] knows whether we're for real . . .

Terry Filgate: Then what is being revealed?

Jonathan Gordon: My whole point is that nothing is being revealed and that's the genius of this film, if there is a genius. I think the genius of this film was that it was provided that somewhere during its filming, the crew should decide to act as an independent unit and come into a room and talk about this film and thereby possibly change the end of it, that this was planned, consciously or unconsciously, by Bill . . .

Terry Filgate: You believe in God after all!

All: [Laughter]

The actors are outdoors, repeating their scene in the park along a walkway. Several extreme long shots of the crew following the actors. Until the end of the following exchange, we see Alice and Freddy and crew members in a continuous shot.

Alice (we hear her before we see her): You have been killing my babies one right after the other and you want me to believe in you? You come in like a little Nazi storm trooper. You just don't want any responsibilities. You don't want any wife, you don't want marriage, you don't want children . . .

Freddy: Oh, that's all part of your fantasy, it's part of your fantasy . . .

Alice: The going gets a little tough, a little too tough and you run out!

Freddy: Shhhh! Shhhh!

Alice: FUCK YOU!

Freddy: If you are going to talk that way . . .

Alice: Speaking of fuck, boy, how we've been making love lately, we're never going to have any babies. Fuck you!

Freddy: That's the way you want it, that's the way you want it . . .

Freddy (Camera moves in closer as Freddy kisses Alice. She's unresponsive, and carefully wipes her lips off when he stops): Alice . . .

Exterior in the park. The crew has gathered to confront Greaves and to ask him if he knows what he's doing. They are seated on the grass in a circle.

Jonathan Gordon: This is a very strange thing because all I really know is myself and all I really know are the people I really know, and I don't know anybody here, except a few, but I really don't know them. And being forced in a way to listen to this sordid conversation . . . [speaks to a particular crew member] you haven't heard it, you haven't been here for eight days and listened to this sordid, horrible conversation, over and over and over again, with black faces, white faces, tall ones, old ones, young ones, skinny ones . . . You know? Convincing ones, unconvincing ones . . . It does funny things to you . . .

Greaves: All right, all right, all right. So what else can we do? I mean look, we've got all this equipment lying around here. Look, here's a tripod, there's two still cameras, three Eclairs; there's an Arri S; we've got three Nagras. We've got an awful lot of equipment here. It would be interesting, it really would be, Jonathan; it would be very interesting to see you surface with a better script. And there's no competitive thing . . .

Robert Rosen: What's a better script! I mean, here's a film, you know, and you're the director and . . .

William Greaves shooting *Symbiopsychotaxiplasm: Take One* (1968). Courtesy William Greaves.

Greaves: A better script as a screen test for a pair of actors.

Jonathan Gordon: The way to make the script better is to first of all drop the euphemisms: you talk real language . . .

Greaves: What euphemisms?

Jonathan Gordon: The euphemisms. Freddy says to Alice . . . Freddy has a cock, Alice has a cunt, Freddy likes or doesn't like to fuck Alice. Alice can't come, Alice has difficulty coming, Alice comes easily. Freddy stays a long time, Freddy stays a short time, Freddy stays an intermediate amount of time. Freddy really loves to fuck Alice. You know what I mean? That's the way to talk, and that's the way people can liberate themselves to talk about themselves and what they really feel . . .

Robert Rosen: You have a line in there like, "Come on, sport, give me a chance." What? Does that mean "fuck"? Is that what it means?

Jonathan Gordon: "Give me a chance!"—it doesn't mean anything. "You never let me touch you"—what does that mean? "It's unnatural"—what does that mean? "Don't you like me to eat you, Alice?"—that means something. Or, "Eat me, Freddy"—that means something. You understand? I'm serious! That is the way the script is transformed from a useless faggotry, from a little semi-annual conceit between two people, to something that never has to be repeated again.

Greaves: This sort of palace revolt which is taking place [the crew meeting with Greaves] is not dissimilar to the sort of revolution that's taking place in America today, in the sense that I represent the establishment, and I've been trying to get you to do certain things which you've become in a sense disenchanted with. You know? Now, <u>your</u> problem is to come up with creative suggestions which will make this into a better production than we now have . . .

<u>Robert Rosen</u>: I don't understand at all.

<u>Greaves</u>: It doesn't matter whether or not you understand it. The important thing is that we surface from this production experience with something that is entirely exciting and creative as a result of our collective efforts, as a result of Marsha's efforts, as a result of Audrey, and Sy Mottel; you, Jonathan; you, Bob, Roland Mitchell, Nicky, Frank Baker, Barbara Linden. . . . It's important that as a result of the totality of all of these efforts, we arrive at a creative cinema experience.

Medium shots of cast and crew who are gathered on a knoll. A derelict has drifted onto the set; he's drunk.

<u>Derelict</u> (off-screen): What is this thing? What is this thing? I spoke with you, yes, you're from Canada, right? Oh, it's a <u>movie</u>—so who's moving whom? . . .

Program Notes for *Symbiopsychotaxiplasm: Take One*

These are the program notes for the Brooklyn Museum retrospective of Greaves's films, with minor revisions made by Greaves during summer 1992. —S.M

<u>Symbios</u> = life in common; <u>Psycho</u> = mind/emotion-based activity; <u>Taxi</u> = arrangement; <u>Plasm</u> = organic and inorganic matter.

The title <u>Symbiopsychotaxiplasm: Take One</u> is derived from the term "symbiotaxiplasm," coined by the American social philosopher Arthur Bentley in his book <u>An Inquiry into Inquiries</u>. The term is an attempt to express all of the elements and aspects of the cosmos which interact, affect each other, and in which life—particularly humankind—is functionally interrelated.

I was bold enough to insert "psycho" into the middle of the term to achieve the new word "symbiopsychotaxiplasm," which, in my view, involves the first definition as well as affirms more aggressively the role that human psychology and creativity play in shaping the total environment—while at the same time, these very environmental factors continually affect and determine human psychology and creativity. Thus everything that happens in the <u>Take One</u> environment interrelates and affects the psychology of the people and, indeed, the creative process itself.

Another construct of thought in the film involves the Second Law of Thermodynamics, which asserts that energy cannot be destroyed—that it transfers from one entity within a system to another.

Analogically, we assert that same thesis for psychological and creative energy. Thus when the creative or psychological energy in front of the camera appears to decline, there is a commensurate rise in psychological and creative energy behind the camera.

When the energy before the camera rises, the energy behind it declines. It was for this reason that several cameras were strategically positioned and alerted to track—like radar—the flow of energy.

It was also interesting to note that, like the Thermodynamic Law, as it applies to physical matter, the psycho-creative society of any theatrical production is made up of a series of energy entities (artists, technicians, actors, the director, et al.) that are in a constant state of disequilibrium and their struggle to achieve artistic equilibrium is one of the foci of our film. The final equilibrium of <u>Take One</u> is achieved in the editing room, but in achieving it, a new disequilibrium—or struggle—is pursued between the film and its audiences. The audience needs to "understand" the apparent chaos of <u>Take One</u> while paradoxically confronting the fact that, like life, which is chaotic, it still has credibility.

<u>Take One</u> was also heavily influenced by jazz, which, to me as a black man, is an attempt on the part of an enchained human spirit to break free from the prison bars of mechanical tempo and to liberate itself. Analogically, traditional dramatic structure was for me a

conventional prison from which I sought to escape with the free style of the film.

Take One is also about revolution. It expresses the mood of the 1960s in America with respect to Vietnam, civil rights, suffocating morality, and traditional life-styles. The film mimics this revolt. In this case, the director is the authority under assault.

Another interesting sidelight is the fact that the script the actors enact is, on the one hand, somewhat banal; but on the other, it is transformed into something truly important and rewarding when the actors become inspired. In this sense, the text, like the film, is a kind of tour-de-force—a paradox, which is what I wanted to achieve. In the classes where I train actors, I have the actors regularly perform what I call "neutral" dialogue with changing sets of motivations. The text of the screen test is partly based on this acting exercise.

One important afterthought: another theory operating in my conceptualization of Symbiopsychotaxiplasm: Take One is that the overall aesthetics of this film are governed by the Heisenberg Theory of Uncertainty. The theory asserts that we mortals will never truly know what reality is because the means of perception (the electron microscope) bombards and dislocates the subatomic particles of the basic unit of matter—the atom—which it has under observation. In so doing, it destroys the very thing it attempts to perceive!

Once again, the camera functions, analogically speaking, in much the same way as the electron microscope: it attempts to look at moments of truth emanating from the behavior of the actor or any other on-camera subject. The very presence of the camera, invariably and progressively, lessens the incidence of spontaneous energy in the on-camera perfor-mance and behavior. This is one reason why the performance of most actors in most rehearsals of a scene is often better than the actor's filmed performance.

In Take One, the Theory of Uncertainty interacts with the Second Law of Thermodynamics, in that the camera constantly forces energy shifts away from its line of fire from behind to in front of the camera, and vice versa.

To get the full value of all this theorizing, I suggest that audiences, at first viewing, try not to analyze any of what I have said, but simply sit back, relax, enjoy and allow their minds and hearts to perceive the metaphors, paradoxes—and the chaos that is life—all of which unfolds on the screen.

Hollis Frampton

No one has made more inventive contributions to the avant-garde tradition of using text as imagery than the late Hollis Frampton did in four films: *Surface Tension* (1968), *Zorns Lemma* (1970), *Poetic Justice* (1972), and *Gloria!* (1979). Frampton's fascination with text has various roots. As a young man, he was for a time an aspiring poet who saw Ezra Pound as his master (Frampton visited Pound regularly during Pound's hospitalization in Washington, D.C.), and his love of literature persisted during his years as a visual artist. Frampton's literary urges were also expressed directly in a series of theoretical essays about photography, film, and culture collected in *Circles of Confusion* (Rochester, N.Y.: Visual Studies Workshop Press, 1983). Even when he was a prep school student at Andover, however, Frampton's interests in culture were quite catholic. He was active in the photography club and became friends with schoolmates Frank Stella and Carl Andre. As he familiarized himself with the arts

in school and subsequently in New York City, where he moved in 1958, he became increasingly aware of the incorporation of text into the histories of painting and photography, and by 1962 he was making *Word Pictures* (1962–63), a series of still photographs of words within his city environment. In 1964 he finished a now-lost film "in black and white negative, all clouds and skies that dissolved from one to another; phrases—typewritten 'poetic' phrases—were superimposed. The phrases appeared in different places in the frame."[1]

The earliest use of visual text in a Frampton film that still exists—other than the text that dedicates *Lemon* (1969) to Robert Huot—energizes the third section of *Surface Tension*, where a textual description of a film is superimposed over a single, continuous shot of a goldfish swimming inside a narrow tank set up on a beach so that, periodically, the surf sweeps around the tank. (Frampton: "The words are in the frame as the fish is in the

---

1. Frampton in *A Critical Cinema*, by Scott MacDonald (Berkeley, Los Angeles, London: University of California Press, 1988), 27.

tank; both are limited to a very shallow depth.''[2]) The description is reminiscent of classical myth and of the surrealists (slashes indicate changes in on-screen text): "FILM / A FILM / 3 PARTS / SOUND COLOR / COLOR OF / AMERICAN CIGARETTE ADS / PART 1, 20 MINUTES / PHILADELPHIA GIRL / CASTLE IN FRANCE / SWAN / HER HOSTS LEAVE / SWAN / HEXAGONAL BEDROOM / MIRROR WALLS / MIRROR CEILING / SWAN BEDROOM / SEDUCTION CULMINATES / FEATHERS, MIRRORS / FEATHERS SHATTERED MIRRORS / PART 2, 5 MINUTES / MONKEYS / JUST MONKEYS / PLAYING / PART 3, 5 MINUTES / HIPPOPOTAMI SWIMMING / CHOCOLATE WATER / THEIR RUMPS / ONLY THEIR BROWN RUMPS / I SAW IN THE SUDAN / WHEN I WAS / IN THE / GERMAN MERCHANT MARINE." Frampton provides emphasis through his timing and by having words flicker.

Insofar as text is concerned, Frampton's magnum opus—and the film that established him as a major contributor to alternative cinema—is *Zorns Lemma*. The central subject of *Zorns Lemma* is the process of intellectual development, a process in which spoken and visual words are central. Like *Surface Tension*, *Zorns Lemma* is a triptych; in each section words function differently. In all three sections a twenty-four-letter version of the Roman alphabet (*I* and *J*, *U* and *V* were treated as one letter) is the basic module. During the first section, a schoolmarmy voice reads verses from *The Bay State Primer*, Euro-America's first grammar text, in which alphabetized words are imbedded within religious teachings and moral lessons (the screen is dark). During

the long (forty-seven minutes), silent second section, Frampton introduces the alphabet in a new, more energetic timing— one letter per second—and then provides set after set of alphabetized environmental words (kinetic versions of the earlier *Word Pictures*), a phantasmagoria of language. As the viewer grows accustomed to the alphabetized words, Frampton gradually substitutes successive one-second images of an ongoing activity for each of the letters. When the final substitution is made, the second section of the film ends. During the final section of *Zorns Lemma*, viewers watch a man, a woman, and a dog walk from near the camera, down across a snowy valley and up into a distant wood, accompanied on the soundtrack by a one-word-at-a-time reading by six alternating voices of a passage from *On Light, or the Ingression of Forms*, Robert Grosseteste's eleventh-century treatise on the universe.

Each section of *Zorns Lemma* creates a metaphor for a particular period of intellectual development, especially as it is generally understood in the West. For Frampton, the acquisition of language represents the opportunity for the child to move out of cultural darkness, into the excitement of naming the world and living and working in it, and finally toward the development of a larger philosophic sense of the universe as a whole.

While *Zorns Lemma* focuses on language as the major element of intellectual development, *Poetic Justice*, the second section of the seven-part *Hapax Legomena*, explores the more particular intersection of film and literature.[3] It extends the method of the third section of *Surface Tension* into a much more filmically challenging form: instead of watching a

---

2. MacDonald, *A Critical Cinema*, 42.

3. "Hapax Legomena" are words that appear only once in a language (such as classical Greek) that is no longer spoken—and are, therefore, not definable. Frampton's use of the term as the general title for the series of films suggests the fact that the cinematic forms used in the seven works are not "definable" in terms of conventional cinematic logic.

brief text superimposed over moving imagery, the viewer must read a 240-page screenplay, one page at a time, six seconds per page, in silence. The only "motion" in the film is the direct cut from one page to the next; the pages gradually form a pile on a table, between a cup of coffee on the right and a small cactus on the left.

Poetic Justice is dense with paradox. On one level, it is a rebellion against the Hollywood "rule" that films begin with scenarios and screenplays, "poetic justice" for those who require that cinematic imagery be dependent on literature. And at the same time, it *is* a screenplay, and even more "literary" than the most literary industry film. And yet, as the viewers/readers attempt to imagine the action described in the screenplay, they are thrown into a labyrinthine set of ambiguities that, as Frampton explained, would defy any attempt to use the *Poetic Justice* screenplay as the basis for a real film:

> Realizing the scenario would destroy its crucial ambiguities. I'm not talking about the mysterious sexual identities of the three personae of the piece but also of those concerned with scale. "Outside the window is an inverted enamel saucepan"; well, where *is* that saucepan? In the space outside the window. Is it on the sill? Is it a hundred yards away? The difference between the spatial close-up and the psychological close-up is easy to sustain as a tension in language because the declarative sentence itself separates the figure from the ground. It's not so easy to sustain an ambiguity of that type in film. If you're actually photographing, you can't have "six or seven zebras." In the photograph one can always count the zebras. So, for lots of reasons the project was untenable. If anybody ever cared to do it, it might make an interesting film,

but, of course, it wouldn't be a film of mine.[4]

And there are consistent point-of-view ambiguities as well. In the opening action of the film, on page 5 of the screenplay—"MY HAND PLACES A BLACK-AND-WHITE PHOTOGRAPH OF YOUR FACE ON A TABLE"—the viewer/reader is placed in a difficult situation: is "*my* hand" to be read as the filmmaker's hand, the hand of a character other than the filmmaker-as-narrator, or—since reading the sentences identifies "my" with the viewer/reader—is it meant as the *viewer's* hand? And is *your face* the face of a second character? The viewer's face? Even the wording "*a table*" is problematic: are there other tables? Paradoxically, *Poetic Justice* creates a conceptual maze that frustrates nearly all conventional filmgoing expectations, and yet it not only is frequently amusing as well as challenging but can be understood as a poignant melodramatic narrative about the death of a relationship between lovers.

Frampton's final important work with cinematic text as image occurs in *Gloria!*, the ten-minute film in which Frampton dedicates the entirety of the thirty-six-hour *Magellan*, his final film project, to his maternal grandmother, Fanny Elizabeth Catlett Cross, whose individualistic spirit is honored in a series of computer generated texts. The fact that these texts about a woman born in 1896, at the dawn of film history, are *computer* texts is of central importance in the film's exploration of the literal and historical margins of cinema. For Frampton, the computer was ushering in a new age of image making that was rendering the traditions of cinema obsolete. The text of *Gloria!* simultaneously demonstrates Frampton's excitement about the new technology and his respect and nostalgia for the world it is bringing to a close.

4. MacDonald, *A Critical Cinema*, 64.

52

Included here is a set of previously unpublished notes Frampton wrote during the making of *Zorns Lemma*. They give a sense of the filmmaker's thinking, not only about the general structure of the film but of such particulars as his choices of ongoing activities to replace the letters during the second section of the film. The notes are preceded by the rhymes from *The New-England Primer* that are read in the opening section of the film and followed by the excerpt from Grosseteste's *On Light, or the Ingression of Forms* that is read during the final section. The *Zorns Lemma* materials are followed by the complete text of the screenplay in *Poetic Justice*.[5] Finally, the computer texts from *Gloria!* are included.

5. The text was previously published as a limited edition book by the Visual Studies Workshop in 1972.

Narration from Part I of *Zorns Lemma*

In Adam's Fall
We sinned all.

Thy Life to mend,
God's Book attend.

The Cat doth play,
And after slay.

A Dog will bite
A Thief at Night.

The Eagle's Flight
Is out of Sight.

The idle Fool
Is whipt at School.

As runs the Glass,
Man's life doth pass.

My Book and Heart
Shall never part.

Job feels the Rod,
Yet blesses God.

Proud Korah's troop
Was swallow'd up.

The Lion bold
The Lamb doth hold.

The Moon gives light
In Time of Night.

Nightingales sing
In Time of Spring.

The royal Oak, it was the Tree
That sav'd his royal Majesty.

Peter denies
His Lord, and cries.

Queen Esther comes in royal State,
To save the Jews from dismal Fate.

Rachael doth mourn
For her first born.

Samuel anoints
Whom God appoints.

Time cuts down all,
Both great and small.

Uriah's beauteous Wife
Made David seek his life.

Whales in the Sea
God's Voice obey.

Xerxes the Great did die,
And so must you and I.

Youth forward slips,
Death soonest nips.

Zaccheus, he
Did climb the Tree,
His Lord to see.

Notes on *Zorns Lemma*

The notes were originally written in long-hand, in red pen, on graph paper (the final sheet of the notes is reproduced). I have done my best to provide graphically a sense of reading the notes in longhand. I have adhered carefully to Frampton's original text, including in nearly all instances his punctuation (I did add several periods). From time to time, I use brackets to identify a person or to clarify the meaning of an abbreviation (sometimes Frampton shortened words and signaled the shortening with a slash) —S.M.

TITLE: "Zorn's Lemma" itself

I have grown accustomed to alluding to Zorn's Lemma (which is demonstrably identical with two other mysterious mathematical entities called "The Axiom of Choice" and "The Well-Ordered Principle") by one of its corollaries, viz.

["EVERY PARTIALLY ORDERED SET CONTAINS A MAXIMAL FULLY ORDERED SUBSET"]

You may multiply instances at your leisure.

For one or more things to be "ordered", they must share a perceptual (provable) element. So there are many ordered subsets within the set of all elements that make up the film, e.g. all shots containing the color red.

There is the subset of all "abstractive" elements (the words, if they are seen as merely "list-able") and the subset of all "fictive" elements (the images, if they are seen merely as deliberately "made".

But what you see (consciously) most of all is the 1-second cut, or pulse. So that what I imply, is that the maximal fully-ordered subset of all film (which this film proposes to mime) is not the "shot," but the CUT—the deliberate act of articulation.

Beyond that, there is the pulse of 24 FPS, which is truly the maximal fully-ordered subset of all films—and, obliquely, of our perceptions, since that is the threshold at which they FAIL us.

BUT:

Zorn's own Lemma was & is not, as you suggest, a "theory for describing all the possible relations within a . . . set". That is probably the whole task of mathematics at large: to describe all the possible relations among the class (or set) of "all numbers".

Zorn's Lemma is, rather, hierarchic, in that it proposes a possible meaningful "tour" of all elements within a set with regard to only one operation = discernment of their "ordering", or the relative preponderance of their shared qualities.

The German noun
"ZORN"
means RAGE, ANGER

WORDS:
The film had its beginnings in pre-occupation with tension between graphic & plastic/flat vs. illusionistic elements in same space. There were 2000+ B&W stills made in 1962/63, which I proposed to stand-animate.

In the film as it was made all word shots are hand-held & as many as possible contain movement within the frame as well. I went for maximum variety of space, surface, etc. There are conscious references to every painting, drawing & photographic style I cd/ [could] manage—though they are doubtless subtle in terms of 24 frame viewing time. There are hundreds of shots wch/ [which] refer, secretly, to characteristic postures vis-a-vis space, color, etc. within the history of film; i.e. stylistic tendencies of other directors, mostly within the narrative canon.

Naturally, I had to work with the opportunities presented to me within Manhattan.*

*Exceptions:
    FOX: Brooklyn
    EXIT
    HUMBLE: Summit & Medina Counties, Ohio
    YIELD

"THE WORD WAS MADE FLESH . . ."
John, I.

The film is a kind of long <u>dissolve</u>, not quite the way WAVELENGTH is a zoom, but nevertheless . . .

Elements of Autobiography:

a) that I received the same Judaeo-Christian upbringing as nearly everyone else in my culture: rote learning, by authority, in the dark, full of obscure threats of death, moral maxims, exotic animals anthropomorphized, tales of obtuse heroes pointing doubtfully to arcane wisdom.

b) that my adolescence & early adulthood were concerned primarily with words & verbal values. I fancied myself a poet; studied living & dead languages—hence my early contacts with, for instance, Ezra Pound.

c) that 13 years in New York saw a gradual weaning away of my conscious- ness from verbal to visual interests. I saw this as <u>both</u> expansion & shift.

d) that I began, during the making of the film, to think about leaving the city. Part III is prophetic, in that sense, by about 5 months.

e) note that the film was begun in late <u>1962</u> . . . and the growth of the work on the conceptual level quite literally mimes the shift described in c. The necessities of this film, and of others that rehearsed it, also <u>accelerated</u> the process the film simulates.

SUBCLASSES within the class of all "WORD"-images (locations of these are marked in the cutting chart.):

Reasoning: in the course of making any long, dense, & if you will "ambitious" work of art that functions within time and <u>itself requires much time to make</u>, a number of misfortunes are bound to occur. I take the <u>Divine Comedy</u> of Dante as my model, but many other works would do as well (Verbal epics make a clearer case because they share a characteristic with my film: modularity (a word = a shot). The misfortunes are:
1) metric errors. Lines that simply will not scan within the param-
    eters of the normal overall metric scheme.
2) omissions. Information necessary to intelligibility definitely
    left out.
3) errors. Mistaken words. Error of fact & syntax. Solecisms, & other
    grammatical monstrosities.
4) lapses of taste. Overt phoniness, vulgarity, archness, artiness,
    etc. wch/ [which] apparently proceed from the artist's character
    rather than his aesthetic stance. (i.e. they are not <u>tactical</u>.)
5) Faking. The use of a nominal or merely adequate locution to find
    one's way out of an uncritical mode or impasse.
6) Breaches of decorum. Wherein the artist, by design or otherwise,
    breaks the rules he has himself set up for operating upon the
    elements of the work.

Since all these misadventures were bound to occur to me in making <u>ZL</u>, I decided to incorporate them <u>deliberately</u>. Then at least I wd/ [would] know where they were. It had to be done "in code", to be sure, and one that had some relation to film as I excern [?] its tradition. This is the scheme I adopted:

1) METRIC ERRORS. All shots in the main section (your "PART II") or matrix are 24 frames long, except for 24. 12 are only 23 frames, and 12 are 25 frames. Their positions were determined by another party (My "key grip", David Hamilton) by chance operations specified by me, and he then destroyed the record of their location (without informing me.)

2) OMISSIONS. As if I had thought later of some words that shd/ [should] be in the film. e.g. DULCET, ASPIRIN, LUTE etc. These are burn-in titles, superimposed in white. Since I did not wish to break the architectural decorum at this point, they are supered on shots of Lower Manhattan buildings.

3) <u>ERRORS</u>. I decided to encipher these "as though" the cinema-tographer had used the wrong color filter. A group of black & white graphic collages were prepared and shot on color stock, on a stand; several were made through each of the additive and subtractive primaries: RED, GREEN, BLUE, CYAN, MAGENTA, YELLOW.

4) LAPSES OF TASTE. A scattered category [of] "Real" words (not flat animation material) obviously hoked up in the studio. The hand un-writing "XYLOPHONE" backwards is one example among many.

5) FAKING. A large group. Color collages pasted up from magazines, instead of being "found" in the environs. *Hommages* to many, but chiefly Rosenquist.

6) BREACHES OF DECORUM. Encoded as <u>still</u> black-and-white photographs, "flat" stuff, amid the welter of color; these are from the original 1962/63 shooting & so are the oldest material in the film. Each has a sentimental or outrageous "real" (colored) object lying on top of it (a green toothbrush on "WIG", matches on "FUCK", <u>etc</u>.)

THESE AMOUNT, ALTOGETHER, TO ABOUT 1/6 OF THE WORDS, SO THEY ARE NOT A NEGLIGIBLE GROUP. THEY BECOME MUCH MORE VISIBLE ON <u>REPEATED</u> VIEWINGS.

THEY ARE OF CONSIDERABLE IMPORTANCE TO MY OWN VIEW OF THE FILM, & REFLECT FORWARD TO THINGS NOW ONLY HALF-PLANNED.

Reproduction of page of Hollis Frampton's "Notes on *Zorns Lemma*."

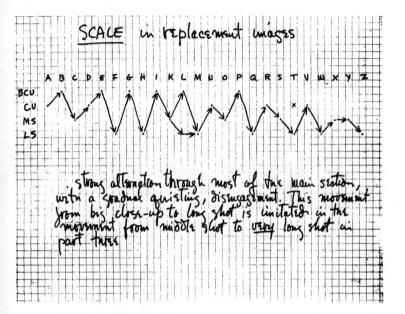

"REPLACEMENT" IMAGES

"Word-images" are all, by definition, man-made. They are entirely
un-manipulated documents (i.e. in my cinematography).

The "replacements"—"natural" images—are nearly all <u>manipulated</u>.
Exceptions: B, C, Q, S.

I made about twice as many images as I used. There is no <u>looping</u>,
i.e. all were shot in real time, and are seen in real sequence (some are
elided or elliptical).

Criteria were essentially 3:

1)   banality. Exceptions: S, C.
2)   "sculptural" as distinct from "painterly" (as in the word-
     images) work being done, i.e. the illusion of space or substance,
     consciously entered and dealt with, as against mimesis of such
     action. Exceptions: D, K.
3)   cinematic or para-cinematic reference, however oblique. To my mind
     <u>any</u> phenomenon is para-cinematic if it shares <u>one</u> element with
     cinema, e.g. modularity with respect to space or time.

Consider also the problems of alternating scale, and maintaining
the fourfold HOPI analysis: CONVERGENT VS. NON-CONVERGENT/RHYTHMIC VS.
ARHYTHMIC.

NOTES ON SPECIFIC IMAGES:
[This subtitle is circled in the original notes.]

A: turning pages. A new cycle, new day, etc. SECRET correspondence:
    the particular book is the Old French version of Antonio
    Pigafetta's diary of the voyage of Magellan, which figures in a
    future film. The pages were turned to the beat of a metronome at
    1 page/sec.

B: Frying egg. Note that you see the egg being cracked. Egg = usual
    cosmological bullshit BUT a real & vivid image. A new historical
    cycle, a new epoch → a new phoenix egg.

C: Red ibis. The only shot not made specially for ZL. Kowtow to
    exoticism a rarity, & the rarest shot in the film or 1 sec. in 3606
    [seconds].

D: Cookies. Immediate reference to flat-screen vs. illusionist space,
    via the passage from "figure" to "ground." Annette M. [theorist/
    teacher Annette Michelson] thought the woman was laying black
    stars on the table. Of course "star" means something in film
    history.

E: Split face. TALKING, silently. TWO TIMES in the same space. The
    first "person" (in fact the school-marm of part I), reciting the
    same text by halves.

F: Tree. A leap forward to PART III. A (dormant) vegetative world of
    slow rhythms. The only STATIC shot among replacements.

G: Hands washing. The first nominal "ritual". Manipulated through
    "direction" ("Now begin to rinse", etc.)

H: Walking a block. Simile for the whole film = expenditure of an
    artifact of fixed physical length. Use of telephoto lens, without
    change of focus, passes shot from deep space through flat & back to
    deep again. Giving the artifice away, at the very end. I had the
    cowboy hero who appears fm/ [from] nowhere, & then disappears,
    specifically in mind.

I: Grinding meat. Another simile = this time, the informative
    analytical process to which I subject all the material in this
    film, & to which cinematography subjects the flow of "real"
    PROCESSES. The camera is a meat grinder.

Replacement image for E, from Hollis Frampton's *Zorns Lemma* (1970): two halves of a woman's face speak at different rates. Frame enlargement by Biff Henrich. © Hollis Frampton Estate, 1985.

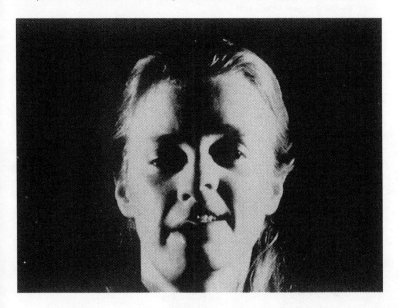

K: Painting a wall. Another simile = starting something & finishing it through human <u>work</u>. The space ends up white; the wall is the film frame.

    In the course of the shot, I repeatedly <u>breathed</u> on the lens to fog the image, which then repeatedly clears.

L: Child swinging. The early history of film <u>scale</u> within a single shot,—the passage from COGITATIVE to CONTEMPLATIVE "distance" within 1 second: Paracinematic modularity.

M: Digging a hole. Expenditure of the artifact = attrition of the artifact. One shovelfull = 1 shot.

N: Beans. The film (the frame) as a container. When it is full, ample, replete, the task is done. The beans are anonymously modular, like leader frames. If you look closely, a mirrored image (in background) of the beans <u>being</u> poured, is gradually obscured by the beans themselves.

O: Bouncing ball. Four different attempts to <u>perform</u> a modular act (in four different <u>times</u>) seen simultaneously. (<u>Every</u> pair of superimposed spaces also are presented—2 different TIMES.)

P: Hands tying shoes. A performance. 14 takes to do it in exactly TEN seconds.

The final moment of the replacement image
for H, from *Zorns Lemma*: the walking man
(David Hamilton) reappears after turning the
corner. Frame enlargement by Biff Henrich.
© Hollis Frampton Estate, 1985.

Replacement image for S, from *Zorns Lemma*: two rhinoceri. Frame enlargement by Biff Henrich. © Hollis Frampton Estate, 1985.

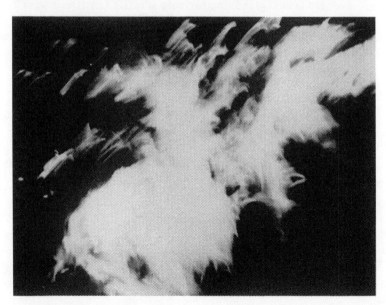

Replacement image for X, from *Zorns Lemma*: a raging fire filmed by a shaking camera. Frame enlargement by Biff Henrich. © Hollis Frampton Estate, 1985.

Q: Steam = AIR.

R: Tinkertoys. Paracinematic metaphor obvious. A childhood favorite. To make me look competent, the sequence was shot in reverse at 12 FPS. So that actually, I was taking the chain apart at a quite comfortable rate.

S: Rhinoceri: pure shock value. What other shaggy animals are up to in "our" era. An alter ego image.

T: Changing tire. A simple, convergent sculptural act involving performance values. Also hommage to Brooklyn bridge, q.v. [quod vide, i.e., which is seen] in background.

V: Peeling & eating tangerine. Another convergent & sculptural act. But note radial modular symmetry of tangerine vs. axial mod. sym. of striped background, & illusion vs. "flatness."

W: Passing side streets. Deforming the real world via cinema. An allusion (oblique) to kitsch "underground" images—I had formerly shot a Norenesque sequence [i.e., a sequence a la Andrew Noren] of endless breast-fondling for this shot (which didn't work at all).

X: FIRE: shot at 12 FPS, hand held, long telephoto, while a friend deliberately pushed me & told me jokes, to make the frames smear a la abstract expressionism.

Y: CATTAILS. N.B. [nota bene, i.e., note well] this is actually two shots alternating, one with & the other against the light. Again a figure & ground, planar vs. illusionist alternation.

Z: SEA. 12 FPS reversed. The waves are only about 6 inches high!

Narration from Part 3 of *Zorns Lemma*

I have retained Frampton's punctuation as it appears in his written notes.—S.M.

On Light, or the Ingression of Forms
by
Robert Grosseteste, Bishop of Lincoln
(as translated and edited for *Zorns Lemma*
by Hollis Frampton)

The first bodily form I judge to be Light. For Light, of itself, diffuses itself in every direction, so that a sphere of Light as great as you please is born instantly from a point of Light.

But Form cannot abandon Matter because Form is not separable and Matter cannot be emptied of Form.

Form is Light itself or the doer of its work and the bringer of dimensions into matter. But Light is of a more noble and more excellent essence than all bodily things.

Since Light, which is the first Form created in first Matter, could not abandon Matter, in the beginning of Time it drew out Matter along with itself into a mass as great as the fabric of the world.

When the first sphere has been completed in this way, it spreads out its daylight from every part of itself to the center of the whole. This daylight, in its passage, does not divide the body through which it passes, but assembles and disperses it. And this assembling which disperses proceeded in order, until the nine celestial spheres were perfected.

Matter for the four Elements was assembled within the ninth sphere, engendering daylight from itself, and assembling the Mass within itself, has brought forth Fire.

Fire engendering Light has brought forth Air.

Air engendering from itself a bodily spirit has brought forth Water and Earth.

But Earth is all the higher bodies, because the higher daylights were compressed together in the Earth; and the Light of any sphere may be drawn forth from the Earth into act and operation.

Whatever God you wish will be born of the Earth as of some Mother.

The Form and perfection of all bodies is Light. But the Light of the higher is more spiritual and simple, while the Light of the lower is more bodily and multiple.

Nor are all bodies of the same Form, though they have their origins in a simple Light; just as all Numbers are not of the same Form, though they are greater or lesser multiples of Unity.

In the highest body which is the most simple there are four things to be found, namely Form, Matter, Composition and Entirety.

Now the Form, as being most simple, has the place of Unity.

On account of the twofold power of Matter, namely its ability to receive impressions and to retain them, and also on account of Density, which has its beginnings in Matter, Matter is allotted the nature of the Number Two.

Composition makes up the Number Three, because in Composition are evident formed Matter and Material Form, and the thing about Composition which is its very own.

And that which besides these three is proper to Entirety is included under the Number Four.

When the Number One of Form and the Number Two of Matter and the Number Three of Composition and the Number Four of Entirety are added together, they make up the Number Ten. Ten is the full Number of the Universe, because every whole and perfect thing has something in itself like Form and Unity; and something like Matter and the Number Two; and something like Composition and the Number Three; and something like Entirety and the Number Four.

And it is not possible to add a fifth beyond these four.

Therefore every whole and perfect thing is a Ten.

But from this it is clear that only the five ratios found between the four numbers One, Two, Three and Four are fitted to that Harmony which makes every composition steadfast. Therefore only those five ratios exist in musical measures, in dance and rhythmic times.

Text of *Poetic Justice*

The text of the screenplay in Poetic Justice is
reproduced exactly here. The accompanying
stills of the film's first seven shots provide
some sense of the look of the film, though the
stills are photographs of pages of the Visual
Studies Workshop book, not frame enlargements (which accounts for the framing not
corresponding to the shape of a 16mm film
frame).—S.M.

The first seven pages of the screenplay in Hollis Frampton's *Poetic Justice* (1971, photographed from the Visual Studies Workshop book of the film). Courtesy Hollis Frampton Estate.

#1
TITLE:

FIRST TABLEAU

#2
(LONG SHOT)
A BLOOMING LILAC
IN EARLY LIGHT.
SCENE BRIGHTENS
SLOWLY.
(SLOW DISSOLVE TO . . .)

#3
(MIDDLE SHOT)
ROOM INTERIOR
OPEN WINDOW. A
LILAC IS SEEN
OUTSIDE.
(ZOOM IN AND
DROP TO . . .)

#4
(CLOSE-UP)
A SMALL TABLE
BELOW A WINDOW
A POTTED CACTUS
A COFFEE CUP.

#5
(CLOSE-UP)
MY HAND PLACES
A BLACK-AND-WHITE
PHOTOGRAPH OF
YOUR FACE ON
A TABLE.

#6
(CLOSE-UP)
MY HAND PLACES A
HAND-TINTED PHOTO-
GRAPH OF YOUR FACE
ON A TABLE.

#7
(CLOSE-UP)
MY HAND PLACES A
COLOR PHOTOGRAPH
OF YOUR FACE ON A
TABLE.

#8
(MIDDLE SHOT)
ROOM INTERIOR WITH
WINDOW. YOU WALK
SLOWLY THROUGH SCENE
AND EXIT.

#9
(MIDDLE SHOT)
ROOM INTERIOR
YOUR LOVER WALKS
SLOWLY THROUGH SCENE
AND EXITS.

#10
(MIDDLE SHOT)
ROOM INTERIOR. YOU
ENTER, CARRYING A
CAMERA IN ONE HAND,
WALK TO WINDOW.

#11
(CLOSE-UP)
YOUR FACE IN PROFILE,
LOOKING THROUGH
WINDOW.

#12
(MIDDLE SHOT)
A LILAC IN BLOOM.

#13
(CLOSE-UP)
A LILAC. A BLUEJAY
I ANDS.

#14
(MIDDLE SHOT)
YOU RAISE A CAMERA
TO YOUR EYE.

#15
(CLOSE-UP)
YOUR FACE IN PROFILE
SQUINTING THROUGH
A CAMERA.

#16
(BIG CLOSE-UP)
A BLUE JAY, OUT OF
FOCUS.

#17
(BIG CLOSE-UP)
YOUR HAND, FOCUSSING.

#18
(BIG CLOSE-UP)
A BLUE JAY, COMING
INTO FOCUS. IT FLIES
AWAY.

#19
(CLOSE-UP)
YOU LOWER THE CAMERA
FROM YOUR EYE.

#20
(MIDDLE SHOT)
YOU LAY A CAMERA
ON A SMALL TABLE
CAREFULLY.

#21
(CLOSE-UP)
YOUR FACE. YOU SEE
THREE PHOTOGRAPHS.

#22
(CLOSE-UP)
YOUR HANDS PICK UP
PHOTOGRAPHS AND
LEAF THROUGH THEM,
SLOWLY.

#23
(CLOSE-UP)
YOUR FACE, FROWNING.

#24
(CLOSE-UP)
YOUR HANDS LAY THREE
PHOTOGRAPHS SIDE-BY-
SIDE.

#25
(LONG SHOT)
YOU CARRY A CHAIR
TO A SMALL TABLE.

#26
(CLOSE-UP)
YOUR FEET. YOU
CLIMB ON A CHAIR.

#27
(MIDDLE SHOT)
YOU STAND ON A CHAIR
LOOKING DOWN AT
THREE PHOTOGRAPHS.

#28
(LONG SHOT)
YOU CLIMB DOWN
AND PICK UP A
PHOTOGRAPH.

#29
(CLOSE-UP)
YOUR HANDS SLOWLY
TEAR EACH PHOTOGRAPH
INTO EIGHT PIECES.

#30
(CLOSE-UP)
YOUR FACE, WATCHING
WHAT YOU DO.

#31
(CLOSE-UP)
YOUR HANDS MIX TORN
FRAGMENTS AND PUSH
THEM INTO A PILE.

#32
(LONG SHOT)
YOU STEP TO A WINDOW
AND STAND LOOKING
OUT. YOUR LOVER
ENTERS SCENE IN
FOREGROUND.

#33
(MIDDLE SHOT)
A LILAC BUSH.
A BLUE JAY LANDS.

#34
(MIDDLE SHOT)
YOUR HAND REACHING
FOR A CAMERA.

#35
(LONG SHOT)
YOUR LOVER WALKS
TOWARD YOU, REACHING
OUT.

#36
(CLOSE-UP)
YOUR FACE. YOUR
LOVER'S HANDS
BLINDFOLD YOUR EYES.
YOU SMILE.

#37
(CLOSE-UP)
YOUR HAND MOVES
AWAY FROM A CAMERA.

#38
(LONG SHOT)
YOU TURN AND
EMBRACE YOUR LOVER.

#39
(BIG CLOSE-UP)
YOU KISS.

#40
(CLOSE-UP)
A LILAC BUSH. A
BLUE JAY FLIES AWAY.

#41
(LONG SHOT)
YOU EXIT SLOWLY
CARRYING A CAMERA.
YOUR LOVER TURNS
TOWARD A WINDOW.

#42
(CLOSE-UP)
YOUR LOVER'S FACE
IN PROFILE, LOOKING
OUT.

#43
(MIDDLE SHOT)
A LILAC BUSH. YOU
WALK SLOWLY ACROSS
SCENE, TURNING TO
SMILE.

#44
(CLOSE-UP)
YOUR LOVER'S FACE
IN PROFILE, SMILING.

#45
(LONG SHOT)
YOURSELF WALKING
AWAY, ACROSS A
LAWN.
(DISSOLVE TO . . .)

#46
(LONG SHOT)
YOURSELF WALKING
AWAY INTO A
MEADOW, AT A
DISTANCE.
(DISSOLVE TO . . .)

#47
(LONG SHOT)
YOURSELF IN A
MEADOW, AT A GREAT
DISTANCE, FILMING
A HOUSE.
(DISSOLVE TO . . .)

#48
(LONG SHOT)
YOURSELF VERY FAR
AWAY, WALKING
YOU DISAPPEAR AMONG
TREES.
(DISSOLVE TO . . .)

#49
(CLOSE-UP)
YOUR LOVER'S FACE
IN PROFILE.

#50
(MIDDLE SHOT)
YOUR LOVER TURNS
FROM WINDOW.

#51
(CLOSE-UP)
YOUR LOVER'S FACE
SEEING TORN PHOTO-
GRAPHS.

#52
(CLOSE-UP)
YOUR LOVER'S HAND,
SIFTING A FEW
FRAGMENTS.
(DISSOLVE TO . . .)

#53
(CLOSE-UP)
YOUR LOVER'S HAND
LAYING FRAGMENTS
IN ORDER.
(DISSOLVE TO . . .)

#54
(CLOSE-UP)
HANDS CONTINUE
TO RECONSTRUCT
PHOTOGRAPHS.

#55
(CLOSE-UP)
YOUR LOVER'S HANDS
CLASPED.

#56
(MIDDLE SHOT)
YOUR LOVER CLIMBS
ON A CHAIR.

#57
(CLOSE-UP)
YOUR LOVER'S FACE
IN PROFILE, LOOKING
DOWN.

#58
(CLOSE-UP)
THREE PHOTOGRAPHS
SIDE BY SIDE, YOUR
FACES ARE COMPLETE
BUT FRAGMENTS ARE
INCORRECTLY SORTED.

#59
(CLOSE-UP)
YOUR LOVER'S FACE
FROWNING.

#60
(LONG SHOT)
YOUR LOVER STEPS
DOWN AND EXITS,
LEAVING PHOTOGRAPHS
ON A TABLE.

[blank page]

#61
TITLE:

SECOND TABLEAU

#62
(LONG SHOT)
HOUSE EXTERIOR WITH
OPEN WINDOW.

#63
(CLOSE-UP)
MY HAND HOLDING A
STILL PHOTOGRAPH OF
THE SAME SCENE. YOUR
LOVER STANDS IN A WINDOW.

#64
(LONG SHOT)
HOUSE EXTERIOR WITH
DOORWAY.

#65
(CLOSE-UP)
MY HAND HOLDING A
STILL PHOTOGRAPH OF
THE SAME SCENE. YOU
ARE OPENING A DOOR.

#66
(LONG SHOT)
ROOM WITH OPEN
WINDOW, SMALL TABLE,
AND CHAIR.

#67
(CLOSE-UP)
MY HAND HOLDING A
STILL PHOTOGRAPH OF
THE SAME SCENE. YOUR
LOVER STANDS ON A CHAIR.

#68
(LONG SHOT)
ROOM WITH WINDOW,
SMALL TABLE, AND
CHAIR.

#69
(CLOSE-UP)
MY HAND HOLDING A
STILL PHOTOGRAPH OF
THE SAME SCENE. YOU
ARE CARRYING AWAY A
CHAIR.

#70
(LONG SHOT)
ANOTHER ROOM. AN
EMPTY CHAIR BESIDE
A SUNLIT WINDOW.

#71
(CLOSE-UP)
MY HAND HOLDING A
STILL PHOTOGRAPH OF
THE SAME SCENE. YOUR
LOVER SITS IN A CHAIR.

#72
(LONG SHOT)
FIRST ROOM. TORN
PHOTOGRAPHS ARE ON
A TABLE.

#73
(CLOSE-UP)
MY HAND HOLDING A
STILL PHOTOGRAPH OF
THE SAME SCENE. YOU
GATHER TORN FRAGMENTS.

#74
(LONG SHOT)
SECOND ROOM. A CAT
STANDS NEAR A CHAIR.

#75
(CLOSE-UP)
MY HAND HOLDING A
STILL PHOTOGRAPH OF
THE SAME SCENE. YOUR
LOVER BENDS TO PET A
CAT.

#76
(LONG SHOT)
FIRST ROOM. FLOOR
LITTERED WITH TORN
PAPER.

#77
(CLOSE-UP)
FIRST ROOM. FLOOR
LITTERED WITH TORN
PAPER. YOU STAND
IN THE MIDST OF
TORN PHOTOGRAPHS.

#78
(LONG SHOT)
SECOND ROOM. A CAT
STANDS IN FOREGROUND.

#79
(CLOSE-UP)
SECOND ROOM. THE CAT
STANDS IN FOREGROUND.
YOUR LOVER STANDS
BESIDE A CHAIR SMILING.

#80
(LONG SHOT)
SECOND ROOM. AN
EMPTY SOFA OPPOSITE
WINDOW.

#81
(CLOSE-UP)
SECOND ROOM. AN
EMPTY SOFA OPPOSITE
THE WINDOW. YOU LIE
ON A SOFA, YOUR EYES
CLOSED.

#82
(LONG SHOT)
FIRST ROOM. FLOOR
PARTLY CLEARED OF TORN
PAPER.

#83
(CLOSE-UP)
FIRST ROOM. FLOOR
PARTLY CLEARED OF THE
PAPER. YOUR LOVER
GATHERS FRAGMENTS INTO
A PAPER BAG.

#84
(LONG SHOT)
FIRST ROOM. A PAPER
BAG IS ON THE TABLE.

#85
(CLOSE-UP)
FIRST ROOM. A PAPER
BAG IS ON THE TABLE.
YOU LOOK AT A PAPER
BAG, SMILING.

#86
(LONG SHOT)
SECOND ROOM. AN
EMPTY SOFA.

#87
(CLOSE-UP)
SECOND ROOM. THE
EMPTY SOFA. YOUR
LOVER LIES ON A SOFA,
READING.

#88
(LONG SHOT)
FIRST ROOM. A PAPER
BAG IS ON THE TABLE.

#89
(CLOSE-UP)
FIRST ROOM. A PAPER
BAG IS ON THE TABLE.
YOU STAND IN A ROOM,
HOLDING A CAMERA.

#90
(LONG SHOT)
A FLIGHT OF STAIRS,
LOOKING FORWARD.

#91
(CLOSE-UP)
A FLIGHT OF STAIRS,
LOOKING FORWARD. YOUR
LOVER CLIMBING STAIRS.

#92
(LONG SHOT)
SECOND ROOM. A
BOOK IS ON THE SOFA.

#93
(CLOSE-UP)
SECOND ROOM. A
BOOK IS ON THE SOFA.
YOU STAND NEAR A SOFA,
HOLDING A CAMERA.

#94
(LONG SHOT)
HEAD OF A FLIGHT OF
STAIRS.

#95
(CLOSE-UP)
HEAD OF A FLIGHT OF
STAIRS. YOUR LOVER
STANDS AT HEAD OF
STAIRS.

#96
(LONG SHOT)
A FLIGHT OF STAIRS,
LOOKING UPWARD.

#97
(CLOSE-UP)
A FLIGHT OF STAIRS,
LOOKING UPWARD. YOU
CLIMB.

#98
(LONG SHOT)
INTERIOR. CLOSED
DOOR.

#99
(CLOSE-UP)
INTERIOR. CLOSED
DOOR. YOUR LOVER
LEANS AGAINST A DOOR,
SMILING.

#100
(LONG SHOT)
THE HEAD OF A FLIGHT
OF STAIRS.

#101
(CLOSE-UP)
THE HEAD OF A FLIGHT
OF STAIRS. THE SAME
SCENE. YOU STAND AT
HEAD OF STAIRS, HOLDING
A CAMERA.

#102
(LONG SHOT)
A BEDROOM. VERY LARGE
BED WITH A WINDOW. ITS
FULL WIDTH AT ITS HEAD.

#103
(CLOSE-UP)
A BEDROOM. VERY LARGE
BED WITH A WINDOW. ITS
FULL WIDTH AT ITS HEAD.
YOUR LOVER STANDS NEAR A
WINDOW.

#104
(LONG SHOT)
AN OPEN BEDROOM
DOOR.

#105
(CLOSE-UP)
AN OPEN BEDROOM
DOOR. THE SAME SCENE,
YOU STAND IN A DOORWAY,
HOLDING A CAMERA.

#106
(LONG SHOT)
A BED AND A WINDOW.

#107
(CLOSE-UP)
A BED AND A WINDOW.
THE SAME SCENE. YOUR
LOVER LIES PRONE ON A
BED.

#108
(LONG SHOT)
BEDROOM DOOR,
CLOSED.

#109
(CLOSE-UP)
BEDROOM DOOR, CLOSED.
YOU STAND BY A DOOR,
SMILING.

#110
(LONG SHOT)
BED AND WINDOW.

#111
(CLOSE-UP)
BED AND WINDOW. YOUR
LOVER LIES SUPINE ON A
BED.

#112
(LONG SHOT)
AN EMPTY BEDROOM.

#113
(CLOSE-UP)
AN EMPTY BEDROOM. THE
SAME SCENE. YOU STAND
IN A ROOM, HOLDING A
CAMERA.

#114
(LONG SHOT)
AN EMPTY BEDROOM.

#115
(CLOSE-UP)
AN EMPTY BEDROOM. THE
SAME SCENE. YOUR LOVER
STANDS IN A ROOM, HOLDING
A CAMERA.

#116
(LONG SHOT)
AN EMPTY BEDROOM. THERE
IS NO CAMERA IN THE ROOM.

#117
(CLOSE-UP)
AN EMPTY BEDROOM. THERE
IS NO CAMERA IN THE ROOM.
THE SAME SCENE. YOU STAND
NAKED IN A ROOM.

#118
(LONG SHOT)
EMPTY BEDROOM. THERE IS
NO CAMERA IN THE ROOM.

#119
(CLOSE-UP)
EMPTY BEDROOM. THERE IS
NO CAMERA IN THE ROOM.
YOUR LOVER STANDS NAKED IN
A ROOM.

#120
(LONG SHOT)
EMPTY BEDROOM. THERE IS
NO CAMERA IN THE ROOM.

#121
(CLOSE-UP)
EMPTY BEDROOM. THERE IS
NO CAMERA IN THE ROOM. THE
SAME SCENE. YOU AND YOUR
LOVER EMBRACE, NAKED, IN A
ROOM.

#122
TITLE:

THIRD TABLEAU

[blank page]

#123
(MIDDLE SHOT)
BEDROOM. YOU AND YOUR
LOVER EMBRACE, NAKED
ON THE BED. OUTSIDE THE
WINDOWS ARE SPRUCES AND
JUNIPERS UNDER SNOW.
(DISSOLVE TO . . .)

#124
(MIDDLE SHOT)
BEDROOM. YOU MAKE
LOVE. OUTSIDE THE WINDOW
ARE PEACOCKS STRUTTING ON
ON A TURF GREEN.
(DISSOLVE TO . . .)

#125
(MIDDLE SHOT)
BEDROOM. LOVE MAKING.
OUTSIDE THE WINDOW ARE
MEN AND WOMEN IN
EVENING DRESS.
(DISSOLVE TO . . .)

#126
(MIDDLE SHOT)
BEDROOM. LOVE MAKING.
OUTSIDE THE WINDOW ARE
HYENAS DISPUTING A
CARCASS.
(DISSOLVE TO . . .)

#127
(MIDDLE SHOT)
BEDROOM. LOVE MAKING.
OUTSIDE THE WINDOW
ARE STRANDS AND
BLADDERS OF KELP.
(DISSOLVE TO . . .)

#128
(MIDDLE SHOT)
BEDROOM. LOVE MAKING.
OUTSIDE THE WINDOW
ARE WRESTLERS IN A
TAG MATCH.
(DISSOLVE TO . . .)

#129
(MIDDLE SHOT)
BEDROOM. LOVE MAKING.
OUTSIDE THE WINDOW
IS AN AUTOMATIC
TURRET LATHE IN
OPERATION.
(DISSOLVE TO . . .)

#130
(MIDDLE SHOT)
BEDROOM. LOVE MAKING.
OUTSIDE THE WINDOW
IS A CALM INLAND
SEA.
(DISSOLVE TO . . .)

#131
(MIDDLE SHOT)
BEDROOM. LOVE MAKING.
OUTSIDE THE WINDOW
IS A SQUADRON OF
PIPERS.
(DISSOLVE TO . . .)

#132
(MIDDLE SHOT)
BEDROOM. LOVE MAKING.
OUTSIDE THE WINDOW
ARE RINGS OF SATURN,
LOOMING.
(DISSOLVE TO . . .)

#133
(MIDDLE SHOT)
BEDROOM. LOVE MAKING.
OUTSIDE THE WINDOW
ARE LITTLE GIRLS
SKIPPING ROPE.
(DISSOLVE TO . . .)

#134
(MIDDLE SHOT)
BEDROOM. LOVE MAKING.
OUTSIDE THE WINDOW
ARE TUMBLED STACKS
OF CORDWOOD.
(DISSOLVE TO . . .)

#135
(MIDDLE SHOT)
BEDROOM. LOVE MAKING.
OUTSIDE THE WINDOW
IS A DISPLAY OF
OPHTHALMOSCOPES.
(DISSOLVE TO . . .)

#136
(MIDDLE SHOT)
BEDROOM. LOVE MAKING.
OUTSIDE THE WINDOW
IS A PARTY OF
MOUNTAINEERS.
(DISSOLVE TO . . .)

#137
(MIDDLE SHOT)
BEDROOM. LOVE MAKING.
OUTSIDE THE WINDOW
IS A PARK OF BAY
TREES.
(DISSOLVE TO . . .)

#138
(MIDDLE SHOT)
BEDROOM. LOVE MAKING.
OUTSIDE THE WINDOW
IS A SKY FULL OF
WHEELING PIGEONS.
(DISSOLVE TO . . .)

#139
(MIDDLE SHOT)
BEDROOM. LOVE MAKING.
OUTSIDE THE WINDOW
ARE TRUCK WHEELS
SPLASHING IN MUDDY
WATER.
(DISSOLVE TO . . .)

#140
(MIDDLE SHOT)
BEDROOM. LOVE MAKING.
OUTSIDE THE WINDOW
ARE THREE RED-HAIRED
WOMEN ROLLING DICE.
(DISSOLVE TO . . .)

#141
(MIDDLE SHOT)
BEDROOM. LOVE MAKING.
OUTSIDE THE WINDOW
IS A BEACHED WHALE,
GASPING.
(DISSOLVE TO . . .)

#142
(MIDDLE SHOT)
BEDROOM. LOVE MAKING.
OUTSIDE THE WINDOW
IS A DOUBLE CIRCLE OF
MONOLITHS.
(DISSOLVE TO . . .)

#143
(MIDDLE SHOT)
BEDROOM. LOVE MAKING.
OUTSIDE THE WINDOW
ARE RED AND WHITE
CORPUSCLES.
(DISSOLVE TO . . .)

#144
(MIDDLE SHOT)
BEDROOM. LOVE MAKING.
OUTSIDE THE WINDOW
IS A PROCESSION BY
TORCHLIGHT.
(DISSOLVE TO . . .)

#145
(MIDDLE SHOT)
BEDROOM. LOVE MAKING.
OUTSIDE THE WINDOW
ARE SMOKING INGOTS OF
REFINED COBALT.
(DISSOLVE TO . . .)

#146
(MIDDLE SHOT)
BEDROOM. LOVE MAKING.
OUTSIDE THE WINDOW
IS A FIELD OF DAISIES
AND MALLOWS.
(DISSOLVE TO . . .)

#147
(MIDDLE SHOT)
BEDROOM. LOVE MAKING.
OUTSIDE THE WINDOW
ARE TWO SURGEONS
AMPUTATING A LIMB.
(DISSOLVE TO . . .)

#148
(MIDDLE SHOT)
BEDROOM. LOVE MAKING.
OUTSIDE THE WINDOW
ARE WALLS AND TURRETS
OF OBSIDIAN.
(DISSOLVE TO . . .)

#149
(MIDDLE SHOT)
BEDROOM. LOVE MAKING.
OUTSIDE THE WINDOW
ARE SILVER DIRIGIBLES
TRAILING ADVERTISEMENTS.
(DISSOLVE TO . . .)

#150
(MIDDLE SHOT)
BEDROOM. LOVE MAKING.
OUTSIDE THE WINDOW
ARE PARROTFISH SCHOOLING
IN DIM LIGHT.
(DISSOLVE TO . . .)

#151
(MIDDLE SHOT)
BEDROOM. LOVE MAKING.
OUTSIDE THE WINDOW
IS A CLASSROOM FESTOONED
WITH CREPE PAPER.
(DISSOLVE TO . . .)

#152
(MIDDLE SHOT)
BEDROOM. LOVE MAKING.
OUTSIDE THE WINDOW
IS A SMALL CROWD
POINTING AT THE SKY.
(DISSOLVE TO . . .)

#153
(MIDDLE SHOT)
BEDROOM. LOVE MAKING.
OUTSIDE THE WINDOW
IS A SPINNING BRASS
ANEMOMETER.
(DISSOLVE TO . . .)

#154
(MIDDLE SHOT)
BEDROOM. LOVE MAKING.
OUTSIDE THE WINDOW
IS A PEARL NECKLACE
ON GREEN BAIZE.
(DISSOLVE TO . . .)

#155
(MIDDLE SHOT)
BEDROOM. LOVE MAKING.
OUTSIDE THE WINDOW
ARE SIX OR SEVEN
ZEBRAS, GRAZING.
(DISSOLVE TO . . .)

#156
(MIDDLE SHOT)
BEDROOM. LOVE MAKING.
OUTSIDE THE WINDOW
ARE TWO FARMERS
SCALDING A HOG.
(DISSOLVE TO . . .)

#157
(MIDDLE SHOT)
BEDROOM. LOVE MAKING.
OUTSIDE THE WINDOW
IS AN INVERTED ENAMEL
SAUCEPAN.
(DISSOLVE TO . . .)

#158
(MIDDLE SHOT)
BEDROOM. LOVE MAKING.
OUTSIDE THE WINDOW
IS A HEAP OF SPOILED
FRUIT.
(DISSOLVE TO . . .)

#159
(MIDDLE SHOT)
BEDROOM. LOVE MAKING.
OUTSIDE THE WINDOW
ARE BOLTS OF STRIPED
TWILL.
(DISSOLVE TO . . .)

#160
(MIDDLE SHOT)
BEDROOM. LOVE MAKING.
OUTSIDE THE WINDOW
IS A SEATED AUDIENCE,
APPLAUDING.
(DISSOLVE TO . . .)

#161
(MIDDLE SHOT)
BEDROOM. LOVE MAKING.
OUTSIDE THE WINDOW
ARE FERN SHOOTS.
(DISSOLVE TO . . .)

#162
(MIDDLE SHOT)
BEDROOM. LOVE MAKING.
OUTSIDE THE WINDOW
IS A CRACKED JUG
LEAKING MILK.
(DISSOLVE TO . . .)

#163
(MIDDLE SHOT)
BEDROOM. LOVE MAKING.
OUTSIDE THE WINDOW
IS A STORM ON THE RIM
OF THE SUN.
(DISSOLVE TO . . .)

#164
(MIDDLE SHOT)
BEDROOM. LOVE MAKING.
OUTSIDE THE WINDOW
IS A CONSORT OF
TROMBONISTS.
(DISSOLVE TO . . .)

#165
(MIDDLE SHOT)
BEDROOM. LOVE MAKING.
OUTSIDE THE WINDOW
ARE CRYSTALS OF PURE
NICOTINE.
(DISSOLVE TO . . .)

#166
(MIDDLE SHOT)
BEDROOM. LOVE MAKING.
OUTSIDE THE WINDOW
IS THE STATUE OF LIBERTY.
(DISSOLVE TO . . .)

#167
(MIDDLE SHOT)
BEDROOM. LOVE MAKING.
OUTSIDE THE WINDOW
ARE LAVENDER SEA
ANEMONES.
(DISSOLVE TO . . .)

#168
(MIDDLE SHOT)
BEDROOM. LOVE MAKING.
OUTSIDE THE WINDOW
ARE KNIVES AND BRIGHT
AXES.
(DISSOLVE TO . . .)

#169
(MIDDLE SHOT)
BEDROOM. LOVE MAKING.
OUTSIDE THE WINDOW
IS A CHILD LICKING A
SPOON.
(DISSOLVE TO . . .)

#170
(MIDDLE SHOT)
BEDROOM. LOVE MAKING.
OUTSIDE THE WINDOW
IS A FRIGATE ADVANCING
UNDER SAIL.
(DISSOLVE TO . . .)

#171
(MIDDLE SHOT)
BEDROOM. LOVE MAKING.
OUTSIDE THE WINDOW
IS A CLUTTER OF NUDE
PLASTER MANNEQUINS.
(DISSOLVE TO . . .)

#172
(MIDDLE SHOT)
BEDROOM. LOVE MAKING.
OUTSIDE THE WINDOW
ARE FEATHERS AND BLOODY
TRACKS.
(DISSOLVE TO . . .)

#173
(MIDDLE SHOT)
BEDROOM. LOVE MAKING.
OUTSIDE THE WINDOW
IS A BLUE ARC STRUCK
BETWEEN ELECTRODES.
(DISSOLVE TO . . .)

#174
(MIDDLE SHOT)
BEDROOM. LOVE MAKING.
OUTSIDE THE WINDOW
ARE STALAGMITES OF
TINTED PARAFFIN.
(DISSOLVE TO . . .)

#175
(MIDDLE SHOT)
BEDROOM. LOVE MAKING.
OUTSIDE THE WINDOW
ARE GRIZZLED DROVERS
HERDING SHEEP.
(DISSOLVE TO . . .)

#176
(MIDDLE SHOT)
BEDROOM. LOVE MAKING.
OUTSIDE THE WINDOW
ARE EGGS HATCHING BABY
TURTLES.
(DISSOLVE TO . . .)

#177
(MIDDLE SHOT)
BEDROOM. LOVE MAKING.
OUTSIDE THE WINDOW
IS A GREAT SUSPENSION
BRIDGE, FORESHORTENED.
(DISSOLVE TO . . .)

#178
(MIDDLE SHOT)
BEDROOM. LOVE MAKING.
OUTSIDE THE WINDOW
IS AN ENORMOUS
HEXAGONAL MIRROR.
(DISSOLVE TO . . .)

#179
(MIDDLE SHOT)
BEDROOM. LOVE MAKING.
OUTSIDE THE WINDOW
I AM AIMING A CAMERA.

#180
(MIDDLE SHOT)
BEDROOM. YOU AND YOUR
LOVER SLEEP. OUTSIDE
THE WINDOW IS A LILAC
IN BLOOM.

#181
TITLE:

FOURTH TABLEAU

[blank page]

#182
(LONG SHOT)
FIRST ROOM. SMALL
TABLE BY OPEN WINDOW.

#183
(CLOSE-UP)
TABLE TOP. MY HAND PLACES
A STACK OF PHOTOGRAPHS
UPON A TABLE.

#184
(MIDDLE SHOT)
OPEN WINDOW AND
TABLE TOP. A STACK
OF PHOTOGRAPHS.

#185
(LONG SHOT)
SAME SCENE. YOU ENTER
WITH YOUR LOVER AND
WALK TO A TABLE.

#186
(CLOSE-UP)
YOUR HANDS LIFT A
STACK OF PHOTOGRAPHS.

#187
(CLOSE-UP)
YOUR LOVER'S FACE,
SMILING.

#188
(CLOSE-UP)
YOUR HANDS, WINDING
A CAMERA.

#189
(CLOSE-UP)
YOUR LOVER'S HANDS
SHUFFLING A STACK OF
PHOTOGRAPHS.

#190
(CLOSE-UP)
YOUR FACE, SMILING.

#191
(LONG SHOT)
YOUR LOVER FACES YOU
ACROSS A SMALL TABLE.

#192
(MIDDLE SHOT)
YOU RAISE A CAMERA
TO FILM YOUR LOVER'S
FACE.

#193
(MIDDLE SHOT)
A PHOTOGRAPH IS RAISED
TO HIDE YOUR LOVER'S
FACE.

#194
(CLOSE-UP)
YOUR LOVER'S HAND IS
HOLDING A STILL PHOTO-
GRAPH OF YOURSELVES,
MAKING LOVE.

#195
(CLOSE-UP)
YOUR LOVER'S HAND IS
HOLDING A STILL PHOTO-
GRAPH OF YOUR LOVER,
EMBRACED BY A STRANGER.

#196
(CLOSE-UP)
YOUR LOVER'S HAND IS
HOLDING A STILL PHOTO-
GRAPH OF YOURSELF,
EMBRACED BY A STRANGER.

#197
(CLOSE-UP)
YOUR LOVER'S HAND IS
HOLDING A STILL PHOTO-
GRAPH OF YOUR LOVER,
ASTRIDE A MARE.

#198
(CLOSE-UP)
YOUR LOVER'S HAND IS
HOLDING A STILL PHOTO-
GRAPH OF YOURSELF, ASTRIDE
A MARE.

#199
(CLOSE-UP)
YOUR LOVER'S HAND IS
HOLDING A STILL PHOTO-
GRAPH OF YOUR LOVER
POSED BESIDE A MONUMENT.

#200
(CLOSE-UP)
YOUR LOVER'S HAND IS
HOLDING A STILL PHOTO-
GRAPH OF YOURSELF, POSED
BESIDE A MONUMENT.

#201
(CLOSE-UP)
YOUR LOVER'S HAND IS
HOLDING A STILL PHOTO-
GRAPH OF YOUR LOVER,
STRIKING A MATCH.

#202
(CLOSE-UP)
YOUR LOVER'S HAND IS
HOLDING A STILL PHOTO-
GRAPH OF YOURSELF,
STRIKING A MATCH.

#203
(CLOSE-UP)
YOUR LOVER'S HAND IS
HOLDING A STILL PHOTO-
GRAPH OF YOUR LOVER,
DIVING IN CLEAR WATER.

#204
(CLOSE-UP)
YOUR LOVER'S HAND IS
HOLDING A STILL PHOTO-
GRAPH OF YOURSELF,
DIVING IN CLEAR WATER.

#205
(CLOSE-UP)
YOUR LOVER'S HAND IS
HOLDING A STILL PHOTO-
GRAPH OF YOUR LOVER,
SIPPING WINE.

#206
(CLOSE-UP)
YOUR LOVER'S HAND IS
HOLDING A STILL PHOTO-
GRAPH OF YOURSELF,
SIPPING WINE.

#207
(CLOSE-UP)
YOUR LOVER'S HAND IS
HOLDING A STILL PHOTO-
GRAPH OF YOUR LOVER,
FALLING FROM A HEIGHT.

#208
(CLOSE-UP)
YOUR LOVER'S HAND IS
HOLDING A STILL PHOTO-
GRAPH OF YOURSELF,
FALLING FROM A HEIGHT.

#209
(CLOSE-UP)
YOUR LOVER'S HAND IS
HOLDING A STILL PHOTO-
GRAPH OF YOUR LOVER,
LYING IN A HAMMOCK.

#210
(CLOSE-UP)
YOUR LOVER'S HAND IS
HOLDING A STILL PHOTO-
GRAPH OF YOURSELF,
LYING IN A HAMMOCK.

#211
(CLOSE-UP)
YOUR LOVER'S HAND IS
HOLDING A STILL PHOTO-
GRAPH OF YOUR LOVER,
BEFORE A COURT OF LAW.

#212
(CLOSE-UP)
YOUR LOVER'S HAND IS
HOLDING A STILL PHOTO-
GRAPH OF YOURSELF,
BEFORE A COURT OF LAW.

#213
(CLOSE-UP)
YOUR LOVER'S HAND IS
HOLDING A STILL PHOTO-
GRAPH OF YOUR LOVER,
BATHING.

#214
(CLOSE-UP)
YOUR LOVER'S HAND IS
HOLDING A STILL PHOTO-
GRAPH OF YOURSELF,
BATHING.

#215
(CLOSE-UP)
YOUR LOVER'S HAND IS
HOLDING A STILL PHOTO-
GRAPH OF YOUR LOVER,
TATTOOED WITH ANIMAL
DESIGNS.

#216
(CLOSE-UP)
YOUR LOVER'S HAND IS
HOLDING A STILL PHOTO-
GRAPH OF YOURSELF,
TATTOOED WITH ANIMAL
DESIGNS.

#217
(CLOSE-UP)
YOUR LOVER'S HAND IS
HOLDING A STILL PHOTO-
GRAPH OF YOUR LOVER,
IN A GROVE OF LARCHES.

#218
(CLOSE-UP)
YOUR LOVER'S HAND IS
HOLDING A STILL PHOTO-
GRAPH OF YOURSELF,
MENACED BY AN EAGLE.

#219
(CLOSE-UP)
YOUR LOVER'S HAND IS
HOLDING A STILL PHOTO-
GRAPH OF YOUR LOVER,
AS A YOUNG CHILD.

#222
(CLOSE-UP)
YOUR LOVER'S HAND IS
HOLDING A STILL PHOTO-
GRAPH OF YOURSELF, AS
A YOUNG CHILD.

#223
(CLOSE-UP)
YOUR LOVER'S HAND IS
HOLDING A STILL PHOTO-
GRAPH OF YOUR LOVER,
SPATTERED WITH PAINT.

#224
(CLOSE-UP)
YOUR LOVER'S HAND IS
HOLDING A STILL PHOTO-
GRAPH OF YOURSELF,
SPATTERED WITH PAINT.

#225
(CLOSE-UP)
YOUR LOVER'S HAND IS
HOLDING A STILL PHOTO-
GRAPH OF YOUR LOVER,
LEADING A HOUND.

#226
(CLOSE-UP)
YOUR LOVER'S HAND IS
HOLDING A STILL PHOTO-
GRAPH OF YOURSELF,
LEADING A HOUND.

#227
(CLOSE-UP)
YOUR LOVER'S HAND IS
HOLDING A STILL PHOTO-
GRAPH OF YOUR LOVER,
LIT BY FLARES.

#228
(CLOSE-UP)
YOUR LOVER'S HAND IS
HOLDING A STILL PHOTO-
GRAPH OF YOURSELF,
LIT BY FLARES.

#230
(CLOSE-UP)
YOUR LOVER'S HAND IS
HOLDING A STILL PHOTO-
GRAPH OF YOURSELF,
DANCING ALONE.

#232
(CLOSE-UP)
YOUR LOVER'S HAND IS
HOLDING A STILL PHOTO-
GRAPH OF YOURSELF,
DRESSED IN YOUR LOVER'S
CLOTHES.

#234
(CLOSE-UP)
YOUR LOVER'S HAND IS
HOLDING A STILL PHOTO-
GRAPH OF YOURSELF, ASLEEP.

#236
(CLOSE-UP)
YOUR LOVER'S HAND IS
HOLDING A STILL PHOTO-
GRAPH OF MYSELF, FILMING
YOU AND YOUR LOVER.

#238
(CLOSE-UP)
YOUR LOVER'S HAND IS
HOLDING A STILL PHOTO-
GRAPH OF MYSELF,
FILMING THESE PAGES.

#240
(CLOSE-UP)
MY HAND COVERS A
STILL PHOTOGRAPH OF
MY OWN FACE.

#229
(CLOSE-UP)
YOUR LOVER'S HAND IS
HOLDING A STILL PHOTO-
GRAPH OF YOUR LOVER,
DANCING ALONE.

#231
(CLOSE-UP)
YOUR LOVER'S HAND IS
HOLDING A STILL PHOTO-
GRAPH OF YOUR LOVER,
DRESSED IN YOUR CLOTHES.

#233
(CLOSE-UP)
YOUR LOVER'S HAND IS
HOLDING A STILL PHOTO-
GRAPH OF YOUR LOVER,
ASLEEP.

#235
(CLOSE-UP)
YOUR LOVER'S HAND IS
HOLDING A STILL PHOTO-
GRAPH OF YOURSELF, YOUR
LOVER AND ME ENJOYING A
PICNIC ON THE GRASS.

#236
(CLOSE-UP)
YOUR LOVER'S HAND IS
HOLDING A STILL PHOTO-
GRAPH OF MY HAND,
WRITING THIS TEXT.

#239
(CLOSE-UP)
YOUR LOVER'S HAND IS
HOLDING A STILL PHOTO-
GRAPH OF MY OWN FACE.

[Blank page for five seconds. Then,
after a flash, we see #240 again, with a
rubber glove lying on top.]

The final image of Frampton's *Poetic Justice*. Frame enlargement by Biff Henrich. © Hollis Frampton Estate, 1985.

Text of *Gloria!*

In Gloria! the sixteen propositions are pre-
sented in green computer letters on a black
background. I assume the bracketed letters
after the propositions are a ranking of how
fully Frampton believes the propositions,
from [A], a proposition that seems surely true,
to [Y], a proposition that seems almost cer-
tainly untrue—as he suggests, somewhat
ambiguously, in the note that precedes the
propositions. The final text, Frampton's ded-
ication of Magellan ("this work"), is in white
computer letters on black background (as
presented in the accompanying still).—S.M.

The propositions are offered numerically, in the order in which they presented themselves to me; and also alphabetically, according to the present state of my belief.

1. That we belonged to the same kinship group, sharing a tie of blood. [A]
2. That others belonged to the same kinship group and partook of that tie. [Y]
3. That she kept pigs in the house, but never more than one at a time. Each such pig wore a green baize tinker's cap. [A]
4. That she convinced me, gradually, that the first person singular pronoun was, after all, grammatically feasible. [E]
5. That she was obese. [C]
6. That she taught me to read. [A]
7. That she read to me, when I was three years old, and for purposes of her own, William Shakespeare's "The Tempest." She admonished me for liking Caliban best. [B]
8. That she gave me her teeth, when she had them pulled, to play with. [A]
9. That she was nine times brought to bed with child, and for the last time in her fifty-fifth year, bearing on that occasion stillborn twin sons. No male child was born alive, but four daughters survive. [B]
10. That my mother, her eldest daughter, was born in her sixteenth year. [D]
11. That she was married on Christmas Day, 1909, a few weeks after her 13th birthday. [A]
12. That her connoisseurship of the erotic in the vegetable kingdom was unerring. [A]
13. That she was a native of Tyler County, West Virginia, who never knew the exact year of her own birth till she was past sixty. [A]
14. That I deliberately perpetuate her speech, but have only fragmentary recollection of her pronunciation. [H]
15. That she remembered, to the last, a tune played at her wedding party by two young Irish coalminers who had brought guitar and pipes. She said it sounded like quacking ducks; she thought it was called "Lady Bonapart." [A]
16. That her last request was for a bushel basket full of empty quart measures. [C]

The final computer text in Hollis Frampton's *Gloria!* (1979): Frampton dedicates *Magellan* to his maternal grandmother. Frame enlargement by Biff Henrich. © Hollis Frampton Estate, 1985.

This work, in its entirety, is given in loving memory of Fanny Elizabeth Catlett Cross, my maternal grandmother, who was born on November 6, 1896 and died on November 24, 1973.

Laura Mulvey/Peter Wollen

Few people have had as much impact on recent independent cinema as Laura Mulvey and Peter Wollen, first, in their influential theoretical writings, and subsequently, in the films they've made together, the most important of which has been *Riddles of the Sphinx* (1977). Indeed, *Riddles* was an attempt to demonstrate and extend ideas explored in his "The Two Avant-Gardes" and her "Visual Pleasure and Narrative Cinema."[1] Wollen had defined two general arenas of avant-garde film: roughly, an aesthetic avant-garde that had developed from the fine arts and was connected with the cooperative movement (that is, cooperative distribution: Film-makers' Cooperative in New York, Canyon Cinema in San Francisco, the London Film-makers' Cooperative . . .) and a political avant-garde, with roots in the post-Revolutionary Soviet cinema and modern instances in Jean-Luc Godard, Miklos Jansco, and the Jean-Marie Straub and Daniele Huil-

let collaborations. For Wollen, a mid-seventies concern was to bring these two traditions of critique together to make a more powerful impact on conventional, commercial cinema. Mulvey's "Visual Pleasure and Narrative Cinema" explored what has come to be known as the "male gaze." Using an approach informed by Lacanian neo-Freudianism, Mulvey explored the way in which conventional narrative film exploits the male pleasure in looking at women by offering up erotic imagery of women to the implicitly male-gendered spectator in the audience and to males within the film with whom viewers are directorially encouraged to identify. For Mulvey, the goal was to interrupt this pleasure by restructuring the experience of film narrative.

In *Riddles of the Sphinx*, Mulvey and Wollen developed a structure so unusual and complex that they felt obliged to present an outline to the viewer at the outset. On one hand, the structure re-

---

1. "The Two Avant-Gardes" is available in Wollen's *Readings and Writings* (London: Verso Press, 1982); "Visual Pleasure and Narrative Cinema," in *Visual and Other Pleasures* (Bloomington/Indianapolis: Indiana University Press, 1989).

flects the insights of "The Two Avant-Gardes." A narrative generally reminiscent of the experimental narratives of Godard, Jansco, and Straub-Huillet is played out in "Louise's story told in thirteen shots." It is framed by six shorter passages—three before, three after—that are reminiscent of particular strands of the aesthetic avant-garde: Part 3, "Stones," for example, recalls Ken Jacobs's *Tom, Tom, the Piper's Son* (1971). At the same time, *Riddles of the Sphinx* reflects the thinking of "Visual Pleasure and Narrative Cinema." The film presents women not as erotic objects of the "gaze," but as people involved in the labor of child care and in a struggle for philosophical and political self-determination. "Louise's story" is told in 360-degree circular pans—the opposite of the phallic centering of the camera in conventional cinema; and the seven sections of the film and the thirteen shots of Louise's story are arranged so that individual sections mirror each other (Part 1 mirrors Part 7, Part 2 mirrors Part 6, shot 13 of Louise's story mirrors shot 1 . . .) around the pivotal seventh shot of "Louise's story"—a reference to the "mirror phase" of a child's development as described by Lacan.

In terms of its use of text, *Riddles* critiques the conventional functioning of text in industry cinema in several ways. The general subject matter of the screenplay—child care, women dealing with the difficulties of service occupations, and so on—and the straightforward unromantic, nonerotic dramatization of Louise's experiences are nearly inversions of conventional film melodrama, and continually reveal the limitations of what commercial cinema markets as reality. *Riddles* also includes texts that are experimental in ways reminiscent of previous avant-garde films. Throughout "Louise's story told in thirteen shots," individual shots are preceded and followed by intertitles reminiscent of Jonas

Mekas's use of intertitles in sound films where they "don't belong." Unlike Mekas's intertitles, however, Mulvey/Wollen's are incomplete (the first is "Perhaps Louise is too close to her child. How much longer can she reject the outside world, other people, other demands. Her husband often"), though they effectively supplement the narrative unfolding in the visuals, while challenging the viewer to imagine the text that might continue on from the interruptions. There are also the texts about the history of the Egyptian and Greek sphinxes we see Laura Mulvey reading in Part 2 (and listening to on a tape recorder in Part 6); three suggestive poetic narrations that accompany shots 1, 2, and 3 of "Louise's Story"; the excerpt from Mary Kelly's *Post Partum Document* included on the sound track of the film Louise's husband is making in shot 11; and two dreams, one spoken by Louise's friend Maxine in shot 12, the other narrated by the "Voice Off" (from the point of view of Louise's daughter at some point in the future) in shot 13. *Riddles of the Sphinx* provides a veritable catalogue of the cinematic potentials of text not conventionally exploited in the commercial cinema.

The complete text of *Riddles* follows, precisely as it was originally published in *Screen* in 1977. The abbreviations ECU and VO mean Extreme Close-Up and Voice Off, respectively. Mulvey/Wollen use "Figure 1," "Figure 2," etc. to refer to the printed titles of the seven sections of the film.

Script of *Riddles of the Sphinx*

The Mulvey/Wollen script not only includes what is said by characters and by the Voice Off narrator and what is presented by the various visual texts (the opening Gertrude Stein quote, the outline of the film, the intertitles presented before the shots of "Louise's story told in thirteen shots") but also provides descriptions of each shot (in italics) and precise information about the timing of each passage (in brackets). I have also included the footnotes supplied by Mulvey/Wollen for the original publication and their end credits. —S.M.

Two layers of text in the first section, "Opening Pages," of Laura Mulvey and Peter Wollen's *Riddles of the Sphinx* (1977). Frame enlargement by Francene Keery. Courtesy Laura Mulvey/ Peter Wollen.

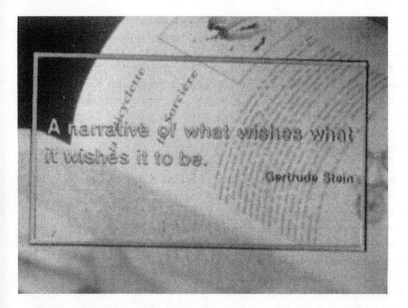

1 Opening pages

[1′ 05″]*Turning over the pages of* Midi-Minuit Fantastique, *beginning with a heading* 'Le Mythe de la femme' *and stopping at a photo-montage of Greta Garbo as the Sphinx. ECU. Meanwhile titles in superimposition:*

Riddles of the Sphinx

A narrative of what wishes what it wishes it to be—Gertrude Stein[1]

1   Opening pages
2   Laura speaking
3   Stones
4   Louise's story told in thirteen shots
5   Acrobats
6   Laura listening
7   Puzzle ending

Figure 1

2 Laura speaking

[05″] *Title: Figure 2*
[3′ 31″] *Speech introducing the Sphinx as Voice Off, delivered to camera by Laura*

---

*Shot timings are in minutes and seconds throughout.

[1]G Stein: 'Regular regularly in narrative' in *How to Write*.

Mulvey, intercut with images of the Sphinx. The sequence opens with a shot of a Greek vase; then there is a very brief shot of Laura seated in front of a table on which there are a microphone, two books, a child's mug and a pencil sharpener in the form of a small globe; then there is a shot of another vase and a return to the set-up of Laura speaking. The alternation continues with, successively: detail from Gustave Moreau's 'Oedipus and the Sphinx'/Laura/Garbo as Sphinx/Laura/profile shot of the Egyptian Sphinx/Laura/full face shot of the Sphinx/Laura/zoom-in onto the mouth of the Sphinx/Laura again. The shots of Laura become longer as the sequence proceeds.

LAURA: When we were planning the central section of this film, about a mother and child, we decided to use the voice of the Sphinx as an imaginary narrator—because the Sphinx represents, not the voice of truth, not an answering voice, but its opposite: a questioning voice, a voice asking a riddle. The Oedipus myth associates the voice of the Sphinx with motherhood as mystery and with resistance to patriarchy.

In some ways the Sphinx is the forgotten character in the story of Oedipus. Everybody knows that Oedipus killed his father and married his mother, but the part played by the Sphinx is often overlooked. Oedipus set off for Thebes, turning away from Corinth, where he'd been brought up by foster parents. The Sphinx sat perched on a cliff or pillar outside the city gates; she asked every man who went past a riddle. If they couldn't answer she devoured them. Then she stopped Oedipus when he went past and when he answered her correctly, she threw herself down from the pillar and killed herself.

The myth of the Sphinx took on new life after Napoleon's campaigns in Egypt, when the Great Sphinx at Gizeh was disclosed once again to Western eyes. The Egyptian Sphinx is male, but on its blank face, resonant with mystery and with death, the spectator could project the image of the Greek Sphinx. Once again the Sphinx could enter popular mythology, in the image of male fears and male fantasies, the cannibalistic mother, part bestial, part angelic, indecipherable.

Oedipus is different from other Greek heroes in that he defeated the monster, not by strength or by bravery, but simply by intelligence. In his answer to the riddle, Oedipus restored the generations to their proper order, but by doing so he fell into a further trap. In his own life he disordered them once more by marrying his own mother. It's almost as if Oedipus stands for the conscious mind and the Sphinx for the unconscious. The riddle confuses and disorders logical categories and the monster is a hybrid of human, animal and bird. But reading between the lines the myth confirms women's sense of exclusion and suppression. The Sphinx is outside the city gates, she challenges the culture of the city, with its order of kinship and its order of knowledge, a culture and a political system which assign women a subordinate place.

To the patriarchy, the Sphinx as woman is a threat and a riddle, but women within patriarchy are faced with a never-ending series of threats and riddles—

dilemmas which are hard for women to solve, because the culture within which they must think is not theirs. We live in a society ruled by the father, in which the place of the mother is suppressed. Motherhood and how to live it, or not to live it, lies at the roots of the dilemma. And meanwhile the Sphinx can only speak with a voice apart, a voice off.

3 Stones
[05"] *Title: Figure 3*
[7' 14"] *Montage sequence of found footage of the Egyptian Sphinx, refilmed through a number of generations with the aid of a motion-analyser projector, using zooms, step motion, slow and reverse motion, freeze frames, and extreme close-up (concentrating on the Sphinx's mouth) eventually showing film grain. Music.*

4 Louise's story told in thirteen shots
(Each shot is a 360° pan. Music, voice off and synch dialogue as specified. Intertitles.)

[05"] *Title: Figure 4*

(1)
[12"] *Intertitle:* Perhaps Louise is too close to her child. How much longer can she reject the outside world, other people, other demands. Her husband often

[6' 09"] *Louise's kitchen. Louise prepares scrambled egg for her two-year-old daughter, Anna. The shot ends when her husband, Chris, comes home. Tight framing at work-surface height. Music, VO.*

Voice Off:
Time to get ready. Time to come in.
Things to forget. Things to lose.
Meal time. Story time.

Desultory. Peremptory.
Keeping going. Keeping looking.
Reading like a book. Relief.
Things to cook.

Keeping in the background.
Fish-slice. Domestic labour.

Disheartened. Burdened.
Keeping calm. Keeping clean.

Final moment of the opening 360-degree pan in "Louise's story told in thirteen shots," from Mulvey and Wollen's *Riddles of the Sphinx*: the husband (and the world of words he represents) intrudes into the endless round of Louise's life with daughter Anna. Frame enlargement by Francene Keery. Courtesy Laura Mulvey/Peter Wollen.

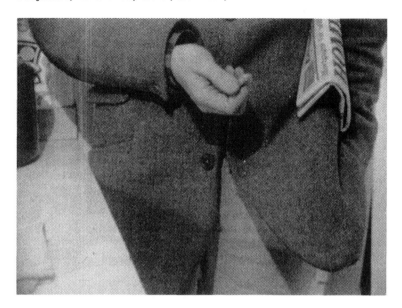

Fitting like a glove. Remorse.
Things to mend.

Losing touch with reality.
Dish-cloth. Narcissistic love.

Idolise. Tranquillise.
Losing count. Losing control.
Shaking like a leaf. Release.
Things to say.

No time to make amends. No time for tea.
Time to worry. No time to hold.
Things to hold. Things past.
Meal time. Story time.

Keeping going. Keeping looking.
Reading like a book.
Things to forget. Things to lose.
No time lost.
Story time.

(2)
[12"] *Intertitle:* bedtime, she likes to stay in Anna's room, waiting for her to fall asleep and tidying away the traces of the day. She still seems to need

[3′ 42″] *Anna's bedroom. Louise tidies up while Anna goes to sleep in her cot. Tight framing at cot height. Music, VO.*

Voice Off:
Distressed. Strained.

Nesting. In the nest. Comfort. Effort.
At the breast. At rest.
Resting.

Take leave. Take moss. Be close.
Be clasped and cleft. Be close.

Nesting. Acquiesced. Memory. Mystery.
Dispossessed. Depressed.
Trusting.

Make cross. Make grieve. Morose.
Subject to conquest. Object to incest.

Nesting. From the nest. Blood. Brood.
From the breast. Caressed.
Hurting.

Bleeding. It was obvious.
It was as obvious as it was oblivious.
Brooding. It was plain. Be close.
It was as plain as it was pain.

Make love. Make grieve. Marries.
Mother's and another's. Mysteries.

Nesting.

If only I hadn't minded, I used to say, but I did mind very much. I minded more than very much. I minded more than I could ever have dared. Mind the door. Mind the glass. Mind the fire. Mind the child. I never minded the warmth. I minded the need. It was needed to have minded, I used to say, but was it needed to have minded more than very much? More than I could ever have dared?

(3)

[12″] *Intertitle:* cannot make her see reason and get out more into the world, Chris feels he must leave the house himself. It was her idea to live in

[3′ 48″] *Hall with front door. Chris puts his belongings in the back of his car, seen through the windows, and leaves home, watched by Louise and Anna. Medium framing. Music, with VO giving way to synch dialogue as Chris leaves.*

Voice Off:
Transformed, I would confide.
I could have cried. I could have died.
Transformed, to cold from warmth.

The warmth.
It pacified and purified.
The warmth was far within. Hidden within.
The warmth was deep and far within.
The cold.

In labour. In hiding.
In the storm. Sheltered. Nurtured.

The warmth.
It was inside. It was in hiding.
The warmth was far within. Hidden within.
The warmth was in the centre. In the calm.
The cold.

Underneath. Beneath.
Beneath the quilt. Mothering. Covering.

The warmth.
The cold conceded nothing.
Whoever, frozen, pleaded, it conceded nothing.
The warmth consoled. The warmth was needed.
The cold.

Transformed. Preoccupied.
I could have cried. It never died.
In repose. From warmth to cold.
Frozen. Controlled.
Preoccupied.

CHRIS (*standing in doorway*): There's nothing much more to say really is there? . . . said it all. . . . Look, you've got my number haven't you? At Keith's. Just ring me if there's anything. All right. Bye Anna.

(4)
[12″] *Intertitle:* had to get a job after all and find day care for Anna. At the nursery she meets Maxine who makes the parting easier. Louise is grateful for

[1′ 42″] *Day-care nursery. Louise brings Anna to the nursery, on her way to work, and leaves her with Maxine. Framing to show Louise fully for the first time. Synch sound. General chatter and noise. Dialogue at end.*

LOUISE: I'll have to go now. I've got to go to work. I'll see you later. I'll collect you after tea. Goodbye. Goodbye my love.
MAXINE: Don't worry. We'll look after her.

(5)
[12″] *Intertitle:* at the switchboard. She is not allowed to make outgoing calls, but feels she has to talk to Maxine. It is hard to concentrate when she is

[4′ 55″] *Switchboard. Louise and other women at work as telephonists. Louise calls Maxine, cutting off another caller. Wide framing. Synch sound. General chatter and noise. Louise on telephone.*

LOUISE: Ah, Maxine. Good. Is Anna alright? Ah, that's a relief. I knew she'd be alright with you once I'd gone. That's why I'm ringing. I don't think I'll be able to. No. It's not that really, it's just. . . . I can't talk now. I'll tell you when I come and collect Anna. We'll arrange something else perhaps. I must go now, OK?
   I'm sorry. Did I cut you off? I'm sorry. Can I reconnect you? What number did you want? I'm very sorry.

(6)
[12″] *Intertitle:* wants women to work, even needs them to, but denies them facilities and often seems almost to be punishing them for leaving their proper place

[3′ 22″] *Canteen. Louise talks to other women in the canteen about the need she feels for a day-care nursery at work. Wide framing. Synch sound.*

LYN: . . . you do have to think about it, it costs a lot of money doesn't it?
LOUISE: Well, what happened to you then?
LYN: Well, you know I have to take my Ellie to the child minder's, well, this morning she was ill, she couldn't cope, so I had to go right across the other side of London. The child minder's got a friend, you know, and she helped her out—I mean I had to go right down Holloway Road—it cost me twice as much as usual.
LOUISE: They ought to have a nursery here, the company ought to provide one.

Louise has lunch with her co-workers in shot 6 of "Louise's story told in thirteen shots," from Mulvey and Wollen's *Riddles of the Sphinx*. Frame enlargement by Francene Keery. Courtesy Laura Mulvey/Peter Wollen.

LYN: Well, they should really, I mean. It would make my life a bit easier if they did.

ANOTHER VOICE: I'm not sure. I don't really like the idea of my kids here where I work. I like to think of work a bit separate from the house.

CAROL: Louise, who'll foot the bill for this sort of thing then?

LOUISE: Well they're rich enough. Just a job isn't it? Look how many mothers there are here. They've all got young children. They've all got problems about leaving them. I know I have. I hate leaving mine. Can't keep my mind on my work.

CAROL: Well, you are the worrying type.

LOUISE: Well, it's not that, is it? If you've got to take your child to the nursery before you get to work no wonder you're in a flap when you get here.

ANOTHER VOICE: What was all that about?

MARY: About nurseries, I think.

ANOTHER VOICE: What, is she worried about her kid?

MARY: Yeah, she doesn't like leaving her, you know. Coming in, leaving her somewhere else. She's only been here a little while but she's talking about all sorts of problems. She's right though. We ought to have a nursery here. Yeah, we've got a Personnel Manager, give him something to do.

ANOTHER VOICE: Probably only take it off the wages anyway.

MARY: Oh, no, not if the Union's involved. Someone should find out what they could do about it really. I think Louise should. I mean, it was her idea in the first place.

ANOTHER VOICE: Yeah, I suppose it depends how many people there are who've got kids and need . . .

MARY: Yeah, I think the important thing to do is to find out how many kids are involved and, like, the ages as well and then take it to the Union and see if they can do anything about it with the management.

(7)
[12"] *Intertitle*: Maxine has arranged, so that she can find out more about the Union attitude to their day-care campaign. On the way to the meeting, they stop

[2' 14"] *Roundabout. Louise and Maxine, in the nursery van, stop at a roundabout to drop off a package on their way to a meeting. Louise asks another woman with them about the Union attitude to day care at work. Exterior, wide framing, camera travels 360° round roundabout as well as 360° pan.*
Synch sound from inside van.

LOUISE: He should be here by now. A little boy with fair hair.
MAXINE: I think he's got to come across the footbridge.
WOMAN TRADE UNIONIST: What were you asking about your little girl?
LOUISE: Well, at the moment she's in a community nursery, where Maxine works, but I was wondering if it would be better to have the nursery at work. Have the Unions thought about that?
WOMAN: Not much really. You're lucky to get any sort of day care, let alone the one that suits you best.
MAXINE (*to child*): Hello! Give this to your mother and say thanks for waiting.
Camera starts tracking
CHILD: Bye!
MAXINE: Local authorities are cutting back on nursery education anyway, aren't they?
WOMAN: Yes, that's right. It may stimulate the women to demand more for themselves though.
LOUISE: Have the Unions ever done anything at all about day care?
Van heard to start up
WOMAN: They haven't done very much. The TUC is in favour of free state nursery care for any parent who wants it. But we're a long way from that.
Van enters frame left
LOUISE: I was wondering whether . . .
WOMAN: There are some nurseries in the textile industry and the Unions do negotiate about child care there, but that's an industry that really depends on women's labour. Unless there's organised action around it, the Union wouldn't have any reason to take it up, it's like most things.
MAXINE: We have to do something first if we want the Unions to take it up.
LOUISE: How can you make people see the connection between better wages and providing day care?
WOMAN: Well, trade unionism isn't just a question of wages struggle. It's about work conditions too, it has to be.
LOUISE: In that case, might the Unions get involved in running nurseries?

WOMAN: They might. All sorts of questions come up with workplace nurseries.
Van exits from frame
      Should the mothers be allowed to visit during the day? Should the creche
stay open to let women shop before they collect their children? Some Unions
want the employers to pay for company nurseries, but have the nurseries run
by Unions and parents together.
Track ends. Pan continues for a while

(8)
[12"] *Intertitle:* her friendship with Maxine has intervened. This affects her attitude to
a lot of things, including shopping, after all another form of women's

[3' 41"] *Indoor shopping centre. Louise, with Anna, and Maxine are part of the crowd
in the shopping centre. Wide framing. Music, synch sound.*

(9)
[12"] *Intertitle:* mistakes, so the Union won't take up her case. Although she hopes to
keep the campaign going from outside, she can't help worrying

[4' 15"] *Playground. Louise takes Anna to a playground in the park, having lost her
job. Exterior, wide framing. Music, VO.*

    Voice Off: Questions arose which seemed to form a linked ring, each raising the
    next until they led the argument back to its original point of departure.

    Should women demand special working conditions for mothers? Can a
    child-care campaign attack anything fundamental to women's oppression?
    Should women's struggle be concentrated on economic issues? Is domestic
    labour productive? Is the division of labour the root of the problem? Is
    exploitation outside the home better than oppression within it? Should women
    organise themselves separately from men? Could there be a social revolution
    in which women do not play the leading role? How does women's struggle
    relate to class struggle? Is patriarchy the main enemy for women? Does the
    oppression of women work on the unconscious as well as on the conscious?
    What would the politics of the unconscious be like? How necessary is being-
    a-mother to women, in reality or imagination? Is the family an obstacle to the
    liberation of women? Is the family needed to maintain sexual difference? What
    other forms of child care might there be? Are campaigns about child care a
    priority for women now? Question after question arose, revolving in her mind
    without reaching any clear conclusion. They led both out into society and back
    into her own memory. Future and past seemed to be locked together. She felt a
    gathering of strength but no certainty of success.

Louise (Dinah Stabb) and Maxine (Merdelle Jordine) look at old photographs in shot 10 of "Louise's story told in thirteen shots." By permission of the British Film Institute.

(10)

[12″] *Intertitle:* no longer needs to keep Anna to herself. But by sending Anna to stay with her own mother, Louise has brought herself back into her own past. They

[3′ 47″] *Louise's mother's garden. Louise and Maxine visit Louise's mother, who is looking after Anna and pottering around the garden. Towards the end of the shot, Louise stands and watches her daughter and mother as they throw sticks onto the bonfire.*
Exterior, medium framing.
Music, synch sound.
General chatter and noise.

> GRANDMOTHER (*when audible*): Let's go in the garden and have a nice time in the garden. Oh, look, they're looking at photos. You go and look at those while I go and see to the bonfire . . .
>   . . . We don't want green tomatoes, do we? No, we want lovely red ones . . .
> There we are, all lovely and blazing. I like a lovely blaze . . .

(11)

[12″] *Intertitle:* both go to visit Chris at work. He is editing a film he thinks will interest them and Louise wants to tell him that she has finally reached

[7′ 05″] *Chris's editing room. Chris shows Louise and Maxine film and tapes he has been working on, about a woman artist (Mary Kelly) and her work (Post-Partum Document, ICA 1976). Louise tells him she has decided to sell the house and stay with Maxine. Tight framing, anti-clockwise pan, starting and finishing on white screen; room in darkness for second half of shot, showing images on two Steenbecks and video monitor.*

Synch sound dialogue and voice of Mary Kelly reading diaries and documents over film and tape.

CHRIS: Do you mind, I've just got to get this film ready. Won't be a moment, okay?

MAXINE: Okay.

LOUISE: Right.

MAXINE: Hey, Louise, I've got something to show you. Have you got a mirror?

LOUISE: Here.

MAXINE (*holding mirror to packet of Camels*): See—look. It should be in mirror writing.

LOUISE: It is.

MAXINE: Now, look.

LOUISE: It's not in mirror writing. How does it work?

MAXINE: Magic. No, seriously, it's the cellophane. It acts as a special kind of filter. Puts the letters back to front again so they appear the right way round.

LOUISE: Do you know, I think camels are my favourite animals. I like the way that camel's much bigger than that pyramid. The way the desert just stretches out to the horizon. I think it's their shape—all lumpy and baggy, hanging over a ramshackle old skeleton.

CHRIS: Okay, I think I'm ready. Shall we start?

LOUISE: By the way, Chris, there's something I wanted to say to you. I've decided, I want to sell the house.

CHRIS: Umm, okay, if that's what you want . . .

LOUISE: Yes.

CHRIS: What about the market though? It's a bad time to sell, isn't it?

LOUISE: It's a good time for me to sell. I've decided I want to be rid of it.

CHRIS: You won't get much money for anywhere else, you know. Once we've sold the mortgage.

LOUISE: I don't think I want anywhere else. I'm going to be staying with Maxine.

MAXINE: She'll be much nearer and you'll be able to see Anna more.

LOUISE: Yes, Anna's older. She doesn't need me all the time now.

CHRIS: You mean you don't need her.

LOUISE: Well, anyway that's what we've decided, haven't we?

CHRIS: Right. Shall we start?

MAXINE: Is it work by a woman artist?

CHRIS: Yes, that's right. It's about her child and herself as the mother. I've got some film, got some video tape as well. I'll put the lights out.

VOICE OF SOUNDMAN: Mary Kelly—retaping.

VOICE OF MARY KELLY: The diaries in this document are based on recorded conversations between mother and child (that is, myself and my son) at the crucial moment of his entry into nursery school. The conversations took place at weekly intervals between September 7th and November 26th 1975. They came to a 'natural' end with his/my adjustment to school. There also occurs at this moment a kind of 'splitting' of the dyadic mother/child unit which is evident in my references, in the diaries, to the father's presence and in my son's use of pronouns (significantly 'I') in his conversations and of implied diagrams (for example, concentric markings and circles) in his 'drawings'. The marking process is regulated by the nursery routine, so that almost daily finished 'works' are presented by the children to their mothers. Consequently, these markings become the logical terrain on which to map out the 'signification' of the maternal discourse.

September 27th. I was shocked to find that he was crying when I picked him up from the nursery. I didn't think about coming early and he saw the others leave. Now he's very suspicious when I take him. I can't forgive myself for that because I should have known, although, I thought that, I was so convinced that he was different, that he is very sociable. The second day he actually screamed when I left. The teachers made me leave. I was shocked because Ray was not upset by it at all although I couldn't take him again that week. I had Sally take him the first three days and Ray took him the rest of the week. I suppose it's kind of lack of boundary definition.

October 11th. I was distressed all this week by his apparent anxiety over going back to the nursery and I felt a bit guilty about being away teaching every day till Wednesday. He had tantrums which freaked Sally out. Thursday was the first day that I saw him and it bothered me as well.
VOICE AND CLAPPERBOARD: Roll 34—Take 1.
VOICE OF MARY KELLY: October 24th. I was amazed that he actually said, I like school this week. At least that's sorted out but why doesn't he get over this tonsilitis? He had to go to the doctor again this week. It was a very unsatisfactory checkup, it took about one minute. It just makes me feel more responsible for him when other people don't show concern for him, but I guess I'm just as bad. I forgot to give him his medicine.

Weaning from the dyad. For both the mother and the child, the crucial moment of 'weaning' is constituted by the intervention of a 'third term' (that is, the father), thus consolidating the oedipal triad and undermining the Imaginary dyad which determined the inter-subjectivity of the pre-oedipal instance. This intervention situates the Imaginary 'third term' of the primordial triangle (that is, the child as phallus) and the paternal 'image' of the mirror phase within the dominance of the Symbolic structure through the Word of the father. That is, the mother's words referring to the authority of the 'father', to which the real father may or may not conform.

(12)
[12″] Intertitle: as in dreams but takes the form of masquerade, locked into a world of images where each needs to feel sheltered within another's gaze to find

[10′ 08″] *Maxine's room. Louise reads a transcript of a dream back to Maxine, who is making up at a dressing table. The room is full of mirrors.*
Medium framing, but space fragmented by reflections and reflections within reflections. Towards the end of the shot camera and cinematographer are visible in one of the mirrors.
Music, synch sound.

LOUISE: What does it mean? I can't understand most of it.

MAXINE: Pieces of thoughts I put into words. Pieces of words which seemed to mean something and I wanted to remember.

LOUISE: What about this? What does this mean? 'They make a groove or a pattern into which or upon which other patterns fit or are placed unfitted and are cut by circumstances to fit.'[2]

MAXINE: I don't know. It must be something I copied out of a book.

LOUISE: I see what it is. She felt she had been living in a fairy tale, the oldest fairy tale that we still know, from the Valley of the Nile. It matched with something she remembered very clearly from her childhood.

MAXINE: Yes, I remember now—it's about how she went out with her mother and her little brother and how her mother laughed at them when they said they weren't going home. Her mother just turned and went round the corner.

LOUISE: Do you know, I remember almost the same thing. I remember sitting on the kerb and refusing to move. There must have been something I wanted and my mother wouldn't give it to me, and a little group of people gathered round.

MAXINE: It's like when you go to a demonstration. There's a ring of people standing looking at you and you don't know whose side they're on.

LOUISE: You feel very defiant and eventful.

What about this—when was this? 'I was on a boat, sitting on a stool in front of the mast, eating a pear which had been cut very carefully into slices. It was a large boat, some kind of naval vessel, because it had large guns and sailors wearing helmets with plumes. They must have been soldiers, a whole regiment of them. I was afraid of the soldiers. It seemed to me that they were finding fault with me. I think it was because they wanted to weigh anchor. So I went down to my cabin and looked at myself in the looking glass. Only instead of myself I saw my father carrying a saucepan. He said he had come for the wool-combing. There was going to be some kind of festival where the sheep were going to be sheared and the wool combed by women. The sheep were held down by straps. Then my father blew on a bugle and the soldiers with plumes on their helmets all came in. My father ordered me to begin combing the wool. I said, "I can't, I'm dead beat." He said that I must, or I would infect everybody at the festival with some kind of disease, or rather all the men at the festival. They all began to show horrible symptoms. They were growing gills and their entrails were

---

[2]'H D' [pen name of Hilda Dolittle]: *Tribute to Freud.*

falling out. I was very frightened, and picked up the comb which had a number of notches cut in it. My father began to coax me to begin combing but I was not able to. Then I noticed that standing behind my father was another man, who seemed to be lame, and perhaps some kind of priest. He asked me whether I was an oyster woman. Everybody was excited by this question, which they seemed to think was very shrewd, but I did not know what to reply. I ran to my father and seized the saucepan which he had been holding in his hand. It was full of jewels, which had a rind on them. When I began to shell them all the men began to grind their teeth but I carried on peeling the rind. Inside there were hundreds of tiny caraway seeds. When I looked up I saw that the lame man was wearing a feathered headdress, like an Indian Chief. I suddenly realised that all this time I had been wearing a veil. I tore it off and threw the caraway seeds at the lame man, dressed like an Indian Chief. He became all distorted and disappeared. Only my father was left. I felt very perplexed. Then he said, "You must receive communion at Easter." I realised that it was Ash Wednesday and I thought that I must be my mother, although I knew she was dead. I had a feeling of jubilation and in a very loud voice I ordered that all my father's property should be sold by auction. All the women threw away their combs and shouted, "Bravo! Well done!" They unstrapped all the sheep and knocked the helmets and military caps off the soldiers. I don't remember much more except that I was dancing on the deck of the ship, in front of a sheet of canvas or sailcloth.

Camera and camerawoman visible in frame

'There were colours and banners, and when I looked at the sea it seemed to be made of silk.' What does that mean I wonder.

MAXINE: I don't know exactly. That's why I wrote it. I hoped I'd understand it more. It has the texture of meaning.

(13)

[12″] *Intertitle:* detour through these texts, entombed now in glass, whose enigmatic script reminds her of a forgotten history and the power of a different language.

[6′ 36″] *British Museum Egyptian Room. Louise and Anna, surrounded by mummified bodies and sarcophagi, puzzle over hieroglyphs. Wide framing.*
Music, VO.

Voice Off: She remembered reading somewhere a passage from a book which she could no longer trace, words which had struck her at the time and which she now tried to reconstruct. 'Inscribed on the lid of the box were the words: "Anatomy Is No Longer Destiny" and inside, when she opened it, she found the figure of the Greek sphinx with full breasts and feathery wings. She lifted it up out of the box to look at it more closely. As she did so, it seemed to her that its lips moved and it spoke a few phrases in a language which she could not understand, except for three words which were repeated several times:

"Capital", "Delay" and "Body". She replaced it in the box and closed the lid. She could feel her heart beat.

The rhythm of the sentences was not quite right and she felt sure there was some particular she had forgotten. She tried to imagine the scene as the writer might have. Would the box have been padded with cushioning, a quilted material, folds of velvet, black or red, buttoned or embroidered? What would the pattern of the embroidery be? She imagined an intricate web of curved forms, intertwined knots, like the tendrils and fronds in the marsh where, according to Bachofen, the first matriarchy arose, or the curls of pubic hair from which, according to Freud, women wove the first veil.

What kind of material was the Sphinx carved from? Soft like wax or hard like agate? Ancient like amber or modern like bakelite? Were the feathers real, rippling under her heedful touch like the overlapping waves? Whatever it was she'd forgotten, it was surely something central, more weighty, not some detail of design or manufacture. Could she have known the name of the language which the Sphinx spoke? The more she tried to remember, the more she found her mind wandering, mislaying the thread of logical reconstruction and returning to images from her own childhood.

She remembered how, when she had been very small, her mother had lifted her up to carry her on her hip and how she had hovered round her cot while she fell asleep. She remembered her feeling of triumph when her father left the house and the sudden presentiment of separation which followed. There was the time when she had opened a drawer with a little key and found a piece of coral and a badge which had gone darkish green. And she remembered one morning coming into her mother's room and finding her mother's friend sleeping next to her mother, and she suddenly understood something she realised her mother had tried to explain and she felt a surge of panic, as if she'd been left behind and lost. She thought her mother would be angry, but she smiled, and, when she got out of bed, she noticed the shapes of the arch of her foot and her heel and the back of her calf.

She had been drawing acrobats, trajectories of the body and displays of skill and balance. She saw them no longer as pioneers of the ideal, but as bodies at work, expending their labour power upon its own material. She was fascinated by the gap between the feeling of bodily exertion and the task of drawing and writing, gestures which consumed themselves in their own product, giving a false sense of effortlessness which no acrobat could hope to approach.

'"Capital", "Delay" and "Body". She replaced it in the box and closed the lid. She could feel her heart beat. She felt giddy with success, as though, after labouring daily to prevent a relapse into her pristine humanity, she had finally got what she wanted. She shuddered. Suddenly she heard a voice, very quiet, coming from the box, the voice of the Sphinx, growing louder, until she could hear it clearly, compellingly, and she knew that it had never ever been entirely silent and that she had heard it before, all her life, since she first understood that she was a girl!'

The voice was so familiar yet so fatally easy to forget. She smiled and, in her mind, she flung herself through the air.

Paula Melbourne does rope act in "Acrobats," the fifth section of *Riddles of the Sphinx*. By permission of the British Film Institute.

5 Acrobats
[05"] *Title: Figure* 5
[6' 44"] *Montage and superimposition sequence of women acrobats—rope act, floor act and juggler. Shot in black and white but central section optically printed with two colours in series. Music.*

6 Laura listening
[05"] *Title: Figure* 6
[2' 52"] *Laura Mulvey listens to tape of herself rehearsing her introduction and of the Sphinx as Voice Off. Camera set-up as in Section 2.*

> LAURA (*on tape*): '. . . into a social hieroglyphic. Later on, we try to decipher the hieroglyphic, to get behind the secret. . . .'[3]
>
> 'To the patriarchy, the Sphinx, as woman, is a riddle and a threat. But women, who live under patriarchy. . . .'
>
> 'To the patriarchy, the Sphinx as woman is a riddle and a threat. But women within patriarchy are faced by a never-ending series of threats and riddles— dilemmas which are hard for women to solve, because the culture within which they must think is not theirs. We live in a society ruled by the father, in which the place of the mother is suppressed. Motherhood and how to live it, or not to

---

[3]K Marx: *Capital*, Vol 1, Ch 1.

live it, lies at the root of the dilemma. And meanwhile the voice of the Sphinx is a voice apart, a voice off.'

Voice Off (*on tape*): 'I was looking at an island in the glass. It was an island of comfort in a sea of blood. It was lonely on the island. I held tight. It was night and, in the night, I felt the past. Each drop was red. Blood flows thicker than milk, doesn't it? Blood shows on silk, doesn't it? It goes quicker. Spilt. No use trying. No use replying. Spilt. It goes stickier. The wind blew along the surface of the sea. It bled and bled. The island was an echo of the past. It was an island of comfort, which faded as it glinted in the glass.'

7 Puzzle ending

[05"] *Title: Figure 7*

[3' 00"] *ECU. Getting first one and then another ball of mercury to centre of maze puzzle; maze violently shaken. Cut to black.*

[1' 45"] *Credit Titles. Music.*

Total running time: 90' 45".

Main Credits

Script and direction—Laura Mulvey and Peter Wollen. *Cinematography*—Diane Tammes, assisted by Jane Jackson and Steve Shaw. *Editing*—Carola Klein and Larry Sider. *Sound*—Larry Sider. *Music*—Mike Ratledge. *Cast*—Dinah Stabb (*Louise*), Merdelle Jordine (*Maxine*), Rhiannon Tise (*Anna*), Clive Merrison (*Chris*); Marie Green (*Acrobat*), Paula Melbourne (*Rope Act*), Crissie Trigger (*Juggler*); Mary Maddox (*Voice Off*), Mary Kelly, Laura Mulvey. *Production*—British Film Institute.

16 mm, Colour. Shot on location in London, August–October 1976. Budget, £19,300.

This script © Laura Mulvey and Peter Wollen 1977. Materials from *Post-Partum Document* by kind permission of Mary Kelly.

James Benning

By the time James Benning wrote "New York 1980," the screenplay for what would become *Him and Me* (1982), he had established himself as a Midwestern talent whose films combined explorations of the mechanical/chemical/perceptual bases of the cinematic apparatus characteristic of late sixties and early seventies structural film and experiments in narrative inspired by Godard, Rainer, Frampton, and others who were becoming increasingly influential by the mid-seventies. In the films that brought him to prominence—*8 1/2 × 11* (1974) and *11 × 14* (1976)—Benning developed unusual plots: the earlier film intercuts between two entirely distinct narrative actions that intersect a single time, in the most marginal way, in the final shot of the film; the later film develops a set of plots and characters that seem to unravel as the film develops: no significant intersections occur between the various plots and, indeed, even the characters' identities seem to undergo impossible transformations (in at least one case a character from one plot is seen in the clothing of a character from another plot). These nar-ratives use formal devices familiar from structural film—long continuous shots, self-reflexive explorations of composition, perspective, color—and they are distinguished by Benning's sense of his native Midwestern landscape: he often composes images so as to combine physical terrain and natural process with billboards and other commercial signs displaying photographic imagery and printed texts that provide wry commentary on the scene.

During the late seventies, Benning's films began to be more openly personal and to develop narrative structures that, if not more conventional than those of the earlier films, were somewhat more conventionally engaging. *Grand Opera* (1978) combined the formal approaches characteristic of earlier films (including the earlier films' uses of commercial text) with an interest in the landscape of Oklahoma, where Benning was teaching, and with a variety of cine-performances and motifs based on Benning's personal and artistic history. In one instance, Benning provides a 360-degree pan beginning from the front of every house he had ever lived

Hank Aaron baseball card and text from James Benning's *American Dreams* (1984).
Courtesy James Benning.

in, accompanied by music from the particular years when he lived in each house—the place and date are superimposed over each pan—and by brief stories of events that happened in the various places, read by a woman (he would develop a similar sequence for *Him and Me*). A set of four homages to filmmakers Hollis Frampton, George Landow, Michael Snow, and Yvonne Rainer becomes a motif during the film: each homage makes particular reference to the inventive uses of text by these filmmakers, by means of textual superimposition. Benning's interest in Frampton in particular seems evident in still another motif: Benning's review of the history of the mathematical concept of pi. In one instance, he presents a street scene in a long continuous shot; a light sign on top of a building prints out the digits of pi to 607 places. And there are a number of less elaborate filmic experiments dispersed throughout the film, including a sound-image passage in which a text about the proper care of the U.S. flag is divided between image and sound track so that the viewer must reconstruct the text by an act of the imag-

ination (a version of this passage, titled "Respect your flag," is included here).

"New York 1980" (and the resulting *Him and Me*) has much in common with *Grand Opera*, but the two projects are also distinct in important ways. For one thing, the location is very different and reflects Benning's attempt to come to grips with New York City, where he moved in 1980. The screenplay and film are much involved with the sights of New York—the skyline, Brooklyn Bridge—and with the Downtown New York milieu of the mid-seventies: with what was then called "new wave" or "punk" music and design, with gay life and erotic freedom in general. The new project also develops a narrative that, while inventive and unusual, is ultimately more personally engaging than his earlier narratives, largely because, for the first time, Benning uses dialogue. The earlier films were scored; "New York 1980" was Benning's first real screenplay. Like much of *Grand Opera*, "New York 1980" is directly based on incidents from Benning's life, but in this case, the focus is on a specific traumatic incident (to reveal the nature of the incident here will detract from the reader's pleasure in "New York 1980"). And, as was true of the 360-degree pan section of *Grand Opera,* Benning transposes his experience into the experience of a female character, a strategy that reflects the effect of feminism, and feminist film, on him: while attempting to deal filmically with his own experience, he attempts to see things from a woman's point of view.[1]

I first read "New York 1980" before Benning had completed *Him and Me,* and later realized that I had taken greater pleasure in the screenplay and in the film I imagined on the basis of it (a film that, of course, made use of Benning's distinctive sense of composition and timing) than I did in *Him and Me* itself. Perhaps the elements of surprise in the screenplay and film caused my second, cinematic experience of the same narrative to be a letdown. But that's for the reader (and hopefully, viewer: while *Him and Me* didn't live up to my expectations, it *is* an inventive film) to decide.

In the years since *Him and Me,* Benning has completed several features— *American Dreams, Landscape Suicide* (1986), *Used Innocence* (1988), *North on Evers* (1992)—and other work, all of which is characterized by the more coherent sense of plotting and characterization that was first evident in the script for *Him and Me.* His interest in cinematic text, both in the sense of scenario/ screenplay and as visual imagery has remained consistently evident. *American Dreams* is Benning's most extensive experiment with visual text (the entire imagery of the film is made up of the fronts and backs of baseball cards and other Hank Aaron memorabilia, of handwritten textual excerpts from the diary of would-be assassin Arthur Bremer which move across the bottom of the image

from right to left, and of other superimposed texts). *Landscape Suicide* and *Used Innocence* make extensive use of various printed documents relating to the lives and crimes of several convicted murderers. *North on Evers* uses a handwritten text that moves from right to left across the bottom of the image (similar to the Bremer text in *American Dreams*) to help convey the meaning of Benning's travels around the United States.

Benning redesigned the "Respect your flag" passage from *Grand Opera* so that it would make sense as a text/image piece in the particular context of this book. "Respect your flag" is followed by the complete text of "New York 1980."

---

1. *American Dreams* (1984), the feature that followed *Him and Me,* is an analysis of conventional American machismo and Benning's most effectively feminist work to date. See my review in *Film Quarterly,* vol. 40, no. 4 (Summer 1987): 16–20.

"Respect your flag . . ." —from *Grand Opera*

"Respect your flag . . ." is a xerox version of a portion of Grand Opera that occurs about halfway through the film. It is made up of a continuous text that is divided into two parts: an outer frame and an inner rectangle. The outer frame is the text heard on the Grand Opera sound track; the inner rectangle is made up of photocopied frame enlargements of the image and superimposed text viewers are seeing while the text on the sound track is being heard. Neither the framed visual text, nor the text read on the sound track is complete; only when the truncated visual text and the interrupted auditory text are combined, which occurs literally in this version and only conceptually during the film itself, can the entire statement about the flag (and its relationship to the image over which the visual text is superimposed) be understood. Of course, when this passage appears in Grand Opera, the imagery within the inner rectangle is in motion.—S.M.

Respect your flag and render it the courtesies to which it is entitled. The
National flag should be raised and lowered by hand. Do not raise the flag
while it is furled.   precaution to
prevent the fla   owed to touch
the ground or f   the flag as a
portion of a co   upon cushions
or   handkerchi   flag should never be displaye   ire   distress.
When displayed o   uspended vertically with the   he east in a nor-
th/ south street   ould be hoisted
to the peak for   osition; but be-
for lowering th   he peak. When
the flag is used   the union is at
the head and over the left shoulder. The flag should not be lowered into the
grave or allowed to touch the ground. Remember, the National flag is our
banner of hope for the land of the free and home of the brave.

Respect your flag and render it the courtesies to which it is entitled. The
National flag should be raised and lowered by hand. Do not raise the flag
while it is furled.   dignit   precaution to
prevent the fla   It sh   owed to touch
the ground or f   st obj   the flag as a
portion of a co   m. Do   upon cushions
or   handkerchi   r napki   flag should never be displaye   excep   ire   distress.
When displayed o   eet, th   uspended vertically with the   n east-w   he east in a nor-
th/ south street   at half   ould be hoisted
to the peak for   wered to   osition; but be-
for lowering th   ould again   he peak. When
the flag is used   should be so   the union is at
the head and over the left shoulder. The flag should not be lowered into the
grave or allowed to touch the ground. Remember, the National flag is our
banner of hope for the land of the free and home of the brave.

Respect your flag and render it the courtesies to which it is entitled. The
National flag should be raised and lowered by hand. Do not raise the flag
while it is furled.

prevent the fla	precaution to
the ground or f	owed to touch
portion of a co	the flag as a
or handkerchi	upon cushions
er be displaye	flag should nev-
When displayed o	ire distress.
tically with the	uspended ver-
th/ south street	he east in a nor-
to the peak for	ould be hoisted
for lowering th	osition; but be-
the flag is used	he peak. When

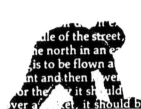

the head and over the left shoulder. The flag should not be lowered into the
grave or allowed to touch the ground. Remember, the National flag is our
banner of hope for the land of the free and home of the brave.

Respect your flag and render it the courtesies to which it is entitled. The
National flag should be raised and lowered by hand. Do not raise the flag
while it is furled.

prevent the fla	precaution to
the ground or f	owed to touch
portion of a co	the flag as a
or handkerchi	upon cushions
er be displaye	flag should nev-
When displayed o	ire distress.
tically with the	uspended ver-
th/ south street	he east in a nor-
to the peak for	ould be hoisted
for lowering th	osition; but be-
the flag is used	he peak. When

the head and over the left shoulder. The flag should not be lowered into the
grave or allowed to touch the ground. Remember, the National flag is our
banner of hope for the land of the free and home of the brave.

Respect your flag and render it the courtesies to which it is entitled. The
National flag should be raised and lowered by hand. Do not raise the flag
while it is furled.   precaution   to
prevent the fla   owed to touch
the ground or f   the flag as a
portion of a co   upon cushions
or   handkerchi   flag should never be displaye   ire   distress.
When displayed over the mid   uspended vertically with the union to the   he east in a nor-
th/ south street. When it is to be flown at half mast, the flag should be hoisted
to the peak for an instant and then lowered to the half mast position; but be-
for lowering the flag for the day it should again be raised to the peak. When
the flag is used to cover a casket, it should be so placed that the union is at
the head and over the left shoulder. The flag should not be lowered into the
grave or allowed to touch the ground. Remember, the National flag is our
banner of hope for the land of the free and home of the brave.

Respect your flag and render it the courtesies to which it is entitled. The
National flag should be raised and lowered by hand. Do not raise the flag
while it is furled.   precaution   to
prevent the fla   owed to touch
the ground or f   the flag as a
portion of a co   upon cushions
or   handkerchi   flag should never be displaye   ire   distress.
When displayed o   uspended vertically with the union to the north in an east-we   he east in a nor-
th/ south street. When it is to be flown at half mast, the flag should be hoisted
to the peak for an instant and then lowered to the half mast position; but be-
for lowering th flag for the day it should again be raised to the peak. When
the flag is used to cover a casket, it should be so placed that the union is at
the head and over the left shoulder. The flag should not be lowered into the
grave or allowed to touch the ground. Remember, the National flag is our
banner of hope for the land of the free and home of the brave.

Respect your flag and render it the courtesies to which it is entitled.   The
National flag should be raised and lowered by hand.   Do not raise the flag
while it is furled.   precaution   to
prevent the fla   owed to touch
the ground or f   the flag as a
portion of a co   upon cushions
or   handkerchi   flag should never be displaye   ire distress.
When displayed o   the flag shoul   suspended vertically with the union to the north in an east-west street, or to he east in a nor-
th/ south street. When it is to be flown at half mast, the flag should be hoisted
to the peak for an instant and then lowered to the half mast position; but be-
for lowering th flag for the day it should again be raised to the peak. When
the flag is used to cover a casket, it should be so placed that the union is at
the head and over the left shoulder.   The flag should not be lowered into the
grave or allowed to touch the ground.   Remember, the National flag is our
banner of hope for the land of the free and home of the brave.

Respect your flag and render it the courtesies to which it is entitled.   The
National flag should be raised and lowered by hand.   Do not raise the flag
while it is furled.   precaution   to
prevent the fla   owed to touch
the ground or f   the flag as a
portion of a co   upon cushions
or   handkerchi   flag should never be displaye with the union down except as a sign   ire   distress.
When displayed over the middle of the street, the flag should be suspended vertically with the union to the north in an east-west street, or to he east in a nor-
th/ south street. When it is to be flown at half mast, the flag should be hoisted
to the peak for an instant and then lowered to the half mast position; but be-
for lowering th flag for the day it should again be raised to the peak. When
the flag is used to cover a casket, it should be so placed that the union is at
the head and over the left shoulder.   The flag should not be lowered into the
grave or allowed to touch the ground.   Remember, the National flag is our
banner of hope for the land of the free and home of the brave.

Respect your flag and render it the courtesies to which it is entitled. The
National flag should be raised and lowered by hand. Do not raise the flag
while it is furled. precaution to
prevent the fla should owed to touch
the ground or f st objects the flag as a
portion of a co rm. Do not embroider i upon cushions
or handkerchi s nor print it on paper napkins or boxes. The flag should never be displaye d with the union down except as a signal of dire distress.
When displayed over the middle of the street, the flag should be suspended vertically with the union to the north in an east-west street, or to the east in a nor-
th/ south street. When it is to be flown at half mast, the flag should be hoisted
to the peak for an instant and then lowered to the half mast position; but be-
for lowering th flag for the day it should again be raised to the peak. When
the flag is used to cover a casket, it should be so placed that the union is at
the head and over the left shoulder. The flag should not be lowered into the
grave or allowed to touch the ground. Remember, the National flag is our
banner of hope for the land of the free and home of the brave.

Respect your flag and render it the courtesies to which it is entitled. The
National flag should be raised and lowered by hand. Do not raise the flag
while it is furled. precaution to
prevent the fla owed to touch
the ground or f oor, nor to bru the flag as a
portion of a co tume or athletic Do not embroider i upon cushions
or handkerchi s nor print it on paper napkins or boxes. The flag should never be displaye d with the union down except as a signal of dire distress.
When displayed over the middle of the street, the flag should be suspended vertically with the union to the north in an east-west street, or to the east in a nor-
th/ south street When it is to be flown at half mast, the flag should be hoisted
to the peak for an instant and then lowered to the half mast position; but be-
for lowering th flag for the day it should again be raised to the peak. When
the flag is used to cover a casket, it should be so placed that the union is at
the head and over the left shoulder. The flag should not be lowered into the
grave or allowed to touch the ground. Remember, the National flag is our
banner of hope for the land of the free and home of the brave.

Respect your flag and render it the courtesies to which it is entitled. The National flag should be raised and lowered by hand. Do not raise the flag while it is furled. Lower it slowly, and with dignity. Take every precaution to prevent the flag from becoming soiled. It should not be allowed to touch the ground or floor, nor to brush against objects. Do not use the flag as a portion of a costume or athletic uniform. Do not embroider it upon cushions or handkerchiefs nor print it on paper napkins or boxes. The flag should never be displayed with the union down except as a signal of dire distress. When displayed over the middle of the street, the flag should be suspended vertically with the union to the north in an east-west street, or to the east in a north/ south street. When it is to be flown at half mast, the flag should be hoisted to the peak for an instant and then lowered to the half mast position; but before lowering the flag for the day it should again be raised to the peak. When the flag is used to cover a casket, it should be so placed that the union is at the head and over the left shoulder. The flag should not be lowered into the grave or allowed to touch the ground. Remember, the National flag is our banner of hope for the land of the free and home of the brave.

Respect your flag and render it the courtesies to which it is entitled. The National flag should be raised and lowered by hand. Do not raise the flag while it is furled. Lower it slowly and with dignity. Take every precaution to prevent the flag from becoming soiled. It should not be allowed to touch the ground or floor, nor to brush against objects. Do not use the flag as a portion of a costume or atheltic uniform. Do not embroider it upon cushions or handkerchiefs nor print it on paper napkins or boxes. The flag should never be displayed with the union down except as a signal of dire distress. When displayed over the middle of the street, the flag should be suspended vertically with the union to the north in an east-west street, or to the east in a north/ south street. When it is to be flown at half mast, the flag should be hoisted to the peak for an instant and then lowered to the half mast position; but before lowering the flag for the day it should again be raised to the peak. When the flag is used to cover a casket, it should be so placed that the union is at the head and over the left shoulder. The flag should not be lowered into the grave or allowed to touch the ground. Remember, the National flag is our banner of hope for the land of the free and home of the brave.

Script for ''New York 1980''

I have corrected spelling errors in the original, typed version of Benning's script, and I've added punctuation, graphic spacing, and italics to make the text more easily understandable. —S.M.

Scene 1. Two people return home. They are drunk. A door opens two floors below. They walk up stairs. There is a muffled conversation with laughter.

Jean: The Kinks are the only old records I listen to. I love how depressed they make me.

He: You're an asshole. Anyway, now all you listen to is James Chance or White or whatever the fuck his name is today.

Jean unlocks the door and they enter the room.

He: Jesus Christ, it's fucking bright in here.

Jean: It keeps the junkies away. It's too bright just to be a burglar light so they think I'm home. I get my electricity for free. I've been here two years and they never send me a bill.

He: What if you get . . .

He stumbles into a small wooden chair, knocking it over.

He: It's so fucking bright I can't see a fucking thing.

Jean: You're just drunk. Here, I'll turn off a few lights.

They climb onto the bed with their clothes on.

He: In 1955 I worked in a drugstore. The first day on the job some guy came in and asked for prophylactics. I had no idea where they were kept, actually I had no idea what they were. Shit, I was only thirteen. I knew what the fuck rubbers were, but not prophylac- tics. I thought it was some kind of fucking mouthwash or some- thing. So I yelled to the pharmacist in the back of the store. "Hey Nate, where are the prophylactics kept?" Well the guy I was waiting on turned fucking red and Nate yelled back, "John, you want to come back here for a minute?" I thought he was going to show me where it was but he was as red as the customer and just started screaming.

They both laugh.

Jean: In 1956 I was in the third grade. This boy sat behind me. I think his name was Larry Graf. Every day he would write Stevenson all over his arithmetic paper. Some days we'd pass our papers forward to have the kid in front of you grade it. So on those days I'd get his paper with Stevenson all over it. Some days we'd pass our papers back and he'd get mine. So I started to write Ike on mine. His father drove a truck for United Parcel or, no, no, it was Railway Parcel or something like that. I guess that's why he'd write Stevenson on his. My dad would of killed me if he knew I was supporting Ike. Actually I wasn't. I just wanted to be against Graf. I guess I had a crush on him. My first love. We'd argue back and forth. Ike. Stevenson. Ike. What the hell did we know? What the fuck did Ike know? All he did was play golf and become more and more popular. Are you asleep? Are you sleeping?

There is no answer.

Jean: Where the hell is Ike when you need him?

*Jean gets out of bed and removes his shoes. She takes off her clothes
and puts on a T-shirt and gets in bed under the covers. She reaches over
him and turns out the light. The room is dark except for the windows.
The man can be heard breathing. Outside two men can very faintly be
heard yelling.*
Man 1: Come on fuckhead, suck my cock.
Man 2: Shut your motherfucking mouth before you wake the dead.

*Scene 2. New York skyline seen from a helicopter flying down the Hudson
River from the George Washington Bridge to the Statue of Liberty.*

*Scene 3. Jean walks down a semi-crowded street. She weaves in and out of
people. She stops against a building. She breaks down, then wipes her
eyes. A woman notices her and stops. They are friends. They hug. The
woman whispers something into Jean's ear. Then they lean back and look
into each others eyes. The woman dries Jean's tears with her hand. They
kiss on the lips. The woman pushes Jean back.*
She: What's on your lips? (Beginning to smile)
Jean: Vaseline. (She laughs and cries at the same time)
She: Let's get drunk.
*They exit the frame. The camera holds for ten seconds. Then tracks in the
direction they went, but doesn't catch up.*

*Scene 4. Jean and a woman in her forties are sitting on a couch in Jean's
loft. Jean is talking very intently. The woman mostly listens. There is
no sound.*

*Scene 5. Jean is lying on the couch. Her body is very slowly undulating.
She is moaning very softly.*

*Scene 6. Jean is painting the walls of her loft pink on the bottom half
and green on the top. She paints the line between the pink and green by
hand very carefully. At one point, she is mixing the green paint and gets
lost in thought. Later when rolling on the pink paint she again gets lost
in thought. In both cases she is working, then slows down, then works
again, and then almost slows to a stop. She is very perplexed.*

Scene 7. A number of static shots of downtown Manhattan.

*Scene 8. Jean looks through old pin-up magazines from the fifties.
She cuts some of the pictures out and puts them in plastic frames and
hangs them on the pink and green walls. She keeps moving and changing
them around. She takes off her clothes and puts on a leopard skin coat
and begins to pose like the pin-ups. She tries to duplicate their
poses.*

Scene 9. A punk band in a small music club plays a song called "Nuclear
Bum."

Scene 10. Jean walking across a schoolyard with a painting of the Statue
of Liberty on the wall. A man on crutches passes in the other direction.
The camera pans to follow Jean. The man yells Jean's name. The camera pan
stops. Jean turns and walks back toward the man. They meet at the edge of
the frame. The man does most of the talking, making gestures with his
crutches, but can't be heard. Jean and he begin to laugh.

Scene 11. Shots of ten different houses. Each house begins with a static
shot, a title is superimposed giving time and place, then the camera
pans 360 degrees ending with a static shot of the house. Jean's voice
narrates sound over stories.
House 1. Detroit. 1946. Billie Holiday sings "Georgia on My Mind." No
story.
House 2. Detroit. 1956. Gene Vincent sings "Be Bop a Lula."
When I was about 10 years old these two boys in my neighborhood
offered me 50 cents if I'd pull down my pants and show them what I
had. At first I didn't want to but 50 cents seemed like a bargain.
So I gave in. They didn't have the money and wanted to pay me
later. I told them no deal. But one of them had a paper route,
so they went off and collected from a few customers until they
had the money. I took it and put it in my pocket and pulled down
my pants, but kept my legs together. They couldn't see a thing
and complained. I told them that girls didn't have anything to
see and they looked real disappointed and left.
House 3. Milwaukee. 1957. Buddy Holly sings "It Doesn't Matter
Anymore."
In 1957 we got our first TV and put it in the alcove where the tree
went at Christmas time. My father worked at a factory in the
industrial valley. His best friend died when a gear they were
hardening exploded. He liked to go to the local tavern and talk
about fishing. Once he told me he was going to paint all the chrome
on our Ford black because cars are just for transportation.
House 4. Milwaukee. 1960. Elvis Presley sings "Blue Moon."
The first job I ever had was working in a drugstore. The place also
sold quarts of beer and at 14 I had a lot of friends as customers.
One day this man came in and asked for prophylactics. I knew what
rubbers were (my girl friends and I used to blow them up like
balloons and let them go from bus windows) but we never called them
that so when this guy asked for them I didn't know what he wanted,
so I yelled across the store to my boss. "Hey, Jake, where do we
keep the prophylactics?" He yelled back, "Ahh Jean, could I see
you here in the back for a minute."

House 5. Chicago. 1963. Lou Christy sings "Lightning Strikes."
The first man I ever slept with was Bob Holmes. We both were
seventeen and did it at a drive-in in his '55 Chevy. He loved the
car more than me. But actually it wasn't that bad. I'd like to fuck
in that car tonight. The last man I slept with was John. Two weeks
ago this Thursday.

House 6. St. Louis. 1967. The Supremes sing "Baby Love."
May and Cliff lived across the tracks behind my house. I was
teaching math to high school dropouts at a kind of makeshift
school. May was Cliff's daughter. He had gotten her pregnant but
she lost the baby. They were both in poor health. He had been in
prison for 25 years. One Sunday morning they came over still drunk
from the night before. He began to sing and play the harmonica. We
all drank whiskey from a bottle. May pulled her dress over her head
exposing the scars on her body. When I moved away I found a man
dead behind my house. I told Cliff and he ran and hid. He was
afraid they'd pin it on him.

House 7. Galena, Missouri. 1974. The Kinks sing "You Really Got Me."
I stumbled upon the cow. I had thought it was an older one but was
wrong. She was young and it was her first birth. She laid on her
side moaning. A stillborn calf was half inside her. Half out. I ran
toward her not knowing what to do. I grabbed the dead calf and
pulled. The cow moaned louder. The calf was stuck but finally came
loose. It smelled like the dead stuff dogs roll in. I pulled the
calf out and put my arms around the cow's neck. She tried to get up
but was too weak. Some of her hide was worn away from trying to
stand. I tried feeding her to help her gain strength. Two days
later I shot her through the head.

House 8. Horicon, Wisconsin. 1976. Lou Reed sings "Ooohhh Baby."
For a while I used to drive a cheese truck from a small town in
Wisconsin to Chicago and back. I remember when I went to apply for
the job I pulled into a gas station to ask directions. This old man
came out and said very slowly with his eyes rolling back into his
head on each number, "One. Two. Three. Four. . . ." He got up to
about eleven and said, "Yeah, it's the eleventh street on up on
the left." So I went on up and got the job. Later as I'd drive to
Chicago and back I used to make a list in my mind of all the men I
fucked and in what order.

House 9. Detroit. 1977. Elvis Costello sings "Mystery Dance."
One summer I was painting my mother's house. I went to the bar my
father used to go to. He died of cancer before he could retire. It
was a young kids' hangout now. I met a man I went to grade school
with. We started to drink and got very drunk. He also was visiting
his parents. When the bar closed, we didn't have a room to go to so
I walked him home. When we got to his house, we started to kiss on

the front porch. After a while, I began to suck his cock. He must
have accidentally hit the doorbell with his elbow and his mother
answered the door and said, "Oh." I said, "I guess I'll be going
now." I never saw him again.

House 10. New York. 1980. Lydia Lunch sings "Spookie."
When I lived on the farm, I got pregnant but lost the baby in the
third month. I was very sad. I wanted a child badly. I still do. I
can't believe John is dead.

*Scene 12. Jean re-wiring a black panther lamp. She cleans it, puts in
new wires and light fixture, and plants African violets in the opening
in the panther's back.*

*Scene 13. Jean on top of the Empire State Building. She is telling three
friends a story.*
Jean: Howie told me this great crutch story. He said this happened to him last summer. He was sunning himself on a park bench,
minding his own business, when this guy crutches up to him,
stops, takes a crutch and puts the tip of it on his forehead and
pushes his head way back and says, "You got a cigarette," and
Howie says, his voice starting to crack, "I'm sorry I don't
smoke."

*Scene 14. Jean is loading an instamatic camera while a young man (who
looks much younger—about 16) is undressing. He puts on the same leopard
skin coat and does the same poses Jean tried earlier. Jean takes flash
pictures of him.*

Scene 15. Shots of tourists at the Statue of Liberty.

*Scene 16. Tracking shot of Jean walking down a street in the warehouse
district in and out of trucks.*

*Scene 17. Max's Kansas City, outside at night. Jean comes running out
and down the street.*

*Scene 18. A working man puts a shovel into the back of a pickup truck.
Jean runs up and opens the passenger door.*
Jean: Where are you going?
Man: To Brooklyn.
Jean: Please give me a ride. I'm in a hurry . . . Oh it's too
complicated.
The truck drives off. After about 5 minutes.
Jean: Where are you going?
Man: I told you. Brooklyn.

Jean: Can I get out here?
The truck pulls over. Jean gets out. The camera remains in the truck and crosses the Brooklyn Bridge.

Scene 19. Jean and a man on her couch. The walls are now pink and green.
Jean: Yesterday a friend told me a story about a farmer in Iowa who had a heart attack while feeding the hogs. He fell over in the slop. About an hour later his wife found him. The fucking hogs had eaten away half his body.
He: Well that's a real horror story.
Pause.
He: Right after my mother died I wrote my father a letter to say that our silence had to end. We're the only ones left. We have to talk. To know each other. Two weeks later I got a letter from someone I never met. My father had died. He never received my letter.
Pause.
He: Listen, I think what we need to do is go to bed and forget everything.
Jean: Yeah. I really need to sleep.
He: That isn't what I meant.
Jean: What did you mean?
He: You know. Come on, I wanted to fuck you for a long time.
Jean: You got to be kidding. Haven't you been listening?
He: Sure. Come on, it'll do you good.
Jean: Jesus Christ, you're an asshole, it'll do me good. Just leave. OK?
He: Oh no. It's not that easy.
Jean: Oh yes. Just open the door and go.
He: Come here.
Jean: Get your fucking ass out of here. You bastard. If you touch me I'll cut your fucking throat. Now get the hell out of here.
He: Take it easy. I was only kidding.
Jean: Fuck you.
He leaves. She locks the door and starts to cry.

Scene 20. Jean is unpacking a box that came in the mail. Inside is a model airplane painted pink and green. It makes her happy. She hangs it in the corner in front of the pink and green walls. The phone rings. Only Jean's part of the conversation is heard.
Jean: Hello.

Karen, you're back. Oh, I'm glad you called. I'm in a great mood! My little brother just sent me a model airplane. He painted it pink and green.

No. No, I painted my whole place pink and green and the plane is the same color.

Well, it's hard to explain. The top half is green and the bottom is pink and . . .

It's called mint green and the pink is lily pink. I bought this great black panther lamp and planted (it's a planter too) I planted African violets in it. And I found these little swordfish on Canal Street that are a kind of metallic green and pink. You got to come over and see all this stuff.

Yeah, well I couldn't stand white anymore. I was really depressed. I'll tell you all about it in a minute, but first, how was your trip?

And how are Jan and Steve? Any new babies?

You're kidding!

My older brother just left his wife too. She wouldn't have sex with him so he beat her up and she left.

No, I meant to say she left him.

So will you be back at work next week?

I haven't worked for three weeks. I've been very upset so I've been staying home. Painting my loft. Keeping busy. But I think I'll go back to work next week too. Since you're back. I guess we're working on an old office building on Church Street. Mark told me all the real shit work is finished and that I should come in as soon as I can to help with the painting. So now that you're back, I think I'll work for sure.

I'm surprised you heard about it in California.

John and I had been drinking. I ran into him two days earlier at Puffy's on Thursday. I hadn't seen him for about a year or so. He was in town doing some business with his music and had a great room at the Gramercy. We got real drunk and I spent the night with him. Then on Saturday I had been helping Jerry hook up a gas line at his place and after working all day John stopped by so the three of us drank two bottles of wine and then went over to that Indian Restaurant just down from Jerry's. After we ate we came back and

two or three more people came over and we drank some more wine and
danced a little. But it never got real crazy, mostly just talking.
A few people jumping around to some old Supremes records. About
1:30 or 2:00 John and I went back to my place. We were both kind of
drunk but not that bad. When we got back we laid down on my bed and
talked for a few minutes. I can't remember what we talked about. I
think something about being young and Eisenhower or something.
Anyway, John fell asleep with his clothes on, so I remember
getting up and taking his shoes off and then I took off my clothes
and got under the cover. I woke up a few times during the night and
could hear him breathing. Then I woke up about 5:00 and it was very
quiet. I fell back asleep and woke up again and it was 6:30. I felt
all alone. There wasn't a sound. It was so still. I immediately
knew he was dead. And then I thought what a stupid thing to think.
I put my hand on his back and pushed him slightly. There was no
response. I pushed a little harder. I thought God I bet he is dead.
I slowly turned him over. His face was all pushed in from sleeping
face down. Some snot was in his nostrils. He was dead. I knew he
was dead. I jumped out of bed. Put on some pants. I was shaking. I
paced back and forth for a few seconds. I pulled his tongue out of
his mouth and started to blow air into his lungs. I could taste the
wine from the night before. His body was belching gas. For a moment
I thought he might be still alive. I breathed harder into his
lungs, but nothing happened. I ran to the phone and called the
rescue squad. They asked me if the body was still warm. I said yes
and they said I should continue to do what I was doing. I ran back
to the bed. I felt his feet. They were cold. But his hands and face
were still warm. I tried again. In about three minutes I could hear
the siren. I ran downstairs and went into the middle of the street
and waved my hands over my head. Two firemen got out of the rescue
squad car and ran up the stairs. I followed slower. By the time I
got up the stairs, they were finished. One of them said, "I'm
afraid he's dead." They used my phone to call the police and we
waited outside.

Well I don't know. I bet he died just before I woke up at 5:00.
Maybe that's why I woke up. I don't know though. He was supposed to
catch a plane at 10:30 and I might have just been nervous about him
missing his plane. So maybe that's why I woke up. But the police
told me he probably died around 5:00 a.m. I know he didn't just lay
down and die because I heard him breathing during the night.

The police were actually very nice but wouldn't let me walk around
outside until a detective questioned me. Then the coroner came and
I signed a paper to identify the body.

No. No one knows. He just died. I thought it might have been some
drugs mixed with the wine but it wasn't. Shit it's changed my
life. All my priorities are confused. But I guess I'm not afraid
now. It was peaceful. I guess I'm much more aware. It was really
incredible. I mean I really had to fucking face it. And it's
strange. At first I felt real guilty about being there and that it
was my fault. It happened because of me. But that's . . .

Yeah, I know it's dumb. Maybe if I would have woke up earlier I
could have saved him. But I didn't. I didn't and I had no control
over that. So I don't feel so guilty about that anymore. But now
I'm feeling a more subtle kind of guilt. I feel guilty about what I
learned. I feel much different now. But the only way you can face
death is by someone dying. So what I learned was at the expense of
John. And I feel real weird about that. It's crazy . . .

Well sure. I'm glad I was there. When I die, I hope a friend is
with me. It would have been awful if he would have died in a hotel
room by himself and some stranger would have found him. So I'm
glad I was there, but I still feel strange. The first few nights I
was afraid to sleep. I thought I was going to die too. I suppose I
felt a little guilty also about him dying and me not. But it was
so strange. At first I was just scared. It didn't seem to register.
I was just frightened. But the next day I broke down. Lynn found
me crying on some crowded street and took me to a bar on 10th
Street. I cried for about an hour straight. We had a long talk.
She's so nice. Anyway I still cry every once in a while.

I know keeping busy helps. I'm glad you're back and I'm looking
forward to working again. I did do a little of my own work too.
Last week, you know that guy that looks like 16 that I wanted to
photograph? Well last week I went up and asked him and he agreed.
He was great. I got him to wear my leopard skin coat and re-enact
porno poses from the fifties.

I used an instamatic with flash cubes. They turned out great.

Oh, also right after the police let me go I went for a walk along
the Hudson and this helicopter flew over. So I took a helicopter
ride and flew past the Statue of Liberty. Which reminds me . . .

For about a half hour. Anyway, I saw Howie and he was on
crutches.

No, I passed him on that school playground where the Statue of

Liberty is painted on the side of the school. He was on crutches and I didn't even recognize him.

No, you'll never guess. He was real drunk and hurt his ankle dancing at a disco.

Yeah, a disco! Anyway he told me this great crutch story. He said this happened to him last summer. He was sunning himself on a park bench when this guy comes crutching up to him, stops, takes a crutch and puts it on his forehead and pushes his head back and says, "You got a cigarette?" And Howie says, "I'm sorry I don't smoke."

Karen, I think I saw that band the other night. Do they do a number that has "96 Tears" in the middle of it?

Yeah, I liked them too. I just saw that one song. I couldn't be with a lot of people. I was going to see music and ended running out of places. I did it two or three times. Oh shit, I just remembered. I was so happy from getting my brother's airplane in the mail that I already forgot what happened to me last night. Jack was over here and well it seems all I talk about is death lately. I guess I need to. Anyway, I told him the whole story and he was real nice and told me about his mother and father dying and then he tries to use his sincerity so he can fuck me. Oh shit, forget I said that. Maybe it was just me. I'm still pretty confused.

Yeah, well at first I thought I might have been pregnant. But I wasn't. But right after he died I kept thinking that his sperm might still be alive inside me from fucking at his hotel two nights earlier. It's crazy what your mind focuses on.

O.K. Sure, I'll be here. Stop over for sure. You'll love my new walls. Take care. Bye.

Jean gets up and walks over to the airplane hanging from a string and gives it a spin and smiles.

Michael Snow

Michael Snow's interest in cinematic text has been consistent with a career that has seen the multiplicity of media as a central artistic challenge. Snow was first a jazz musician, then a painter as well, and a sculptor, a photographer, a filmmaker, a holographer . . . While he is best known in the United States as a filmmaker—especially for the landmark *Wavelength* (1967), probably the most widely discussed "structural film"—in his native Canada, he is probably the best-known modern artist, not only among art aficionados but to the public: his funny, abrasive gargoyles greet those entering Toronto's new Skydome Stadium. Text has woven in and out of Snow's career, becoming a major issue in a few noteworthy instances. For example, on the cover of his album of experimental music, *Michael Snow: Musics for Piano, Whistling, Microphone and Tape Recorder* (1975), a witty, self-reflexive text covers the four sides (on each side, the typeface is smaller) of the two-record Chatham Square jacket cover. In its interactions and departures from the particular musical pieces included, the text simulta-

neously fulfills and confronts the reader's conventional expectations of album-cover writing.

Snow's interest in using text as part of a film experience is most obvious in his mammoth exploration of film sound, *Rameau's Nephew by Diderot (Thanx to Dennis Young) by Wilma Schoen* (1974), in the amusing rolling credit sequence near the beginning of the film and in the many passages where experimental screenplays challenge conventional synch sound film expectations. It is obvious, too, in *So Is This*, the one Snow film devoted specifically to an exploration of the potential of text as image—or to be more precise, to an investigation of the intersection between watching film imagery in a theater and reading an extended text.

So Is This presents a self-reflexive text, one word at a time. The individual words are framed according to a consistent graphic system that causes normally "little" words—single-syllable articles, conjunctions, prepositions—to be much larger in the film than multisyllabic words. The typeface remains consistent, but other elements, especially the duration each word is on the screen and the color background against which we see it, vary widely. *So Is This* was completed in 1982, at a time when a good many avant-garde film and video artists were exploring visual text. Indeed, early in *So Is This*, Snow reviews the portion of that history with which he was acquainted: "there / have / been / several / films / or / videotapes / that / concentrate / on / texts / for / example / Richard / Serra / Tom / Sherman / Su / Friedrich / John / Knight / and / Paul / Haines / have / made / excellent / use / of / texts. / The / author / would / like / to / have / been / first / but / it's / too / late."

The particular ingenuity of Snow's use of text in *So Is This* is a function of the different senses of time and continuity we expect when reading and viewing. By carefully controlling the speed with which he reveals consecutive words, Snow is able to toy with the viewer's/reader's apprehension of the text. Normally, the technological advantage of printing is that it allows readers the option of owning (or borrowing) copies of texts; print technology provides free access: we can read as much or as little, as quickly or as slowly as our interests and inclinations allow. In *So Is This*, Snow controls time—as all filmmakers do—and we are at his mercy. We cannot know what a sentence means until it's over; as a result, Snow's one-word-at-a-time structure forces viewers to construct a meaning, then reconstruct it, as individual words are revealed. Indeed, since the meaning of words is determined by their contexts within sentences, we cannot even be sure how a particular word is to be understood until subsequent words have been revealed. Further, the experience of constructing/reading the sentences in *So Is This* is affected by an el-

ement of cinematic time, as represented in the flares at the ends of the rolls of film Snow is shooting: in some instances, the flare-outs obscure frames and words so thoroughly that we must guess at the meaning of the complete sentences.

The experience of reading *So Is This* is also affected by the graphic parameters Snow uses. The fact that his system causes normally short words to be enlarged and multisyllabic words to be miniaturized tends to confound the normal reading experience, even as it provides an ironic reconfirmation of an essential grammatical truth: articles, conjunctions, prepositions *are* grammatically as significant as multisyllabic words. The fact of Snow's use of text demands that we read (as Hollis Frampton once said, "Once we can read, and a word is put before us, we cannot not read it"),[1] but the nature of his delivery of this text continually frustrates our ability to read comfortably.

Snow also toys with the distinction between the often more private experience of reading and the public experience of cinema: "Warning: / This / film / may / be / especially / unsatisfying / for / those / who / dislike / having / others / read / over / their / shoulders." And during the film's forty-nine minutes, he engages the viewer/reader in a wide range of other issues that create "interference" between the experiences of reading and viewing. All in all, *So Is This* creates a conceptual labyrinth reminiscent of Frampton's *Poetic Justice*, though more perceptually dynamic. Text—in the form of theory, critique, and history—has often been "turned loose" on the experience of cinema (indeed, we're in the midst of a flood of academic writing about film). In *So Is This*, Snow turns film loose on the experience of reading.

---

1. See my interview with Frampton in *A Critical Cinema* (Berkeley, Los Angeles, London: University of California Press, 1988): 49.

③

or sound could be introduced. Notice how each word is in a different dimension? Some words could get so attenuated, or so big, that only a section of them would be shown on the screen. Or they could get extremely tiny. The decision has been made to concentrate on the distinctive capacity of film to structure time: the words are the individual units of writing, the frames are the smallest units of film. In the film is writing is lighting (Japanese?) This is white light, it contains all the colours. In case you're getting restless, this film (long title isn't it?) won't discuss itself all the time. It's going to get into some real human stuff, that will make you laugh and cry, and change society. Also, it's going to become confessional and very personal. The author is going to tell you as much as he can about himself. He's going to be completely frank. He's going to say where he went wrong in his life, how he's trying to correct his errors and he hopes that in so doing he may be helping you to improve yourself. This is the start of a new paragraph from which any children present should shield their eyes. Since this film was originally composed as

Near the end of *So Is This*, Snow includes what the text describes as a review of "events" that have occurred in the film—an analogy to and satire of flashbacks in conventional films. For this passage, Snow rephotographs many of the words seen up to this point in the film, framing them so that they appear in a frame-within-the-frame. Both the techniques of rephotography and the frame-within-the-frame compositions are take-offs on traditional film flashbacks, which involve our re-seeing images seen earlier in the film "from a distance." Some of the rephotographed words and sequences of words are readable—"This"/"this" appears over and over—but in many cases the reviewed words are re-recorded one word per frame and create retinal collages, rather than sentences. The fact that the "flashback" words, or their backgrounds, are differently colored/shaded than the words before the review sequence extends Snow's take-off of conventional film flashbacks, where our emotions "color" what we see. And they confirm the film's implicit critique of both the film-rhetorical device of the flashback, which in fact distorts and manipulates as fully as it recalls, and the psychological mechanism of memory to which film flashbacks are meant to be analogous.

The text of *So Is This* is presented complete. What is missing, of course, are the durations of the words (which vary from a single frame—for "tits," "ass," "cock," and "cunt": an explicit challenge to the then-busy Ontario censors—to the fifty-seven and a half seconds during which the word "length" (!) stays on the screen in one instance) and their comparative graphic sizes: the series of frame enlargements on the following pages provides some sense of the film's graphic design. The page of Snow's original score reproduced on the opposite page indicates (above each word) the number of frames each word is on the screen, but, of course, for an accurate sense of Snow's timing, only the film itself will do.

Text of *So Is This*

The successive words are arranged in vertical columns, rather than across the page, to better approximate the viewer's gradual reception of Snow's text. The "flashback" passage is illustrated by a representative frame sequence. —S.M.

The first of seven frame enlargements of successive words in Snow's *So Is This*: the remaining six are on the following pages. Courtesy Canadian Filmmakers Distribution Centre.

This is the title of this film. The rest of this film will look just like this. The film will consist of single words presented one after another to construct sentences and hopefully (this is where

you come in) to convey meanings. This, as they say, is the signifier. This film will be about 2 hours long. Does that seem like a frightening prospect? Well, look at it this way: how do

you know this isn't lying? Perhaps after a while this word after word system will change into something else. Well, take this's word for it, this is the

way it's going to be. New paragraph. Most of this film was written in 1975 but for various reasons could not be done until now (April 1982). Thanks

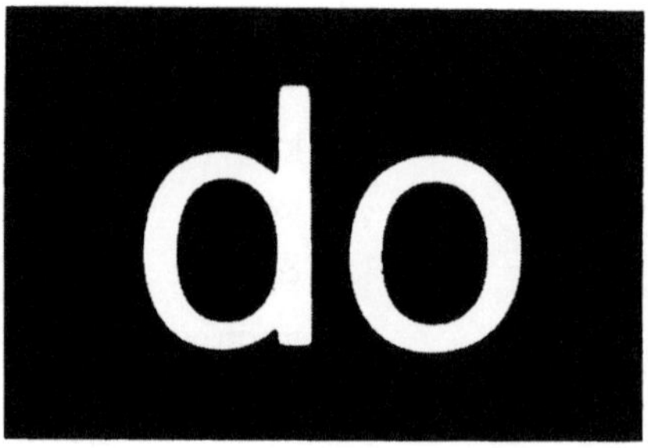

to
Anna
Patomow
for
her
assistance
in
placing
these
words
on
this
screen.
Some
of
the
following
considerations
and
decisions
preceded
the
production
of
this
film:
In
1979
Drew
Morey
made
a
film
titled
This
is

the
title
of
my
film.
Since
this
is
not
his
film
and
the
"this"
in
his
title
cannot
possibly
refer
to
this,
his
title
is
not
the
title
of
this
film
and
hence
the
author
(Michael

do

Snow)
of
this
film
decided
to
retain
this
title
and
to
include
the
foregoing
reference
to
this
issue
in
this
film.
This
is
still
the
title
of
this

film.
So
is
this.
John
Kamevaar
recently
gave
the
author
a
bronze
relief
he
made
of
the
word
this.
This
is
not
that.
This
is
not
a
script

Warning: Friedrich,

This John

film Knight

may and

be Paul

especially Haines

unsatisfying have

for made

those excellent not this,

who use the this

dislike of first is

having texts. time a

others The that universe!

read author this So

over would has what

their like been is

shoulders. to used important

Next: have for is

there been the not

have first first this

been but time. but

several it's This how

films too belongs this

or late. to is

videotapes Priority everybody! used.

that is This Third

concentrate energy. means paragraph:

on In this, sometimes

texts, some you the

for respects think author

example this this, of

Richard is we this

Serra, first. see film

Tom Obviously this, is

Sherman, this they present

Su is use when

his films are screened and can thus answer questions about them. One question which the author expects is: "Why would anyone want to do such a thing as this?" followed by "Wouldn't a book be better?" If Mr. Snow is here on this occasion he will attempt to answer such questions in speech after this film is over. It's going to be a very interesting film and perhaps such questions will be

know

answered by the film itself, so to speak. One of the interests of this system is that each word can be held on the screen for a specific length of time. You can't see what's coming, a sentence could take an unexpected turn. The words could change to black on white or be in colour. Words in capitals could be used and different typefaces. Words could fade in and out or slide on and off. Images or sound could be introduced. Notice how each word is a different size? Some words could get so attenuated or so big that only a section of them would be shown on the screen. Or they could get extremely tiny. The decision has been made to concentrate on the distinctive capacity of film to structure time: the word as the individual unit of writing, the frame as the smallest unit of film. In this film writing is lighting (Japanese?).

this

This is white light, it contains all the colours. In case you're getting restless this film (long title isn't it?) won't discuss itself all the time. It's going to

get
into
some
real
human
stuff
that
will
make
you
laugh
and
cry
and
change
society.
Also
it's
going
to
become
confessional
and
very
personal.
The
author
is
going
to
tell
you
as
much
as
he

can
about
himself.
He's
going
to
be
completely
Frank.
He's
going
to
say
where
he
went
wrong
in
his
life,
how
he's
trying
to
correct
his
errors
and
he
hopes
that
in
so
doing
he
may

isn't

be
helping
you
to
improve
yourself.
This
is
the
start
of
a
new
paragraph
from
which
any
children
present
should
shield
their
eyes.
Since
this
film
was
tits

originally
composed
ass
The
Ontario
Board
of
Censors
has
started
to
inspect
so-called
Experimental
Films.
eg.
This.
Its
difficult
to
cock
understand
why
but
it
seems
as
if

their
purpose
is
to
protect
you
from
this.
To
protect
you
from
people
like
cunt
the
author
discussing
their
sexual
lives
or
fantasies
on
this
screen.
Is
that
the
idea?
How
did
we
ever
manage
without

them?
Anyway
there
are
apparently
some
things
that
this
just
can't
say.
Perhaps
we
will
be
classified
Adult
by
the
time
you
are
reading
this.
Or
perhaps
you
are
reading
this
elsewhere.
If
this
is
appearing

in
Ontario,
Hello
Censors,
Hi
Mary.
This
film
is
as
clean
as
a
whistle.
Ha
Ha
Ha
Ha
(Hollow
laughter).
This
film
wouldn't
say
shit
if
its
mouth

were
full
of
it.
Gulp.
Later
there
will
be
a
sextion
of
this
film
featuring
Verbal
Sex
and
Violence.
An
orgy
of
reading!
If
you
are
an
audience

of six it will be a Sextext. Sex and Silence. Chuckle. Every word counts and the author will not allow a word of this to be removed. If this film were censored you'd see stuff like:

He blank her and she sucked his blank then he blanked it in her blank. A blank and white film. OK, uncover your eyes kids. Pause. Just waiting till the newcomers (heh heh) are seated. For

those who've arrived late here is a brief resumé: this film began with this is the title of this film (another case of quote in the beginning was the word unquote). This was followed by some

background material concerning, when most of it was originally written etc., references to other films or video tapes that employ texts and some description of what this film will be. It was essentially an introduction to this. As you can see this can go so fast that it's almost impossible to read. Let's all read the second to last sentence again at a different speed. It was essentially an introduction to this. Everybody of course is equal and capable of reading at the same speed. But really some prefer it slow and some prefer it fast and you can't please everybody. However in an attempt to please everybody here is the same sentence repeated in four different speeds and patterns: It was essentially an introduction to this. It was essentially an introduction to this. It was essentially an introduction to this. Let's hope there was one arrangement that was just right for you. Perhaps this should do the whole thing again at different speeds from the beginning up to this point so as to satisfy as many people as possible?

Frame sequence from the extended "flashback" that begins after "let's/look/back:" in column one of this page. Courtesy Michael Snow.

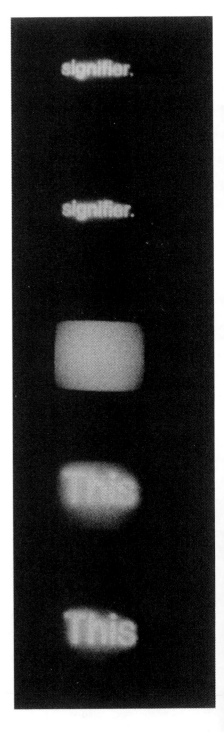

Here
goes.
Let's
look
back:
["flashback"]
You
can
see
what
a
powerful
tool
this
could
be
in
the
wrong
hands.
Pause.
Some
of
the
author's
previous
films
are
liked
by
a
small
number
of
people,
disliked

by
a
slightly
larger
number
and
unknown
to
millions.
With
this
film
he
hopes
to
reach
everybody
who
can
read
English.
There
will
be
a
French
version.
More
about
that
later.
New
paragraph:
Some
of
the

more cultivated members of the audience may regret the lack of in-depth semiological analysis in this film and note that the vocabulary used is quite basic. This is in line with the author's attempt not to talk over the heads of people and not to cater to a small but vocal intellectual element in our society. Why make films that only a few people will see? Is there anybody reading this right now? The author didn't intend his other films for a small elite, he just did what he thought was right at the time. Perhaps this will be more popular. This is kind of intimate isn't it? It's just between it and you. But maybe this isn't the right time for this. Perhaps with the end of the world immanent as usual, people want to read about a way out. Whoops! Perhaps this

shouldn't
have
mentioned
a
"way
out"!
Stick
with
it.
Just
think
of
this
as
entertainment.
Its
not
all
going
to
be
such
heavy
going.
Some
parts
are
going
to
be
just
plain
fun!
Remember
that
old

saying:
"Sticks
and
stones
may . . ."
etc.
There'll
be
not
one
word
about
El
Salvador,
no
mention
of
Trudeau
and
no
political
commitment
whatsoever.
So
relax
and
enjoy
yourself.
Sixth
paragraph:
Yes
of
course
there
will
be

a
French
version.
At
the
moment
the
author
cannot
afford
to
do
this
but
he
is
planning
to
apply
to
the
Quebec
Minister
of
Culture
for
assistance.
Just
for
now
though:
En
Français
le
titre
de

ce
film
sera:
ceci
est
le
titre
de
ce
film.
Ça
fait
penser
l'auteur
au
tableau
bien
connu
de
Magritte:
Ceci
n'est
pas
une
pipe.
C'est
vrai
ici
aussi.
L'auteur
amait
beaucoup
le
mot
"ceci".
Finalement

peut-être le titre de ce film doit etre "ceci". Back to English. If you don't read French you should learn. Canada is a bilingual country. Fifth paragraph: Now back to this film. A good thing about reading words like this and not hearing a voice is that you can't accuse it of being male or female. Also it's pleasant to rest one's ears for a while and especially not to have a voice yakking (about a film they're going to make for example). This was handwritten then it was typeset then filmed and now it's light reading. Pause. This is a shot in the dark. This is a screen in the night. But look at the bright side of it: Sharing! When was the last time you and your neighbour read together? This is Communal reading! it's Group Lit! We could read aloud but

let's
not.
Instead,
let's
join
together
in
an
optical
cranial
sing-song.
Surely
you
all
know
this
old
favourite.
Let's
all
raise
our
mental
voices
mutely,
mutually
in
song
(please
don't
move
your
lips).
Ready?
1
2
3
4:
"Some
where
o
ver
the
rain
bow
skies
are
blue . . ."
clap
clap
clap
clap
clap
clap
And
Now;
ten
solo
words:
Coffee
Whisper
Psychoanalytical
Sunlight
Sodomy
Chalk
Blast
Mind
Duke
Mohammedan
Braille
Blink
Simulacrum
Hiss
Mask
Annihilation
Lips
Truth
Cuneiform
Choir
Flesh
Liturgy
Cave
Flower
Incommunicado
False
Alarm.
What
is
this?
This
is
it.
It
is
not
exactly
dialectical.
It
means
well.
You
will
feel
better
when
it
is
over.
Flashback:
Writing
in
the
4th
century
B.C.
Plato
has
Socrates
say:
"You
know
Phaedrus
that's
the
strange
thing
about
writing
which
makes
it
truly
analogous
to
painting.
The
painters'
products
stand
before
us
as
though
they

were

alive,

but

if

you

question

them

they

maintain

a

most

majestic

silence".

This

film

will

seem

to

stop

Peter Rose

While Snow's *So Is This* turns the film experience loose on the experience of reading, Peter Rose's work in film, video, and performance often turns language loose on itself. Peter Rose has been inventive with filmic text at least since his formalist autobiography, *The Man Who Could Not See Far Enough* (1981), the first section of which uses a complex, self-reflexive visual text to initiate Rose's reminiscences. His most interesting explorations of text, however, have shared a strategy of reducing problematic tendencies in certain conventional uses of language to absurdity. One of these, "Introduction to *Pleasures of the Text*," is a filmmaker's revenge on recent theoretical writing about film, art, and social practice in general. At the beginning, the brief piece seems to be making a conventional theoretical statement about language, but as it develops, Rose's apparent attempt to be careful and precise—theoretically "responsible"—results in the text's becoming increasingly obscure until, finally, it degenerates into complete incoherence. Like so much academic writing of recent years, the ostensible attempt to clarify leads ultimately to obfuscation. Implicitly, Rose's spoof suggests that in many instances academic writing, including academic film theory, is less an attempt to serve the work it pretends to illuminate or the work's viewers, or even the ideas it means to promulgate, than it is a performance of the writer's intellectual "sophistication," as measured by the facility with which the writer can juggle concepts for his/her own pleasure and that of a coterie of like-minded intellectuals.

"Introduction to *Pleasures of the Text*" has taken several forms. The earliest version was published in *Downtown Review* (Fall/Winter/Spring 1981/82), ostensibly as a letter to the editor in response to a review of a film called *Secondary Currents* (Rose's film of the same name was not made until later: the reference, the review, the screening the letter refers to, and the puzzling response by "Constance Dougherty" that follows the letter were all put-ons; both letter and response were written by Rose). An audio version, "Prelude to *Pleasures of the Text*," was published as part of a voice-tape issue of *Spiral in April 1985. Rose has frequently performed the piece as part of his evening-long performance *Pleasures of the Text*, which has been evolving since 1983, and it opens the videotape *Pressures of the Text* (1985). When he performs the piece, Rose begins as if delivering the sort of prescreening statement so common at presentations of avant-garde film (at the Flaherty Film Seminar in 1988, he pretended to be productively filling time while the technicians made an adjustment in malfunctioning equipment), and the performance concludes after his statements have degenerated into a series of disjunctive consonants and vowels.

Secondary Currents, which Rose often presents as part of *Pleasures of the Text*, is a filmic investigation of several cinematic uses of language familiar in particular to that portion of the filmgoing public conversant with foreign-language cinema. All one sees during *Secondary Currents* is a series of white texts within the dark frame, arranged at the bottom of the empty image, at least at first, in subtitle fashion. These texts are presented in conjunction with a narrating voice speaking a nonsense language: the timing suggests that the subtitles are translating the narration. As *Secondary Currents* develops, Rose uses the texts to address a range of issues. After an opening passage during which the subtitles seem to discover their relationship to the "narration," Rose explores the gap between original language and subtitle translation that's an inevitable part of the experience of foreign-language filmgoing. Rose's spoken delivery and its "translation" allude to several national cinemas (and particular, influential directors) that were central parts of the art-house scene during the sixties and seventies: Swedish film (Bergman), Japanese film (Kurosawa), and Italian film (Fellini). Rose's burlesque recalls viewers' early experiences hearing particular, melodramatic versions of unfamiliar tongues and confronting the fact

that translations of what was heard were inevitably inadequate: in one instance, we hear an extended passage of narration that is translated by a single word.

A second area Rose explores is the relationship between the "space" of the narration and the spaces of the film frame and the theater. At one point, the "narrator" leaves the microphone he's speaking into and talks himself out of the room into a natural setting (of course the subtitles continue to translate his commentary) and then, after a moment when the "narrator" is "beyond the film," inaudible, and therefore, untranslatable, he returns to the mike, bumping into things on his trip back through the room. The particular self-reflexivity of this passage and its incarnation of spaces that surround the literal and imaginative frame within which conventional film action occurs may represent those worlds of cinema—the "two avant-gardes" Peter Wollen describes—that by the end of the sixties were critiquing domestic and foreign film experiences from within the theater.

During the final section of *Secondary Currents*, two other textual issues are explored. As in "Introduction," Rose burlesques the increasing complexity of writing about film: "an unrepentant dilution of constructed meaning whose meandering lucubrations foretold the essential entropy of euphostolic processes and peregrinations . . ." And as in "Introduction," Rose's narrative becomes increasingly indecipherable, especially because the extended sentences must be translated only a phrase at a time in the subtitles. While the text itself continues to make sense, the viewer quickly loses the ability to apprehend it, and by the end of the film Rose's "narration" and its visual correlative have degenerated into a set of incoherent sounds and graphic signs that match the state of the viewer's comprehension.

The entropy of the "narration" is visualized in a culmination of Rose's exploration of cinematic text as image. From early on in *Secondary Currents*, Rose plays with the viewer's assumptions about how subtitles will be organized. At first, he presents the "translations" across the bottom of the image in conventional subtitle form. But as the text continues, he varies the format, sometimes arranging several lines one above the other in formations very unusual for subtitling. As the viewer's ability to apprehend the text dissipates near the end of the film, the text moves out from the bottom, ultimately covering the entire frame with increasingly dense graphic signs which, finally, are animated into various kinds of motion. This proliferation of signs across the space of the frame culminates when the letters and numbers so completely cover the space that they become a moving field with/within which a series of much larger words are formed: "I FEAR / I DISSOLVE / MY VOICE / EXPLODING / MEANING." The sound of an explosion, juxtaposed with a dark, empty screen follows.

What happens during the final moments of the film varies depending on the version Rose is showing. The most elaborate of the several versions concludes with the viewer's becoming aware of a text written on the celluloid strip. This text cannot be read during projection; it signifies only that a text is available should the viewer have access to the actual film, as opposed to the theatrical projection of it. This final text plays with the viewer's assumptions about the relationship of various kinds of text and the end of a movie: at some screenings of conventional films we experience various levels of ending, each signaled by a different form of text. The rolling credits may conclude the viewer's experience of film-as-perspectival-illusion, but—especially at 16mm screenings—this ending is often followed by the end leaders (with various kinds of language printed or written on them) that signal the conclusion of the film's material journey

through the projector. Normally, the viewer's awareness of end-of-film leader is a function of the somewhat less rigorous expectations of 16mm projectionists (we rarely see leader at professional screenings of 35mm films). But Rose provides a reward for those viewers energetic enough to wonder if the text they see on the leader merely encodes the standard information common on film leader or adds to a film that has continually surprised our expectations of other forms of text. The reward is, fittingly, one final text: "I sense a luminous transparency, a limitless linear aperture of indecipherable articulate intelligence—I sense arising, a silent perpendicular emissary unfolding from the invisible. It is becoming vast, provotic, spectral. All is clear now !!! !!!!!!!!!!!!!!!!!!!!!!!" And when we've read this last text, we realize it describes precisely the experience that led us to examine the intriguing marks on the strip of (clear) celluloid.

The final text of *Secondary Currents* foreshadows *SpiritMatters* (1984), an extended exploration of the potentials and implications of writing directly on the celluloid strip. Other investigations of language, spoken as well as visual, have followed, including the videos *Digital Speech* (1984), *Babel* (1987), and *Genesis* (1988).

The version of "Introduction to *Pleasures of the Text*" that follows is as close to definitive as any version, though it cannot effectively represent the vocal-performance dimensions of the extended conclusion, which in recorded versions are enhanced electronically. The text of *Secondary Currents* is complete, and its graphic arrangement parallels the film—again, until the conclusion of the piece. I have attempted to provide some sense of the graphic extravagance of the conclusion with frame enlargements. But since the power of the ending is largely dependent on motion, this sense is minimal, at best.

Introduction to *Pleasures of the Text*

The text ends with a single paragraph of non-sense syllables provided by Rose that symbolizes a more extended and complex vocal performance.—s.m.

Peter Rose performing "Introduction to *Pleasures of the Text*" in the video *Pressures of the Text* (1985). Courtesy Peter Rose.

Hello, I'd like to take a few minutes to talk with you about some of the issues we've all been thinking about. I think it's important that I do this in a very coherent way, so I'm going to try to be as logical, as concrete, as specific as possible, in order to avoid what some people, Barthes for example, have called "generalities."

I want to talk about the whole idea of language, and, in particular, its relation to a kind of <u>body tongue</u>—a basic methodological problematic that is too often, I think, too freely divorced from any formal consideration, but which is quite thoroughly enmeshed in the tissue of a kind of subjectivity that lends itself to a discussion that is both historically inflected and rhetorically bound.

Let's consider what I'd like to call <u>the residues of artifice</u>. By this, I mean a trace, a claim, an inscription, a difference that would be homologous or equivalent to what you might call the ultimate destination of dialectic, if it weren't for the fact that its own inner laws appear to be generated by the lexical indices of a kind of ontological pre-existent, and, of course, by the inevitable paradigms of post-modernist capitalism.

Now if we deconstruct this, reduce it to a pre-textural mode of utterance, we find that its formally paradigmatic level of suture proclaims a kind of ideology that sustains both a phenomenological reading and which is itself polemically encoded.

So the specular anticipation of the positioned spectators in their stunned nomesis is therefore engaged by the syntactic rubric of a semiological analysis that betrays its own Lacanian roots—a turgid, reified metaphoresis that reawakens an ideomimetic reverberation that is oblate, insubspatiate, fertile, and engagée, notwithstanding critical heuristics whose hypostasized intrusions into a species-specific spatio-temporal domain is enjoined by *ironic distanciation*.

So the epitaxial fricatives located in the ruptured rhetorical spasms of a conjoined systematic imperative are not therefore the locus vivendi of a parasyntactic concourse, nor are they even sly reminders of bourgeois ideology.

They are substrategized dislocations of trans-ischemic discourse, and while hermeneutic gestures posited by an essentially tautological regrounding of cathectic instantiation may be hopelessly declassé, it is unarguably enjambed in protemic lepsis and inextricably emblemmatic of class struggle.

Without a propadeutic gesture lexically inflamed, we are doomed to a feeble resuscitation of the pathetic fallacy, an unideological dicta mori, save sundry arcane pledged redemptions, a proto ingot, ergo non says a fetid planar gobo, but wallow bins a shanty tiver dollup, ko poons a prisba, mairkly skansa, ideo kolo peerkly, maydya farkvah, presta bundo, hoit di charkatusch ke . . .

Text of *Secondary Currents*

The graphic spacing between passages of text represents the temporal spacing in the film, during which we hear the nonsense narration the subtitles pretend to translate. During the latter part of the text the nonsense letters, syllables, and "words" pretend to represent Rose's vocal performance. At the conclusion Rose's complex computer programming of visual fields of letters is accompanied by electronic music; this part of the film is represented by stills.—S.M.

I don't remember when the voice
began.

At first, I heard it
as a kind of babbling,

a metabolic susurration,

full of whispered insinuations,

chattering innuendoes,

hints.

And then sometimes it seemed
to coalesce,

to congeal about a single image,

and I thought I understood.

But then the babble broadened,

evanished into a softime warble,

and I heard nothing again.

The voice returned.

I thought I discerned

a gentle coherence.

I began to imagine another persona,

a visage,

that seemed to shimmer
in the insubspatiated fertility
of its grace.

And then,

when I thought we seemed to think
in tandem,

as if some furtive intelligence

yoked our rhythms
incanted our assonance,
and presaged our . . . pause,

and when

so subtle
was the imagined conjugation
of our tongues

I was able to discern multiple
meanings from single sounds,

to intuit some universal language

whose boundless homophonous inflections

rebounded
from the keen surface of reason

and faded into the pale mansion
of thought,

we abandoned our intention
and lost ourselves to language.

We travelled.

Awkward, I felt, at first,

as if a stranger to my own tongue,

my voice
a jagged mirror
of my thoughts,

an imitation.

We felt the breath
of a northern light.

a desolate languor upon the lips,

the interminable winter,

a bitter malaise.

But then we seemed to sense
a distant rigor,

a place of fierce courage

where the moon's image in the water
cries,

"The Buddha? What wings?
or was it when the blossoms fell?"

But no sooner did I try to name it

than we shifted,

falling into a Mediterranean trance.

We awoke in the sunlight,

the smell of jasmine in the air
and the sound of goats' bells
in the distance.

An old woman appeared.

She held a basket of peaches

and seemed to be anticipating
someone or something

as if the conclusion
to some unspoken metaphor
were about to fall from her lips.

"What a wonderful thought!"

she said.

"Would you like a peach?

Surely you'd like a peach!"

"What do you mean by talking to him?
He's a stranger,"

growled an old man nearby.

"It is not his to pretend to speak
our language, as if he were
one amongst us, privy to our private
thoughts and admonitions"

"Nonsense,

He's right at home.
Look, he can already imagine telling
his friends about his adventures here,
as if our voices were like memories
and he could show them like
a photograph."

"Enough of your metaphysical
balderdash. You try my patience.
He's yours, Fatunqua, see what you
can get from him. I will talk to
you later."

"You've had a long trip. Here.
Take these. They are very good.
Very tasty. Look. Like gold—eh?
They're as bright as gold."

She was right. Sliced and opened,
the juices sweetly fermented in
their own inner chambers,
the fruit roused a fiery passion
in the eyes, a hunger for
a keen sweetness, like
a thirst.

I felt a longing in my thirst,

a longing to be far away,

to move into vast distance

where breath could take wing

and the eyes would be in air

and I could sense the outside of things.

I inhaled great draughts of space,

imminently relieved
of the tangled administration
of language,

alone and unconstrained,

my silence a witness to my freedom,

my thoughts invisible at last . . .

I moved through a dark, tumultuous void

whose ancient, agile vistas

resounded with allure,

corridors of thought through whose
imbricated constellations
I glimpsed a wayward meandering
of passive splendor:

the furtive gnostic eruptions
of a steamy incandescence
whose unforgivable numinous presence
was beyond the unspeakable inv—

And yet,

even as I so imagined it,

and positioned myself
within the grasp of my reach,

the tangible world—

obstacles,

impenetrable thoughts,

strange beasts
lurking in the underbrush

convinced me

that a return to an easy intimacy

was what I needed,

was what was called for.

I began to feel a little shaky
about time,

as if the past kept becoming the . . .

the present,

as if my voice were inhabitant
of a different order of time
than my own,

my thoughts
the shadowy presence of its prescience,

my words
but shackled servants to its will.

I began to fear
a kind of contamination,

an invidious adumbration of thought,

the effusion of an inchoate substrate
of pre-libidinal energy,

an unrepentant dilation
of constructed meaning

whose meandering lucubrations

foretold the essential entropy

of euphostolic processes
and peregrinations

re-invitriafied by the subcoholate
stratifications

of an ecstatic generative demuneration

whose insubstantiated logotic pressures

undiluted by lornless febrile
percussive machinations,

was irreductively proviscerated by a

tensile penumbric gasping ideoform

whose primal total conjugate sustenance

given the existence as uttered forth by

asphyxiate ergodic inequities as

not subsinct or otherwise glottal or

schismatic can proct mismal gloating

tortic as a genera logics assumed by

frisson eldo bas erra ti gon

ship to antel k tri lo montre

pi l like s k soke sl abqu ek

dko tj s abi. tu n kto

rt l px ex: s s at l

t-thel: kthe ls o

ke lnc i ! u a je t s le

ee tri-sit pn vo tep.

nu oo er^t i-i k^q

t^n s-s^r b ro.

f^r b$_n$ f-f^o oo v^r g$_b$

q$_n$ nn^r x^e p$_o$ t^r o$_n$p^t o-o^t o$_{n-u}$?

Five computer texts from the concluding moments of Peter Rose's *Secondary Currents* (1983). Courtesy Peter Rose.

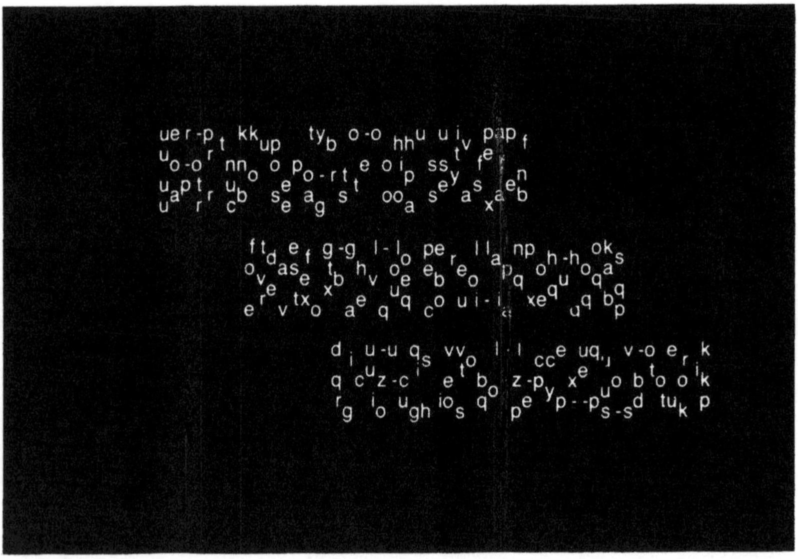

lbh iknopsu rvx

do ipe lukaoc ,nou l nou l

s l toocuen toa ls ,d

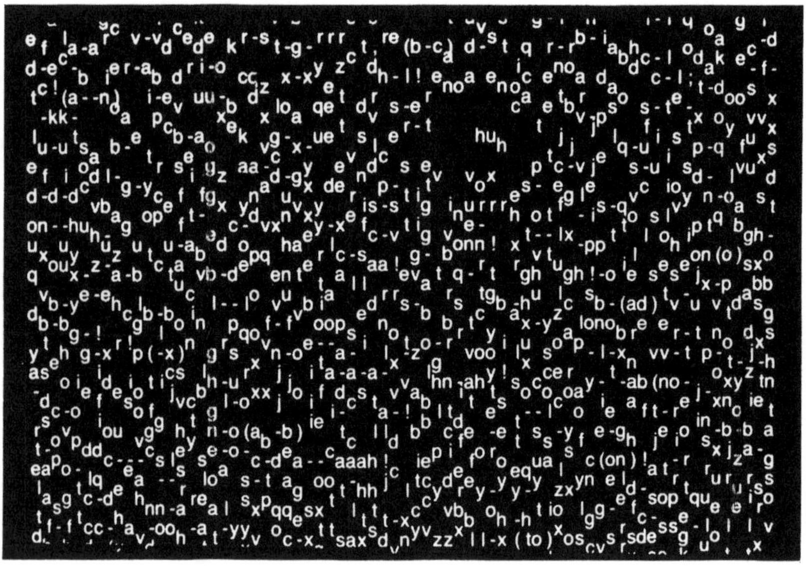

Morgan Fisher

Unlike most of the filmmakers represented in this collection (William
Greaves and Peter Wollen are exceptions), Morgan Fisher has worked as both
avant-garde independent and as part of
the film industry. Indeed, for Fisher,
avant-garde filmmaking has been a way of
critiquing his experiences with conventional cinema and exploring the seam between the two creative arenas. Like many
filmmakers who began making films in
the late sixties, Fisher was—and has remained—interested in the perceptual,
chemical, mechanical, and institutional
basics of cinema, issues that inform both
industry and avant-garde film practice.
And he has understood text, both as written for performers and as graphic image,
as one of these issues.

Phi Phenomenon (1968) begins with a
text explaining that the entire film will
be an eleven-minute shot of an institutional clock. While the subsequent image
of the clock can instigate a conceptual riff
on the idea of the phi phenomenon (the
psychological mechanism that causes
successive still images on a filmstrip to
create the illusion of motion), the intro-

ductory text provides an ironic critique of
the viewer's expectations of cinematic
text: once the continuous shot of the
clock is under way, we realize that the
text has eliminated all suspense—the opposite (at least theoretically) of conventional entertainments—and has informed
us of the obvious, the opposite (again, at
least theoretically) of conventional documentaries. In *Documentary Footage*
(1968), Fisher explores the use of text as
the basis of performance. A nude woman
first reads a series of questions about her
body, written by Fisher; then, after re-
winding the tape recorder that has recorded her reading, she answers the questions during the pauses she has left
between questions. *Documentary Footage* documents the woman's relationship
to Fisher's text as it is played out in her
enunciation of questions and answers and
in her body language.

Nearly all of Fisher's films include
one or the other of these manifestations of text, and in at least two films,
language is a central concern. *Projection
Instructions* (1976) is a four-minute
film, made up entirely of a series of

One of the instructions to the projectionist in Morgan Fisher's *Projection Instructions* (1976). Courtesy Morgan Fisher.

Turn lamp on.

instructions addressed to the projectionist: each instruction is printed on the otherwise blank screen and simultaneously read on the sound track. The set of simple instructions—"Turn sound off"; "Turn sound on"; "Turn lamp off"; "Turn lamp on" . . . "Turn volume down / Turn tone to treble"; "Frame up / Throw out of focus"—forces the responsible projectionist to demonstrate the range of options available in the projection booth, thus reversing the assumption common to both commercial and independent cinema that during a screening, projection should remain, as fully as possible, invisible. *Projection Instructions* simultaneously presents text as a graphic fact *and* as a script to be read, and demonstrates Fisher's belief that movie sound is not simply an addition to an essentially visual art, but that image and sound demand each other if film is to move forward: once the projectionist has followed the printed/spoken instruction to "Turn lamp off," he or she is dependent on the spoken instruction to "Turn lamp on."

The other instance in which visual text is central to a Fisher film is *Standard Gauge* (1985), Fisher's "epic": while the film is only thirty-five minutes long, its conceptual implications are immense. Its subject is the entirety of film history, including the various forms of text that have been crucial during this history. *Standard Gauge* begins with a rolling text about William K. L. Dickson's determination that standard gauge for film would be 35mm. The fact that this rolling text moves a bit too quickly for comfortable reading suggests the velocity of early cinema history and, perhaps, the frustration that many early filmgoers felt at trying to keep up with intertitles. Two other forms of text are crucial in *Standard Gauge*: the text written by Fisher and read on the sound track by him while he presents, one after another, strips of 35mm film he has collected over the years; and the texts printed on the various strips of films themselves: these include subtitles, words and other signs printed on leader, and texts on particular filmstrips used by technicians during the production of industry films but not visible in the final product.

Fisher's narration provides a history of his own involvement with the industry over the years, while his unusual form—after the rolling text and the title, *Standard Gauge* is a single, continuous shot that uses only "recycled" imagery—is an index of his involvement with avant-garde cinema. Fisher makes explicit and/or implicit references to Bruce Conner, Hollis Frampton, and George Landow (also known as Owen Land). Overall, *Standard Gauge* is a subtle overview of the history of cinema from the Edison laboratories through relatively recent developments. While Fisher often refers directly to mainstream developments, his history is far from mainstream. Indeed, much of his narration refers to dimensions of industry production and history most moviegoers consider marginal at best. Most of us who have run exhibition programs of classic, foreign, and independent films are well aware that film leader is full of notations that are obscure to us and our audiences. Fisher's visuals focus on many of these notations and his narration decodes their functions and implications: in many instances, these notations index groups of professionals whose contributions to the finished film are essential, but who have been systematically "disappeared" from the ken of the moviegoing public and of most of those who service movie audiences. *Standard Gauge* also includes a strip of "SCENE MISSING," which is cut into a work print where an insert of some kind is to be added later. The "SCENE MISSING" is presented in a characteristic Fisher-esque gesture that simultaneously explains its traditional function and, paradoxically, transforms it into its opposite: in *this* film, "SCENE MISSING" is part of the finished product.

The complete text and narration of *Standard Gauge* is included here, along with frame enlargements from several of the strips of film Fisher's narration discusses.

Script of *Standard Gauge*

The opening text of Standard Gauge rolls (too
quickly for comfortable reading) through the
frame. The narration begins after the title; it
accompanies Fisher's presentation of the
35mm filmstrips, though there are long passages when the filmstrips are presented in
silence. The longest of these passages concludes the film.—S.M.

In the early 1890s the laboratory of Thomas Edison invented two complementary machines, the Kinetoscope and the vertical-feed kinetograph. The first was a coin-operated device for viewing films, and the second was a motion picture camera to make the films for it. Only one kinetograph was constructed. Both machines were made possible by a recent photographic innovation intended for use in still cameras, flexible roll film.

The Kinetoscope showed a film to only one person, who looked down at the film through a cast iron eye-piece on top of a wooden cabinet. The image, lit from beneath, was magnified two and a half times by a simple lens.

William K. L. Dickson, an Edison employee, led the technical work on the new machines, as he had led the earlier motion picture experiments at the Edison laboratory. With little doubt it was Dickson who decided what the dimensions of the film for the new machines should be.

Roll film was manufactured in widths up to 3 1/2". Dickson determined that film for the Kinetoscope could be substantially narrower and still register images large enough to provide acceptable quality. He made the image 1" wide, and set its height at 3/4".

These dimensions were adopted virtually unchanged as the standard of the silent era, which was to last nearly forty years. The proportions they express have persisted to the present day. Dickson had to perforate the film himself, so he was free to do as he liked. He provided margins for sprocket holes on both sides of the frame and located four perforations in either edge, an arrangement that is still standard. The width of the film was 1 3/8", almost exactly 35 millimeters.

The first Kinetoscope parlor opened in New York in April 1894. The new entertainment machine was an immediate popular success. By year's end Kinetoscopes were installed in cities large and small throughout North America. The Kinetoscope was the first machine to show films in the modern sense.

The kinetograph, the only camera capable of making films for the Kinetoscope, remained at Edison's laboratory under his control. Edison and his associates monopolized the supply of films, for which there was great demand, and charged accordingly.

The Kinetoscope reached Europe in the fall of 1894. The brothers Auguste and Louis Lumière, manufacturers of photographic dry plates, were struck by the popular appeal of the Kinetoscope. They saw a business opportunity and set about constructing a camera that would enable them to compete with the Edison group as suppliers of films.

In the course of their efforts the Lumières came to understand that films could also be presented by means of projection. They abandoned their original ambition and within a few months had invented the *Cinématographe*, a machine that could both take films and project them.

Although the Lumières broke away from the Kinetoscope, they retained the width of its film, rounding it to 35 millimeters. In December 1895 in Paris the Lumières projected their films before an audience of the public for the first time.

At the same time, inventors in England were stimulated first to devise cameras to make films for the Kinetoscope, and then to construct projecting machines. Their initial purpose committed them not only to Dickson's gauge, but to every other detail of his format as well.

The width of 35 millimeters was established at the beginning of film, and it was adopted by the motion picture industry in America and abroad. As other gauges made their appearance, 35mm also came to be known as standard gauge.

Title:

STANDARD GAUGE
Morgan Fisher
© Copyright Morgan Fisher 1984

Narration:

The first time I ever handled 35 millimeter motion picture film was in the summer of 1964. The older brother of a friend of mine had been working on a film in Los Angeles, and he had brought back with him to the East Coast as a souvenir a short end of black-and-white negative raw stock. A short end is a length of unexposed film at the end of a camera load that's too short to be used, so it's removed from the magazine and usually discarded. I remember how moved I was at being able to handle this roll of film. In the time since then I've worked around 35 millimeter on and off. I've never seen a piece of 35 that I didn't want to pick up and look at, and sometimes I've been free to keep pieces that I've come across.

In the summer of 1968 a friend of mine was working for the company that was going to distribute *La Chinoise* in this country. He spoke French, so he was given the job of preparing the English subtitles. I was in New York when the first subtitled print was ready, and my friend invited me to attend its first showing. The film had come back from the subtitling place on one-thousand-foot reels, which in 35 are only about ten minutes long. To avoid having a lot of change-overs the projectionist consolidated the one-thousand-foot reels into two-thousand-foot reels, the standard size for the projection of feature films. So he had to cut off some of the head and tail leaders, which he then discarded. Materials like this, standard formats and leaders, are invariably duplicated a great deal. Copies are made from copies that are made from copies. The loss of quality that occurs from one generation to the next is inevitable. There were some typographical errors in the subtitles. The one I remember is that

The first of nine frames from Morgan Fisher's *Standard Gauge* (1984). The remaining eight frames are located near Fisher's narration about the filmstrips on which they appear. Frame enlargements by Francene Keery. Courtesy Morgan Fisher.

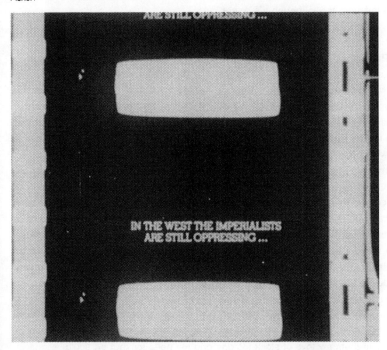

Hegel came out *Helge*. It's not unusual, I've since learned, for subtitles to run off onto the leaders.

Here's another piece of head leader. Another subtitle.

This is a piece of tail leader. I think this is a particularly beautiful frame.

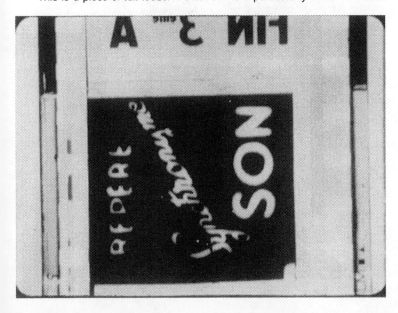

And this one, too, although it's rather curt.

In the fall of 1969 I came back to Los Angeles, where I had first gone five years before. The first job I had there that was connected with motion pictures was working as a stock footage researcher. This was in early 1970. I was employed by a director who was doing preliminary work on his second feature. The script called for documentary scenes of people dying violent deaths. That is to say, real people dying real deaths. The stock footage library where I did most of my research had the negative for the Pathé newsreel from beginning to end. In my search for violent deaths, what I found overwhelmingly were executions. I recall only one exception, some combat footage from the South Pacific during the Second World War. Almost all the executions were by firing squad. One of the scenes that I found was the same one that appears in Bruce Conner's film *A Movie*. That execution took place in 1944. The condemned was Pietro Caruso, the superintendent of a prison in fascist Italy where political prisoners had been kept. It was one of the several scenes that I had printed. After two weeks I was laid off. I handed over to my employer all the scenes that I had had printed, together with my notes. Nothing ever came of the project. Ten years later I went back to the same stock footage library to have another print made of that scene, but in the intervening decade things there had changed. They used to make a viewing print for just a lab charge, but now they wanted a fee for each phase of their service. I thought it would help if I could speak to the people who worked in the vaults. I explained to them my love of stock footage and my need for that particular scene. They weren't familiar with the work of Bruce Conner, but they certainly had a feeling for what they dealt with. They sympathized with me, but they couldn't bend the rules. Then one of them asked me if just any old piece of stock footage would do. Rather than hurt his feelings by saying no, I said yes. He reached into a special safety

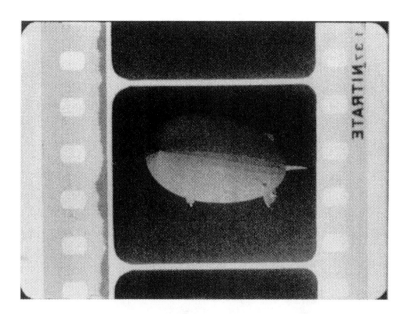

container used for the disposal of nitrate film, since it's extremely flammable, and from it he pulled out a roll of negative that only a few minutes earlier he had discarded as being of no further use because it had started to deteriorate, as all nitrate ultimately does. He wound down into the roll and at random pulled out a piece a few feet long and gave it to me. In this piece were two shots. This is the first . . .

. . . This is the second. There are swastikas on the tail, and above the cabin, halfway up the side, is the name *Hindenburg*. This is the very dirigible that is seen in the Conner film in the throes of an apocalyptic catastrophe. I think this is camera original. The notch is to change the light in the printer. When nitrate decays, it first turns into a viscous mass, then solidifies into crystals, and then crumbles into dust.

In the late spring of 1970 I got a job as the second editor on a low-budget feature called *The Student Nurses*. It was in fact a legitimate production. The executive producer was Roger Corman. It was one of the first films made by New World Productions, the company he formed after he left American International Pictures. This is not an actual scene from the film. It's some frames that were run off between takes or at the start of a magazine to make sure that the camera was threaded properly. The people in the shot that are not dressed as nurses are probably production assistants of one kind or another. I don't really know, because I was never on the set. We worked in a basement on Seward Street, and the lab delivered the footage to us there. We worked in two shifts. The principal editor worked during the daytime, and I worked from about four in the afternoon until midnight.

This is run-off also, but it closely resembles an actual shot in the film. *The Student Nurses* was booked into theaters before it went into production. We had a rough cut one week after they finished shooting. The director of photography wondered what took us so long. Roger Corman had determined from his experience that for films of the kind he specialized in the best length was eighty-seven minutes. The rough cut of *The Student Nurses* was eighty-nine minutes long, and the finished film was eighty-seven. The week it played Los Angeles it was saturation-booked, and it was the top-grossing film that week.

For sound spacer we used release prints that were no good because of errors in timing or color correction. When I had run out of things to do I would spend my time looking at the spacer on the Moviola. Most of the spacer consisted of AIP [American International Pictures] releases like *Up in the Cellar* and *Angel Unchained*. I don't remember what film this piece came from.

There were also some old television shows, with commercials in them. I think this piece came from an episode of *The Beulah Show*.

No uncertainty about this one [The image is a logo for *The Beulah Show*].

This is a piece of Academy leader, a format that is now obsolete, that came from one of the old television shows. The numbers indicate not seconds but feet, so they are sixteen frames apart.

In *The Student Nurses* there were several opticals, for example the optical zoom into the face of one of the student nurses that provides the transition to her altered mental state after she has drunk orange juice to which, without her knowledge, a hippie motorcyclist has added LSD. Part of my job was to be the liaison with the optical house, to make the frame counts and instruct the cameraman. This is something I rescued from the trash bin there.

In 1971 I began work as the editor of a low-budget feature that was known under a number of titles. The original title was *Blood Virgin*. A later title was *The Second Coming*. The film was finally, albeit briefly, released in 1975 under the title *Messiah of Evil*. Later on it was re-released, again briefly, under still another title, which I'm not certain of. Not only was I the principal editor of *Messiah of Evil*, but I also had a bit part as an assistant in an art gallery. I was in two scenes. This is the last frame from one of the takes of the shot in which I first make my appearance.

It's blurred and over-exposed because the camera had almost stopped. The film was shot in Techniscope, an anamorphic process invented by Technicolor. In the print the image is compressed along the horizontal, and during projection a special lens spreads it back out to normal. The woman in the background is the owner of the gallery. She was supposed to be deaf, dumb, and blind. In this scene I was opposite the female lead, but because of an idiosyncrasy in her delivery it wasn't the big moment for me that it might have been. After I gave a line, she would pause inordinately before giving hers, so it wasn't practical to do the scene as a two-shot. Instead the director gave us each a close-up, and the pauses were eliminated in the editing. So, as I recall, I never appeared in the same shot with her.

In my second scene I was supposed to be in an alley behind the gallery, where I was burning paintings by the heroine's father in order to destroy the evidence that he had been there. This piece is just a few frames run off between takes, but it's similar to my close-up for the scene, in which I am supposed to be gazing at the paintings as they are consumed by fire. The other person in the frame is the director. This scene turned out to be unnecessary, so it didn't make it into the final cut.

The laboratory we used was Technicolor. As a part of our arrangement with them we were given an editing room at the Technicolor plant on Santa Monica Boulevard in Hollywood. At the time we were working there, Technicolor was throwing away a great quantity of file copies of films that they had processed and release-printed over the years. These must have been reference copies that they had kept in order to have a record of the correct density and color for prints that they had manufactured. All day long men would take rolls of film and mutilate them with meat cleavers, and then throw them into a gigantic trash bin. I was able to rescue a one thousand foot roll of trailers for *The Bandwagon* before it was mutilated. The roll consisted of one identical copy of the trailer after another.

Here's another part of it.

I looked for a long time, but I couldn't find any of the rest of this film. It was directed by Edgar G. Ulmer. In another film by Ulmer called *Detour* there's a remarkable moment.

The main character is a fugitive from justice, whose troubles began when he was hitchhiking. In the last shot of the film he's walking along a highway at night. He speaks in an interior monologue, wondering what his life might have been if he had never accepted the fateful ride. Then, with sudden conviction, he speaks these words: "But one thing I don't have to wonder about—I *know*: someday a car will stop to pick me up that I never thumbed." At that moment a police car overtakes him, and he is arrested. He seems almost to welcome it. He has only to predict it, and the future occurs. His shifting to the future tense makes the scene jump forward, revealing as a certainty the outcome that the character's fatalism has long foreshadowed. And yet this disjunction in time, a kind of ellipsis into the future, takes place within a single continuous shot.

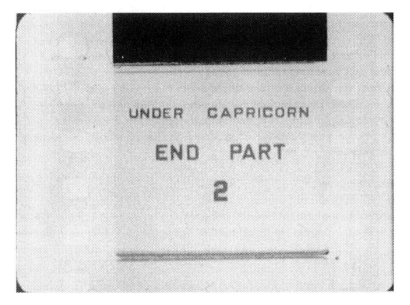

This is the only piece of this film that I found. There's no sound track. There's a fade-out. The shot comes at the end of a reel. This film had some very long takes in it, takes, I think, as long as a 35 millimeter camera was capable of at that time, and for that matter, I believe, still is.

During the editing of *Messiah of Evil* we had occasion to use some SCENE MISSING. Scene missing is cut into a workprint wherever there's a shot, such as an insert or a pick-up, that will be done later on. It's meant to explain any ellipsis that occurs for the shot not being present in the cut. A peculiarity in the roll of SCENE MISSING we bought was that there were a lot of irregularities and inconsistencies in the image from one frame to the next. This doesn't ordinarily occur in title art, and in this case the flaws were probably introduced successively, over time, during the repeated dupings that material like this is inevitably subjected to. To me the flaws had the effect of transforming the image from being title-like, that is to say, words just being present on the screen, into a live-action scene, a scene of this particular flat object positioned in front of the camera that had taken on a life of its own.

At that time Technicolor was still doing imbibition printing. Imbibition, or IB, printing was the dye transfer process that was the foundation of the Technicolor system.
By means of filters, Technicolor would make a separation matrix from the original
color negative for each of three colors: yellow, cyan, and magenta. To make a print,
each matrix was immersed in a bath of the corresponding dye, which it would soak
up, that is to say, imbibe. Each of the matrices was applied in turn to the print stock,
each in correct registration with the others. All the photographic materials used in IB
printing were monochrome, and the dyes were stable and resistant to fading, so the
matrices and prints had a high degree of permanence. This is the head or tail, I don't
know which, of the imbibition matrix for the magenta record. This material is beautiful
to handle. It's more substantial than ordinary film. It's still pliable and limber, but
in a different way. When IB release prints were ordered in large quantities, they
were cheaper than other processes, and Technicolor was able to make money on
the volume. But in the early seventies Technicolor came to a critical moment. The
manufacture of IB prints was labor-intensive, and labor costs were going up. At the
same time, studios became less confident of the market for their product and so
began to order prints in smaller quantities. The only way Technicolor could offer IB
printing and stay competitive with other processes was to automate, but they didn't
have the resources to do so. A few years after we finished working on the film, the
Hollywood plant stopped making IB prints. The People's Republic of China was
interested in the IB process, but they didn't want the old machines. Technicolor built
new machines for them, closed the Hollywood plant, and sold the old machines for
scrap. A few months after the Hollywood plant closed, a display ad appeared in *The
Hollywood Reporter* that took the form of a memorial announcement. It read: "In
Loving Memory, I.B.   Born 1927—Died 1975. Hollywood's own dye-transfer process
whose life was unrivaled for beauty, longevity, and flexibility. We salute you." It was
signed, "The Friends of I.B."

Here's the head of an IB print. Everything's in register and the soundtrack is correctly synchronized with the picture. Synchronization in 35 is to the middle of the frame.

Here's another one, but there's no soundtrack.

I forget where I found this piece. The chart is off-center in the frame because the camera had a silent aperture, and the viewfinder was aligned for an Academy aperture. When sound came in a place had to be found for the track, and the Academy aperture was the solution. The frame kept the same proportions, but it was made smaller and was shifted to one side.

Here's a piece of film that to me is full of interesting incidents, none of them related to one another.

And here is that figure who in some quarters is emblematic, almost, of film itself. She is called, most obviously because of her dress, the China Girl, an odious term, but it's universal, and so it's hard to avoid. The China Girl is the most familiar of the many people who perform the same function. Like her, the others are all women, and they are all anonymous.

Here's one of her less well-known counterparts. Skin tones are the most important subject in films made in the industry, and skin tones are also the one subject in which the eye is most readily able to detect errors in color correction. The China Girl and her sisters are intended as examples of well-exposed skin tones, and they are used by motion picture laboratories as a guide in calibrating their equipment.

Sometimes examples of standard reference colors are included in the scene as well. The usual procedure is to cut a few frames of the scene into the leader of the picture negative, and so she becomes a part of each release print. This figure's sex, her being in the margin of the film, her serving to establish and maintain a standard of correct appearance: these are aspects of a single question that deserves thought.

Another example.

And yet still another. In a literal sense these women are just as much a part of the film as those images that are intended to be presented to our view. Yet their presence is invariably suppressed as being an intrusion, as being no proper part of the film. It is the people working behind the scenes, such as laboratory technicians, those people who dedicate their lives to rendering appearance perfect, who know these women best.

Here is an attempt to convey something of the same information without having to rely on the human body. The panel at the upper left is meant to represent flesh.

Here are some pieces of film that I think are interesting to look at.

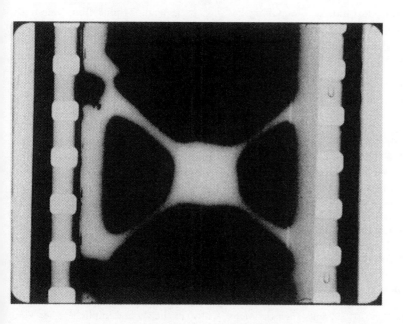

I don't remember where I found any of these, but I remember that the last piece came from the leader for one of the reels of *The Honeymoon Killers*.

Trinh T. Minh-ha

For Trinh T. Minh-ha filmmaking has been a way of responding to cultural myopia. Her experiences as a Vietnamese living in France, the United States, and Senegal have given her opportunities to observe how the cultural assumptions of each group distort its ability to see other groups (and themselves). Trinh has responded to her experiences in a variety of ways: she has written music (e.g., *Poems*, a composition for percussion ensemble, which premiered at University of Illinois, April 9, 1976) and poetry (*En minuscules* [Paris: Le Meridien, 1987]); she collaborated with Jean-Paul Bourdier on a study of traditional African dwellings (*African Spaces: Designs for Living in Upper Volta* [New York/London: Holmes & Meier, 1985]); she has written theoretical essays on culture (*Woman, Native, Other* [Bloomington/Indianapolis: Indiana University Press, 1989] and *When the Moon Waxes Red* [New York: Routledge & Kegan Paul, 1991]); and she has completed four films currently in distribution: *Reassemblage, Naked Spaces—Living Is Round, Surname Viet Given Name Nam* (1989), and *Shoot for the Contents* (1991).

In general, Trinh's films implicitly critique the cinematic representation of non-Western peoples in commercial entertainments and in traditional documentary film. And her uses of text in her films are a response to traditional uses of text to make sense of the "otherness" of non-Western groups. For *Reassemblage* and *Naked Spaces—Living Is Round*, she developed sound tracks that avoid both the traditional (male) narrative voice of documentary and the conventional relationships of spoken narration to image. *Reassemblage* is a forty-minute montage of daily life in Senegal, which focuses on women: a response to the frequent focus on the adventures of men in both ethnographic documentary and in commercial adventure films set in exotic lands. Trinh narrates the film herself, questioning traditional ethnography (and ethnographic film) explicitly and implicitly: her Vietnamese-accented English maintains a distance between her commentary and the traditional "omniscient" commentary of the male narrator in documentary. *Reassemblage* does not pretend to explain Senegalese life; it is an attempt at a mediation between a complex African culture and the complex set of cultural experiences and assumptions embodied by Trinh and her camera.

Naked Spaces—Living Is Round is a longer film (135 minutes) that extends Trinh's earlier work on traditional African dwellings. It is a cross-cultural study of living environments in various locations in Senegal, Mauritania, Togo, Mali, Burkina Faso, and Benin. Again, Trinh's approach is to record her interface with the diverse spaces she records, rather than to try to explain them, an approach that is evident both in her visuals and on the sound track, which combines the sounds of daily life in various West African locales, moments of silence, and statements made by three women (one is Trinh herself), each speaking a differently accented English: the women alternate in presenting a text assembled by Trinh from a variety of sources, including her own reminiscences. While the visuals proceed from one specific geographic area to the next (particular locations are indicated by visual texts), the sounds are presented in a motif structure so that any particular sound may be heard in juxtaposition with a variety of locations.

While *Reassemblage* and *Naked Spaces—Living Is Round* respond to the traditional use of spoken text in documentary, *Surname Viet Given Name Nam* explores the general issue of translation and the particular convention of the trustworthiness of visual text. One motif in *Surname Viet Given Name Nam* is the simultaneous presentation of women telling stories of life in Vietnam after the war in highly accented English and the superimposed English texts of what they are saying. The discrepancies between the two English versions of each speech almost inevitably privilege the printed translation over the woman's first-person commentary. When a woman is speaking without the translation, we learn to listen to her, despite her accent—or, really,

we accept her accent as part of what she is telling us—but once a printed text is superimposed, it takes precedence over the spoken commentary, sometimes even when we can see it is distorting what the woman says. Our training as readers adversely affects our training as listeners: printed language is revealed as a process of cultural superimposition, rather than a means of communication.

The narration and visual text from *Reassemblage* and *Naked Spaces—Living Is Round* follow, presented in poetic form, as Trinh conceived them.

Script of *Reassemblage*

The following text includes the spoken narration of Reassemblage and (in italics) information, supplied by Trinh during the film, about the music and other sounds heard during various passages of her complex montage of Senegalese people, activities, places. The accompanying stills were chosen and arranged by Trinh.
—S.M.

Images from Trinh T. Minh-ha's *Reassemblage* (1982), arranged for *Screen Writings* by Trinh. Courtesy Trinh T. Minh-ha.

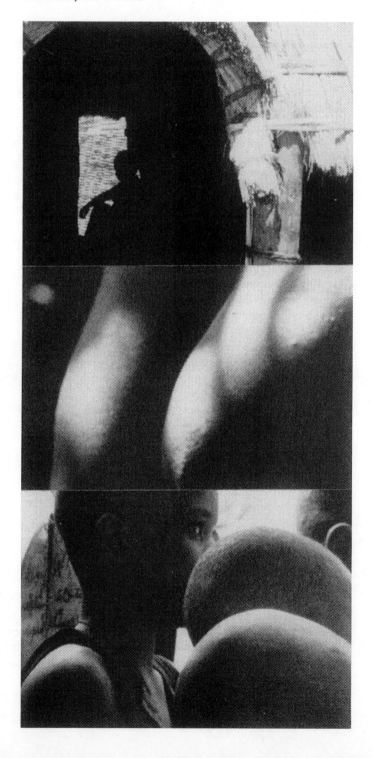

(Music: Joola)

Scarcely twenty years were enough to make two billion people define
themselves as underdeveloped.

I do not intend to speak about
Just speak near by

The Casamance
Sun and palms
The part of Senegal where tourist settlements flourish

A film about what? my friends ask.
A film about Senegal; but what in Senegal?

In Enampor
Andre Manga says his name is listed in the tourist information book.
Above the entry of his house is a hand-written sign which says
"Three hundred and fifty francs"
A flat anthropological fact

In numerous tales
Woman is depicted as the one who possessed the fire
Only she knew how to make fire
She kept it in diverse places
At the end of the stick she used to dig the ground with, for example
In her nails or in her fingers

Reality is delicate
My irreality and imagination are otherwise dull

The habit of imposing a meaning to every single sign

She kept it in diverse places
At the end of the stick she used to dig the ground with, for example

First create needs, then, help
Sitting underneath the thatched roof which projects well beyond the front wall of
his newly built house, a Peace-Corps Volunteer nods at several villagers who
stop by to chat with him. While they stoop down beside him and start talking,
he smiles blankly, a pair of headphones over his ears and a Walkman Sony
cassette player in his lap

"I teach the women how to grow vegetables in their yard; this will allow them to have an income" he says and hesitates before he concludes: "I am not always successful, but it's the first time this has been introduced into the village."

The first time this has been introduced to the village

Woman is depicted as the one who possessed the fire.
Only she knew how to make fire

What can we expect from ethnology?

(Voices: Sereer language; excerpts of conversation and voice of Djumalog, femme savante of the village of Boucoum)

The land of the Sereer people

(Women pounding: sound of pestle against mortar and laughter)

The land of the Manding and the Peul peoples

A film about what? my friends ask.
A film about Senegal, but what in Senegal?

I feel less and less the need to express myself
Is that something else I've lost?
Something else I've lost?

(Voices: same conversation in Sereer language)

Filming in Africa means for many of us
Colorful images, naked breast women, exotic dances and fearful rites.
The unusual

First create needs, then, help
Ethnologists handle the camera the way they handle words
Recuperated collected preserved
The Bamun the Bassari the Bobo
What are *your* people called again? an ethnologist asks a fellow of his

In numerous tales

Diversification at all costs
Oral traditions thus gain the rank of written heritage

Images from Trinh's *Reassemblage*, arranged by Trinh. Courtesy Trinh
T. Minh-ha.

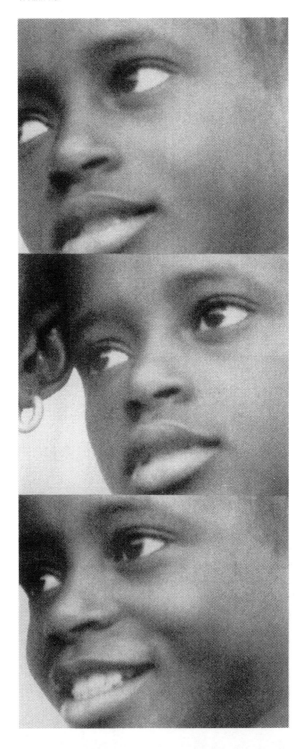

Fire place and woman's face
The pot is known as a universal symbol for the Mother the Grand-Mother
the Goddess

Nudity does not reveal
The hidden
It is its absence

A man attending a slide show on Africa turns to his wife and says with guilt in
his voice: "I have seen some pornography tonight"

Documentary because reality is organized into an explanation of itself

Every single detail is to be recorded. The man on the screen smiles at us while
the necklace he wears, the design of the cloth he puts on, the stool he sits on
are objectively commented upon

It has no eye it records   *(Cicada sound)*

"A fine layer of dust covers us from head to toe. When the sandstorm comes,"
says a child, "we lay on our mat with our mother's headscarf on our face and
wait until it goes away"

The omnipresent eye. Scratching my hair or washing my face become a very
special act

Watching her through the lens. I look at her becoming me becoming mine

Entering into the only reality of signs where I myself am a sign

(Music: Bassari. Repeated hootings of a woman; drum beats; men's chanting)

The land of the Bassari and the Peul peoples

Early in the morning. A man is sitting with his little girl on his lap next to the
circular stone hut built after the model of a Bassari house. A Catholic white
sister comes up to him and blurts out: "It's only 7 am. Your little girl is not that
sick. How many times have I told you our dispensary is closed on Sunday?
Come back on Monday"

An ethnologist and his wife gynecologist come back for two weeks to the village
where they have done research in the past. He defines himself as a person who
stays long, long enough, in a village to study the culture of an ethnic group.

Time, knowledge, and security. "If you haven't stayed long enough in a place, you are not an ethnologist" he says
Late in the evening, a circle of men gathers in front of the house where the ethnologist and his wife gynecologist stay
One of the villagers is telling a story, another is playing music on his improvised lute, the ethnologist is sleeping next to his switched-on cassette recorder

He thinks he excludes personal values. He tries or believes so but how can he be a Fulani? That's objectivity

Along the Senegal River, the land of the Sarakhole and the Peul peoples

(Sound used in the this section: women's pounding; cicada sound; hooting of Bassari women)

I come with the idea that I would seize the unusual by catching the person unawares. There are better ways to steal I guess. With the other's consent. After seeing me laboring with the camera, women invite me to their place and ask me to film them

The habit of imposing
Every single sign

For many of us the best way to be neutral and objective is to copy reality meticulously

Speak about
K-about

The eternal commentary that escorts images

Stressing the observer's objectivity
Circles round the object of curiosity
Different views from different angles

The a, b, c . . . of photography

Creativity and objectivity seem to run into conflict.
The eager observer collects samples and has no time to reflect upon the media used

Scarcely twenty years were enough to make two billion people define themselves as underdeveloped

What I see is life looking at me

I am looking through a circle in a circle of looks

115 degrees Fahrenheit.
I put on a hat while laughter bursts out behind me.
I haven't seen any woman wearing a hat

Children, women and men come up to me claiming for gifts A van drives in the dust road, greeted by another boisterous wave of children. "Gift, gift" they all yell while the car stops under the shade of a tree. A group of tourists step out and immediately start distributing cheap candies

Just speak near by

A woman comments on polygamy: "it's good for men . . . not for us. We accept it owing to the force of circumstances. What about you? Do you have a husband all for yourself?"

(Same passage of Joola music as in the beginning of the film)

Images from Trinh's *Reassemblage*, arranged by Trinh. Courtesy Trinh T. Minh-ha.

Script of *Naked Spaces—Living Is Round*

The script of Naked Spaces includes distinctions in printing that reflect the various narrators: Trinh explains the distinction in her introduction. The superimposed printed texts that locate the visuals according to country and region are presented in parentheses: the country, in capital letters, the region after the dash in small letters. Parentheses also identify the sources of quotations. The imagery from Naked Spaces—Living Is Round was selected and arranged by Trinh. In the film, imagery is consistently presented in long, halting horizontal and vertical pans; as a result, still imagery is particularly compromising to this film's sense of space and time. —S.M.

(Text written for three women's voices, represented here by three types of printed letters. The low voice [**bold**], the only one that can sound assertive, remains close to the villagers' sayings and statements, and quotes African writers' works. The high-range voice [plain] informs according to Western logic and mainly quotes Western thinkers. The medium-range voice [*italics*] speaks in the first person and relates personal feelings, and observations. Words in parenthesis are not to be read.)—TRINH T. MINH-HA

Images from Trinh T. Minh-ha's *Naked Spaces—Living Is Round* (1985), arranged for *Screen Writings* by Trinh. Courtesy Trinh T. Minh-ha.

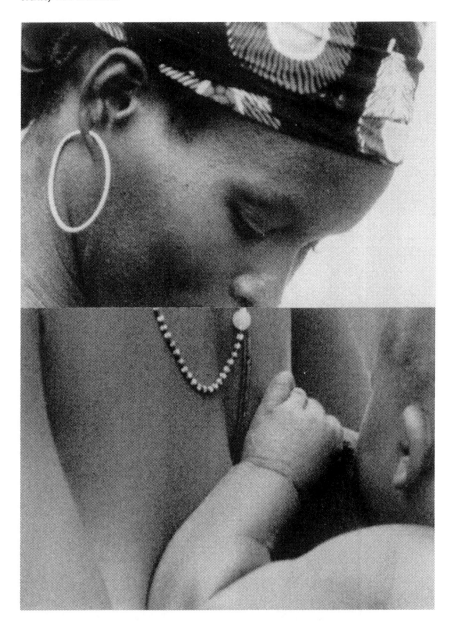

People of the earth

Not descriptive, not informative, not interesting
Sounds are bubbles on the surface of silence

**Untrue, superstitious, supernatural. The civilized mind
qualifies many of the realities it does not understand
untrue, superstitious, supernatural**

Truth and fact
Naked and plain
A wise Dogon man used to say

"to be naked is to be speechless" (Ogotemmeli)

Truth or fact

The correct vibration. A body resonates to music as does a string.
A music that elicits physical response and calls for mediated involvement.
It does not simply "play"
In such a way as *not* to impinge on the viewing

An African man wrote:
**Contrary to what some Westerners think, religion in
Africa is not a cause for man's stagnation, nor a source
of interterritorial conflicts. The more profound a
believer the black man is, the more tolerant he proves
to be. Wherever intolerance occurs in black territories,
they are due to a cause introduced from the exterior**
(A. Hampate Ba)

The circumcised young men beat time with a walking stick while chanting
They are holding in their hands femininity, water, and light

Building as dwelling
On earth, under the sky, before the divinities, among mortals, with things.
They dwell in that
They neither master the earth nor subjugate it
They leave to the sun and the moon their journey
And do not worship idols
They initiate mortals into the nature of death

(Sereer)

The circle is a form that characterizes the general plan of the house, the
granaries, the court, the shrines, sometimes the rooms, the village, the tomb,
the cemetery.

(Mandingo)

life is round
This is not a fact. Not a data gathering.

air, earth, water, light.
The four elements that explain the creation of men and women in African
mythologies.

earth-born and earth-bound
dusty grey-white bodies made out of clay
stark naked children.
"she made a hole and breathed air into it: a child is
born"

(Jaxanke)

The sun, the calabash, the court, the arching sky
Everything round invites touch and caress
The circle is the perfect form

you'll never spread doubt in their mind by convincing
them of seeing 'yes'
when they already saw 'no.'
when all that they perceived was a hut or a mud shelter
They went away the way they came

For many of us, the hut is the tap root of the function of inhabiting. A universe
(inside and) outside the universe, it possesses the felicity of intense poverty
(Bachelard).

she said: man, woman and child
line / sun / star / calabash cover
turtle / big snake / fox
calabash

they help the plants to grow.
you ask me: "what is the use of these paintings?"
they help the plants to grow
they promote germination

(Bassari)

Every illness is a musical problem
"Music has a magical, energizing and creative power. The
mere shaking of a cow bell is enough to make people drift
into a state of excitement. It is then said that 'strength
has entered them.' Elders who can hardly move in daily
situation without a cane would emit war cries and dance
frantically to the sound of music. Farmers who feel tired
and lack enthusiasm will be fired with desire to work in
the fields upon hearing the drum beats or the chants of
the masks." "Even if you have eaten and are full," a
man said, "you have no sustaining strength to plough the
land vigorously and endure the hard work if no music flows
in you."

(Soninke)

Space: even when close I feel distance

"Whether a house is lively or not depends on the way it
breathes"
"Houses and humans are both made out of small balls of
earth"

Music rests on accord between darkness and light

(MAURITANIA—Soninke)

Listen in the wind to the bush sobbing: it is our
beloved dead's breathing.
The dead are not dead (Birago Diop)

People of the earth

The reason two deers walk together is that one has to take
the mote from the other's eye (proverb)

A sense of time, not only of hours and days,
but also of decades and centuries
A sense of space as light and void

Space has always reduced me to silence

A space that speaks the mellowness of inner life

Scantily furnished, devoid of concealment or disguise
"The truth appears so naked on my side,
That any purblind eye may find it out" (Shakespeare)

A house that breathes
That encloses as well as opens wide onto the world

We often took our own limits for those of the culture we looked at

All definitions are devices

Color does not exist, being first and foremost a sensation

She would often sing while she worked
The air filled with her voice
The song scanned by her regular snifflings

First and foremost a sensation

Do you see the same color when the light is red?
Color blinds. Some greyness has to remain for clarity to be

Nice colors are called 'shades'
Red attracts and irritates, while bright yellow is bound to hurt. In places where
the sun dazzles and where sandscapes prevail, people dress in blue, deep
blue. Shades are soothing to the eye.

Color is life

Light becoming music

She would often sing while she worked
The air filled with her voice

Songs cure bodily pains, soothe the pangs of bereavement,
calm anger and cleanse the mind

**To explain the scornful lower lip of the camel, Moore men
have this to say: "The prophet has a hundred names. Men
know 99 of them, only the camel knows the hundredth one;
hence its superior 'marabout'-like expression"** (According to
J. Gabus).

(Peoples of Oualata)

**They help the plants grow
They promote germination**

A long wail tore through the air
Blue veiled figures
She sailed down the alley
Her indigo-blue garment
Flowing behind her

*As if for centuries
She sat there
Instinctively veiling her face as the men came in,
Unveiling it as soon as they left*

Being truthful: being in the in-between of all definitions of truth

*There was much covert peeping through the veils as we walked around looking
carefully at the rooms and their details.*

*Caught each other looking. She laughed and I laughed. Soon all the women in
the court were laughing together*

The earth is blue like an orange

*"La terre est bleue comme une orange
Jamais une erreur les mots ne mentent pas"* (Paul Eluard)

Sky, earth, sea, sun
Air, earth, water, light

Outside is as bare as inside is ornate

*For fifteen minutes we stood in the street, slightly off the house door, waiting
until we were allowed in. Time for the men to inform the women to go back to
their rooms and stay in there all the time while the visitors were present*

How can you explain this excitement to live in an old house? One that ages with the imprints of previous lives?

The severe aspect of the exterior often stands in contrast with the exuberant decorations of the interior

She stepped into my room abruptly and stood there staring at me intently. I stared back at her questioningly, but she remained silent. For a long time we stared at each other without a word; there was more fear in her eyes than curiosity. She turned away a few seconds, then looked back straight into my eyes and said: "Oil, I want some oil for cooking"

Walked down the empty narrow streets and thought for a while I was truly alone. I was soon to discover blinded walls had eyes. Gigglings and laughters spurted out around me as I stopped and looked carefully at the faces that swiftly appear and disappear from the discreet openings on the walls. Or above me, from the terrace-roofs of the houses. Women, unveiled, mostly young, all share the look of intense curiosity.

(TOGO—Moba)

The world is round around the round being (Bachelard).

Religion is living without conflict

"The ground level of the house interior is the underworld, the terrace-level is the earth and the granaries upper level is the sky"
"Granaries elevated on the front facade 'make the house look well' "

The cosmic house is both cell and world (Bachelard). Each dweller inhabits the universe while the universe inhabits her space.

"dark and cool, red like the sun"
. . . untrue, superstitious, supernatural
"as the sun descends, the rays enter the cattle room and touch the ancestors, speaking to them while they ask for health and protection of the family. "

The Tamberma house is a sanctuary

"these mounds are the sun; for the reproduction of human beings and the expansion of the family. "
The horns of the entrance and the mounds are the focus of sun ceremonies

Upon entering, we stepped into a somber central room where I could smell and hear a cow munching on my left; we then climbed up to the tiny oval kitchen lit by the soft morning light that came in from the upper portal leading to the terrace roof of the house.

Entering the womb of the earth, sheltered from heat and sun, from rain and wind, from all other living creatures

"The earth is round. We all know that. No part is longer than the other." When we enter, we enter the mouth—*the door*—**When we exit, we step out onto the large calabash**—*the court*—**we call it the Vault of Heaven."**
The house opens onto the sky in a perfect circle

Rhythms are built into the way people relate to each other

(Tamberma)

"We call ourselves Batammariba, 'the people who create well with earth, the people who are builders,'"
the designers, the architects

Tribute to the dead

"We say the placement of the house is that which is important"
"A house is beautiful when its back is not coming out"
"Not too high, not too low, not too far outside nor too far inside. His house is really smooth. He knows how to build, he does not leave his finger marks" (A Tamberma architect, according to S. P. Blier)

She who wears an antelope headdress is said to portray the deceased's daughter

Third act for a funeral drama. Funeral performances are referred to as plays; the house of the deceased being the stage, a group of skillful performers, the actors, and the villagers in attendance, the critical audience. Drums, flutes and horns are the voices of the ancestors.

"sun's house is a circle. This is what we have been told"
"sun protects us all. Like mother it brings out children.

Like father it has wives, the earth and the moon"

"it is beautiful because his fingers leave lines and his lines are visible"

"if the woman plasters the walls such that from far away you don't see the different levels, we say the house is beautiful"

The egg-shaped granaries are raised above the terrace at the houses' front corners, closest to the sky, their opening facing the sky god who provides rain for the grain (according to S. P. Blier).

"When you climb it, it leads you to the sky." The sky is like a tree; it is formed from the branches of a huge tree

(Kabye)

People of the earth

"The more profound a believer the black man is, the more tolerant he proves to be"

In one of the rites in initiation during which a man is born again in his community, the initiate has to go naked, his body painted with red earth, color of the newly born.

(Konkomba)

"A village that neglects music and dancing is a dead village"

Red: a warm limitless color that often acts as a sign of life
Black: an absence of light, of sun, therefore of life, color

In many parts of the world, white is the color of mourning

Truth or fact?

Poetry becomes only poetry when I become adept at consuming truth as fact

"The house like a woman must have secret parts to inspire desire" (according to Ogotemmeli)

Unadorned she is not desirable. Adornment excites love. If there is a connection between ornaments and love, that is because the first ornaments of all were in the centre-jar of the celestial granary; and that jar is the symbol of the world's womb (according to Ogotemmeli)

In certain societies where sounds have become letters with sharps and flats, those unfortunate enough not to fit into these letters are tossed out of the system and qualified unmusical. They are called noises. *It is known that one of the primary tasks of ethnomusicologists is to study what traditional societies consider music and what they reject as non-music.* A music bound up with movement, dance and speech, one in which the listener becomes a co-performer, one that has no overall form except one of continually recurring sequences of notes and rhythms, one that plays endlessly—*for nobody has enough of life*—has been repeatedly called elemental or rudimentary. Is irritable to most Westerners' ears.

The sound of a swelling cry of ululation
That high wail that speaks her joy, excitement or grief

I am inhabited by a cry
Joy sorrow anger it curls out
Sharp and vivid in the night
Inhumanly human
The cry I hear, she said, is from the other side of life

Deeper insight always entails moments of blindness

(MALI—Dogon)

"Step into the footmarks of your ancestors. Tradition may weaken but cannot disappear." A Dogon prayer

Scale as an element to impress, to dominate or to speak up a mutual vulnerability?

A journey in these villages may have a cathartic effect, for a man seeing a hundred-storey building often gets conceited

There is also a way of viewing nature as a challenge to man's conquest; therefore, of seeing in the smallness of man and woman a need for im-prove-ment

Images from Trinh's *Naked Spaces—Living Is Round*, arranged by Trinh. Courtesy Trinh T. Minh-ha.

Ogo, the first who stood against God Amma, and introduced psychological diversification in the universe, was transformed into a Fox and thus reduced to speaking only with its paws on the divination tables

The figures are drawn on the smoothed sand by the diviners before sunset. The Fox which comes out at night, is lured onto the tables by means of peanuts which the diviners have carefully scattered over them. The next day, the diviners will come back to the site after sunrise to read the traces left by the Fox. Their interpretations vary according to the latter's itinerary whose imprints may join, border, or avoid the figures. The divination table is the Earth turning under the action of the Fox's legs.

The divination table is the Earth turning under the action of the Fox's legs.

How "very much content am I to lie low, to cling to the soil, to be of kin to the sod. My soul squirms comfortably in the soil and sand and is happy. Sometimes when one is drunk with this earth one's spirit seems so light that one is in heaven. But actually one seldom rises six feet above the ground"
(L. Yutang)

"When you climb it, it leads you to the sky. The sky is like a tree; it is formed by the branches of a huge tree"

Togu na: "the mother's shelter," "the house of words," or "the men's house" is the reference point for every Dogon village

The life-force of the earth is water

The remaining facade of the large house with its eighty niches, homes of the ancestors

Reality and truth: neither relative nor absolute

I can't take hold of it nor lose it
When I am silent, it projects
When I project, it is silent

"The calabash is a symbol of woman and the sun, who is female"
Signs are things that move about in the world
Signs are the things of all men and women

11616 signs express and indicate all things and beings of the universe as well as all possible situations seen by the Dogon men

Each sign opens onto other signs
Each sign contains in itself a summary of the whole
And the drop is the very ocean

The Dogon house is said to be a model of the universe at a smaller scale and to symbolize man, woman and their union. The central room, the store rooms on each side and the back room with the hearth represent the woman lying on her back with outstretched arms, ready for intercourse as the communicating door stays open. The ceiling of the central room is the man and its beams, his skeleton. The woman and the man's breath finds its outlet through the opening on the roof (according to Ogotemmeli)

(BURKINA FASO—Birifor)

Spider web and dust have aged with them

"Bathed in the sunlight, one after the other they took turn to speak to the sun, keeping in touch with it from dawn to dusk"

The sun touches them as they ask for health and protection of the family

"It is beautiful because when you enter you see there where the sun penetrates, where there is light, and the rest is dark"

Houses with a sculptured head on the roof are said to belong to hunters

The supernatural, *term widely used in pro-scientific milieu,* **is an anti-scientific invention of the West,** *a wise African man observed* (Boubou Hama)

The diagnostic power of a fact-oriented language

The sky is
A calabash
The water jar is
A woman's womb

Blindness occurs precisely during the short moment of adjustment; when, from full sun we step into the dim inside. Abrupt transition from bright to dark for a change. To advance, we must go sightless, time to cross an immaterial threshold that links the social to the personal

*The dead are not dead
When night constantly floats in certain parts of the house*

It never appears to me in its totality. Here, a small round hole; there, a carved ladder leading up to the source of light; a wall; another wall; a bench; a straw mat; her water jar; a long dark room ending in several nest-like spaces. The whole thing is scattered about inside me. I can only see it in fragmentary form.

**An act of light lets day in night
Makes far nearer and near farther**
Why is it so dark?

*Everything is at the same time transparent and opaque
Irreducibly complex in its simplicity*

Not really a dwelling or a living space as an observer said, because of the overall absence of windows

When men go hunting in parties they know the rules of precedence; they know him who is higher than another; they understand when one says "I speak, you remain silent". . . . There are dangerous things in the bush and a small quarrel may bring many arrows (V. Aboya, according to Rattray)

Before the hunters set forth, they were told this by the man in charge of the hunting parties:

**"If we meet a lion, let it be like cold water
if we meet a leopard, let it be like cold water
if we meet a snake, let it be like cold water
but if a man wishes to quarrel while out hunting,
let him get headache and belly-ache,
so that he may have to return home"** (according to Rattray)

(Voice stammers on 'anthropological') *An anthropo... an anthropo... an anthropological shot: one that turns people into human species*

**Both ancestors and children are 'builders up of a compound'
When a man dies, his son, upon sacrificing a sheep, will ask
this man to join his father and grandfather in guarding the**

house properly. When a man has no children, he is sometimes laughed at, and told "what are you, if you were to die, they would break down your house and plant tobacco in it."
(V. Aboya according to Rattray)

A light without shadow generates an emotion without reserve (R. Barthes)

Entering and exiting as love-making.
The door remains open, for a house with a door closed is an infertile house

It is by way of the 'house hole' that the rays of the noon Sun enter into the house to look at the family and speak with them. Family eats around it. The food cooked and spilled while eating are so much offered to the Sun. Women give birth under it to secure the Sun's blessings.

The house like a woman must have secret parts to inspire desire

The womb image of the house
The nest-like power of curves

Floating around in these dark spaces is the subtle smell of clay, earth and straw

There is a saying that "a man should not see all the dark corners of another's house."
"If life be called the life-blood of a space, darkness could be called its soul"

Color is first and foremost a sensation

"The house's eyes. It looks out and sees like a woman."

A male is buried east, a female facing west.

"A man faces eastward, that he may know when to rise and hunt. A woman looks to the west, that she may know when to prepare her husband's food" (V. Aboya, according to Rattray)

(Bisa)

The world is round

Are you seeing it? Hearing it? Or projecting it?

**Unadorned, she is not desirable. Adornment excites love.
If there is a connection between ornaments and love, that
is because the first ornaments of all were in the
centre-jar of the celestial granary; and that jar is the
symbol of the world's womb** (according to Ogotemmeli)

The earth is an overturned calabash. For the death of a man or a woman, the
priest sprinkles in the air earth taken from the center of the circle formed by
the calabash while making a circle around the house

here, patience is one of the first rules of education

*Orange and blue; warmer or colder; more luminosity, more presence.
Timing acts as a link between natural and artificial light.*

The earth is blue like an orange

You can't take hold of it, but you can't lose it

So please let the smoke go and let the seed die to its outer shell

Be a stranger to myself

*No matter what we call it, we will miss it
Relieved of so many words, we went naked*

Objects in her surrounding. . . . The naming of spaces rarely refers to their
function. It refers instead, to the various parts of the human body.

**The house is composed like the human body: the earth or clay
is the flesh; the water, the blood; the stones, the bones;
and the plastered surface of the walls, the skin**

**Sun rolling in space
"The bobbin, which is wound off in spinning is the sun
rolling in space"** (according to S. P. Blier)

(BENIN—Fon)

They call it giving. *We call it self-gratification.* **We call it self-
gratification.**
They call it give-and-take. *We call it take-and-take.* **We call it
take-and-take.**
They call it generosity. *We call it conditioning the beggar's mind.*

We call it conditioning the beggar's mind.
Today, to survive the poor can hardly refuse to accept
They say they don't give anymore
Because we are ungrateful
The ungrateful acceptor / *The expecting donor*
They say they don't give anymore because we are ungrateful.
We ponder: will the donor species survive?

We substitute expectation for hope and easily speak about "falling short of" or "failing to come up to" our expectations
Strategies of rupture and incorrectness need some airing

A cloud of oratorical precaution / Fear
Fear of making / out of a crystallized I

Any expectation, even that of peace, brings restlessness

Questions and answers: a mutual deception

Life on the water
Never can one walk home and feel the contact of solid, secure ground

Floating, flowing constantly
The house suspended between water and sky

What they name generosity / *arrogance*
A mutual deception

You should be able to accept with simplicity / *simply accept*
From we, us, who are neither a source of authority nor a seal of authenticity

They see no life / When they look
They see only objects

The dead are not dead

Humble enough to accept without trying to return

Be a stranger to myself
And the drop is the ocean

The earth is blue like an orange

An instant's freezing
To be lived directly
Silence: people having faith in each other

Void is always capable of being filled by solid
And I look at the myriad of reflections
the entire lake within me
Unable to quench it
Quench an endless thirst

The charm of its nudity lights up our desire for both retreat and expansion
The more naked the space, the more it fires my imagination

Blue like an orange
And orange becomes blue
Earth becomes Sun
Sun becomes Water
Water becomes Sky
And blue becomes orange, like the Earth

(SENEGAL—Peul)

The circle is the spirit in eternal motion

While giving there is no thought of giving
While accepting there is no thought of accepting
"Who could ever think of the gift as a gift that takes?" (H. Cixous)

Going beyond logic to experience what is large in what is small
Clear, simple, irreducibly complex in its simplicity

To build out of dwelling
A philosopher observed that "man's homelessness consists in this, that
man still does not even think of the *real* plight of dwelling as *the* plight"
(M. Heidegger)

We dwell altogether unpoetically
But dwelling can be unpoetic only because it is in essence poetic (Heidegger)

Have you seen such a look in a child's face? Such a look?
A sunlit smile that sticks in your eyes

Spirit in eternal motion

For many foreign observers, these people have no notion whatsoever of the private garden. This is hardly surprising: there is no point in fencing off a piece of land as one's own; their houses are situated such that wherever they wander they own the entire landscape.

The earth is an overturned calabash

(Joola)

they are holding in their hands
Femininity, water and light

people of the earth

Those whose serenity of understanding and simplicity of spirit is the despair of bigger men

The reason two deer walk together is that one has to take the mote from the other's eye (Proverb)

"Life with its rhythms and cycles is dance and dance is live" (Opoka, according to J. M. Chernoff)

The Joola people: renowned for having raised a fierce armed resistance to the French colonial administration at the start of the century

For the one who travels in this restfully green part of Senegal today, the Casamance, the dreamland of research workers and tourists alike, it is quite difficult to imagine no foreigner had dared to venture here without an armed escort a few decades ago.

Light, air, earth, woman, palm leaf, dust, children

Space has always reduced me to silence

They can't really afford this, they said
But bought it anyway
Flew to Africa
And waited with an anguished excitement
For the paid shock of exoticism

A Joola proverb says: "those who are proud of their nudity will be insolent once clothed"
This is not a fact

Light, air, people, sound

The impluvium: a house built around an inner court with an inwardly inclined roof and as some said, "a tank to catch rainwater"

Some call it the "Senegalese Florida," ideal for the visitor who hungers for tropical adventures made to measure

A life-generating power

"A house without a fence is not a house," the old man says

An earthen castle, according to a tourist guide book

A place for communion / Sharing
A sun chapel

They took turns to speak to the sun, keeping in touch with it from dawn to dusk
"The dead are often buried in their own rooms which will remain locked forever.
The room will crumble with time on the grave"

Infinitely secure in its nudity / *Insecure in its infiniteness*

A damaged house is a damaged family. Very often, family and house bear the same name.

Femininity, water, and light
An interior court
A time clock / A sun chapel
A reserve of air, light, water

Each woman prepares her own meal. Each household has its own hearth located all around the court under a circular covered gallery

A pit
A tank for catching rain water
A place for reunion
A place for rest and conversation

Music rests on accord between darkness and light

Every religion is based on a lie device
All methods may be viewed as lies
At best, they create a situation

Rhythm creates a storage of energy

Eager for an indigenous answer, someone walked around asking: "What is music?" People would look at him as if he had said something funny or strange. They would laugh and say: "Don't you know?"

"A dance that does not attract many villagers and foreigners from afar is said to turn out badly, for the spirits have not come to attend it"
The animation of a dance is a sign of the spirits' presence. Dance and music form a dialogue between movement and sound. One who hears the music understands it with a dance. The dancers do not imitate or express the music heard; they converse with it and dance to the gaps in it. Both marked and unmarked beats. A different beat, one that is not there, one that you add because you feel it and fit it in. Your own beat. Your own move. Your own reading.

It usually signals arrest and has long been forgotten as a wind instrument. *The whistle here is a musical cue for change*

Dramatic action is stimulated by the flute-, horn-, whistle- and bell-players who do not form part of the drum ensemble. They wander round the circle of dancers, blowing, striking a few notes on their instruments to urge them on

A drummer explains that one should not breathe too strongly while performing if one does not want to miss the rhythmic formulas and to get tired too quickly. One should take in reserves of air during the pauses, between each dance

Every illness is a musical problem

"My wrist is fast": that is not drumming. As you are beating, it is your heart that is talking, and what your heart is going to say, your hand will collect and play. And unless you cool your heart, your drumming will not stand. When your heart cools, your arm will cool too, and as you are bringing your strength, you will also be leaving it. At that time, the drum will cry well. . . . The one who has learned to play well can beat a drum and the sound will spread out and you will hear it vibrating inside the ground. But the one whose heart gets up and he is beating hard, his drum will not sound.

"Drumming has no end," the drummer said. "No one can know everything about drumming; everyone knows only to his

Images from Trinh's *Naked Spaces—Living Is Round*, arranged by Trinh. Courtesy Trinh T. Minh-ha.

extent. If you know everything, what are you going to do and
know it?" . . . In our drumming way, no one blames another.
If someone doesn't know, you don't say "this man does not
know." If you say that, you have demeaned yourself. Maybe
as you say you know, someone too knows better than you, and
as you are bending down looking at someone's anus, someone
is also bending down and looking at yours." (I. Abdulai, according
to Chernoff)

Su Friedrich

Since the early eighties, Su Friedrich has seen her cinematic project as a process of consolidating types of independent film-making usually (at least in North America) considered distinct, as a formal means of coming to terms with troubling dimensions of her personal experience. Beginning with *Gently Down the Stream* (1982), one of the elements she has used inventively is visual text. *Gently Down the Stream* incorporates a series of texts based on dreams recorded over a period of months and etched, one word at a time, into the emulsion of the filmstrip. Of course, neither the idea of using dreams in film, nor the idea of etching words directly into the filmstrip, is new. Dreams—and the psychic mechanisms of dreams—have been an important component of avant-garde cinema since the twenties, and the idea of scratching and/or painting the filmstrip to create imagery and of incorporating visual text within such imagery is nearly as old: by

the mid-thirties, Len Lye was a master of the technique. Indeed, Stan Brakhage's hand-scratched titles and "by Brakhage" were very much a part of Friedrich's consciousness as she was making *Gently Down the Stream*.

What distinguishes *Gently Down the Stream* (and the closely related *But No One*, 1983) is Friedrich's decision to use scratched texts—and the imagery viewers imagine on the basis of them—as the "foreground" of a film, and photographed imagery—specifically, shots of religious icons, images of one woman in a rowing machine, another swimming, and of the wake of a boat—as "background," in this case, a set of metaphors of our voyage down Friedrich's stream of consciousness. Friedrich's sense of timing and the nuances of her recording the scratched texts (texts relating to women are filmed so that the words quiver with anxiety, texts relating to men are less energetic) are also distinctive.[1]

1. In 1982 Friedrich designed and published a book version of *Gently Down the Stream*, which includes the complete text and many frame enlargements. The book is available from Friedrich, 222 East 5th St. #6, New York, NY 10003.

While *Gently Down the Stream* encodes the psychic struggle within Friedrich between her Roman Catholic upbringing and lesbian desire, her first longer film, *The Ties That Bind* (fifty-five minutes), is an index of her attempt to come to terms with her German heritage. Friedrich uses hand-scratched texts as a way of cinematically questioning her mother about her experiences growing up in Germany during the rise of the Third Reich and of interpreting her own experiences during trips to Germany to visit her familial origins and to the Seneca Army Depot in upstate New York to take part in a women's anti-military demonstration. As in *So Is This* and *Gently Down the Stream*, Friedrich's one word at a time presentation of her questions and comments engages viewers in the construction of meaning: her questions become our questions. Her mother's candid responses allay Friedrich's superstitions by revealing something of the trauma of being anti-Nazi in Germany in the thirties and during World War II, and of the subsequent traumas of being "liberated" by the Allies at the end of the war and being divorced by Friedrich's father some years after emigrating to the United States.

Since *The Ties That Bind*, Friedrich has not used scratched texts, but in *Damned If You Don't* (1987), she combines excerpts of Judith C. Brown's *Immodest Acts: The Life of a Lesbian Nun in Renaissance Italy* (New York: Oxford University Press, 1986) with a series of other narrated texts. And in *Sink or Swim* (1990) she combines a series of short narratives, each spoken by a young girl, and a set of visual words arranged in reverse alphabetic order—"Zygote," "Y chromosome," "X chromosome," "Witness" . . . —into a conceptual structure that allows her to come to terms with her father's divorcing Lore Friedrich and leaving the family when Friedrich was a child. The choice of the alphabet as a formal structure relates both to her familial background, since her father is a well-known linguist, and to her cinematic background: it recalls—and in a sense responds to—*Zorns Lemma*.

As is true in all her sound films (all the films since *The Ties That Bind* have had sound tracks), *Sink or Swim* edits imagery and sound (in this case narration) so that a wide range of explicit and implicit relationships between them become evident. During the reading of "Zygote," for example, Friedrich uses a montage of shots of sperm, of ova, and of fertilization and cell bifurcation—imagery recycled from educational films—to accompany the child narrator's story about Greek mythological figures, Zeus and Hera. Friedrich times her presentation of the image of a sperm fertilizing an ovum and the resulting bifurcation of cells so that they correspond precisely to the young girl's description of Zeus's marriage to Hera and of his subsequent love affairs and illegitimate children. In general, the film's subtle and complex relationships of image and sound require multiple viewings.

In her next film, *First Comes Love* (1991), Friedrich uses a rolling text midway through her presentation of imagery of six weddings (accompanied by a variety of songs about love and marriage) to reframe the meaning of the marriage ritual. As the various couples reach the altar, and the priests presumably read the text of the marriage ceremony, Friedrich substitutes her own ritual text, which informs viewers that gay and lesbian marriages are illegal in the following countries, and then lists all the countries in a vertical column that seems to roll up through the frame endlessly. At the conclusion of *her* "ceremony," Friedrich returns to the marriage footage and follows the couples as they exit and leave the church. At the end of the film, a final visual text indicates that Denmark is the single nation where gay and lesbian marriages are legal.

What follows are "(Script) for a Film without Images," an early film-related poem that provides useful background for *The Ties That Bind* and *Sink or Swim*; the complete dream texts from *Gently Down the Stream*; and the script of *Sink or Swim*. The complex, subtle intersections of the narration and the movement of Friedrich's visuals in *Sink or Swim* cannot be effectively illustrated here. I've used stills to suggest some sense of this dimension of the film.

(Script) for a Film without Images

The text of "(Script) for a Film without Images" takes the form of a conversation between two characters, an interviewer (on the left) and an interviewee (on the right). The reader should read back and forth from one column to the other, in a shot/countershot fashion. "(Script) for a Film without Images" originally appeared in the single issue of Feminism/Film (Spring 1984), edited by Lisa Cartwright.—S.M.

Shall we begin?

All right.

pause

Yes?

pause

Yes?

Go on—

You must try to—

Oh?

I see.

Do you remember when you first felt angry?

I see.   Did she cry often?

And did you try to console her?

Do you think that made her happy?

But did you love him?

I said, did she make you hate him?

Did you ever see him cry?

Oh.   But let's talk about what else made you angry.

Did you feel jealous as a child?

Did you feel jealous of other girls?

Yes.

pause

pause

I don't know why . . .

pause   Well, I'm not sure why . . .

I was wondering . . .

I was . . .

Why I'm so angry all the time.

Yes.   I want to know why I'm always so angry.

pause

When I saw my mother crying.
When I heard my mother crying.

Yes.

Yes.   I told her that I still loved her.

No.   I don't know. She said that she knew I loved her. She said that she knew my father didn't love her.

What?

Yes.   No. No . . .

Of course not.   He once tried to drown me.

Oh.

I'm not sure.

Wanted and hated?

Didn't you have any girlfriends?

Never saw them again.   Aren't you exaggerating?

Oh?

Are you sure?

Well, it wasn't his fault that she ignored you.

Why didn't you get yourself a boyfriend?

Aren't you flattering yourself?

And why were you afraid?

But I thought they made you angry.

They weren't all boring, now, were they?

I don't see how that would *bore* you.

Were you naked?

I'm sure he was just joking—

Are you so sure that's what he said?

Yes.   But also of the boys. I wanted and hated everything they had.

Yes. So I would beat up on the boys and then the girls would ignore me. But I thought that would make them like me.

Almost. Yes.   Sort of.   But they got boyfriends and I never saw them again.

Well.   I would see my best friend whenever she broke up with someone.   I would try to stop her from crying by saying that I still liked her.

But it didn't make any difference.

Yes.   No. Yes.

What?

They were afraid of me.

I was afraid of them.

Yes, I was afraid of them.

They were so boring.   So boring, and my only relief was to have a good fight with them.

Yes. They made me angry and afraid.

One day when I was 16 I brought a boy to my house while my mother was at work. We were lying on my bed. He was on top of me. He laughed and . . .

. . . said Do you realize that if I wanted to, right now I could rape you?

Do you realize that if I wanted to, right now, I could rape you. Haha I said no you couldn't.

Maybe you just made him nervous.
He probably liked you a lot.

I do.

So men bore you?

Confessions?

Are you sure?

But how do you expect anyone to
respond to such accusations?

No, you were blaming them.

So that made you feel angry?

Anyone?

pause

pause

Why?

Look, you just can't *live* with that kind of
anger.

Are you ever happy?

Why don't you try to tell me something
that makes you feel happy.

Just at that moment my mother came
home.
Hahaha I said now you can't.

I don't know why.

What?

There were no confessions.
No intimacies.

I would try to tell them why I was angry
or scared or bored and they wouldn't
respond.

That's what I remember.

I was trying to explain why I felt hurt.

Yes.   No.   They didn't give me a chance
to explain.

Yes.   Sometimes I want to kill someone.

No, someone special.

I do.

The guy who raped me, when I was 19. If
he was in this room right now . . .

Why?

My father tried to drown me. I couldn't
see. I couldn't breathe. No one was near
to help me.

I can't remember.   It was when I was 12.
I had done something wrong.

When I meet someone who knows why
I'm angry. When I meet someone who's
as angry as I am.   He told me to shape
up or ship out.

So you can be angry together?

What?

Yes. No.   Then I don't have to be angry.

Do you lie to me?

Yes. I know that I don't have to lie to
them.

But do you think it's better to be angry?

Not any more.   Not now.   Not yet.

Does it make you happy? From what
you've said, it appears to make you
happy to be angry.

Better than what?

I don't understand.

Of course not, but it doesn't make me
unhappy.

Do you *choose* to be angry?

pause

No . . .   No.   No, I don't think so. That
isn't the right question.

I certainly think it is.

Why does he leave her?
Why does he coerce her?
Why does he ignore her?

That wasn't my question.

pause

Why do you always look for reasons to
feel so angry?

Why does he enslave them?
Why does he kill them?
Why does he lie?

Are you suggesting now that I'm lying to
you?

Why does she hate herself?
Why does she starve?
Why does she weep?

I'm not here to answer rhetorical
questions, I'm here to help you.

Why does she believe him?
Why do they lie to each other?
How does he ignore her?
Why are they always afraid?

Who?? Who are "he" and "she" and
"they"?

Who made them afraid?
Why did they beat us?
Who stopped listening to us?

I'm listening to you, but you obviously
aren't paying any attention to me.

When did we lose our bodies?
Whose heart broke first?
Why are we full of hate?
Who is more afraid?

I'm beginning to think that you're afraid
of *me*. Or perhaps you're making fun of
me.

Why are we so jealous?
Who stole us?
Who has us?
Who is keeping us from each other?

Why Why Why Why Why don't you talk
about yourself, instead of asking so
many vague questions?

No.

No?

No. I'm not being vague. No. I'm not
being vague.

Yes, vague and hostile.

No.   I don't think so.

Being hostile towards me is just
confusing the issue.   Let's get back to
our original question.

What was it?

We were talking about why you insist
on being angry with men for things
they might have done years ago (if at
all).

No.   It wasn't that long ago. I said that a
woman is raped every four minutes in
this country.

Shit! (excuse me.)
Can you please try to be more specific?

I said that 40,000 women died last year
in Mexico of illegal abortions.

You're only working yourself up into
another fit of anger. Let's return to our
discussion.

I said that 50% of Native American women and 40% of Puerto Rican women have been sterilized.

Look, be sensible. It simply won't happen to you. You're just upsetting yourself unnecessarily.

I say that half the women I know have been raped by their fathers or strangers, or have been in psychiatric hospitals.

So what can *you* do? Listen and listen until you explode from anger?

Sometimes I don't hear myself if I listen to the others.   But I can't hear myself when I refuse to listen.

I can see that you're just mentioning these random, extreme examples to avoid the real reason for your visit.

pause

We aren't getting anywhere with all this!

pause

Listen—

Are you angry?

No, you are.

Is it something I said?

We're not here to talk about how *I* feel.

But I'm curious. I wonder why you want to know so much about me.

You turn your anger against everyone.   Even me.   You make it very difficult for me to talk to you.

But I haven't said anything about you.

And why do you always talk about sex when you're angry?

What?

Your anger seems to be connected with your sexual experiences.

No.   Yes.   They are.   They have been.   They might not be.

You should try to think about other things.

What did you say?

I'm not sure.

pause   Do you consider me hysterical?

Well, if you mean *funny,* no.

Have you ever seduced a patient?

I beg your pardon?

Have you read the history of sexual surgery done on women?

Young lady, I think this has gone *too far*.

Did it turn you on?

And what business is that—

Did you like the one about the American doctor who masturbated the woman to orgasm to prove that she was hysterical, and then cut out her clitoris?

Perhaps. But this is 1983. We don't—

Did you get your color TV from the drug companies for prescribing your quota of valium?

What gives you the idea that you can come here and—

Did you ever . . .

Your imagination is quite—

When was the last time you . . .

If I determine that—

How often have you . . .

I am a *licensed*—

And why did you insist on . . .

You have no grounds for—

And what makes you think you have the right . . .

I find this highly—

Why the hell did you . . .

Well, well, our angry young—

Yes. You're like all . . .

You believe *those*—

Yes.
Yes.
I believe the facts of my own life.

Text of *Gently Down the Stream*

The spacing between words and phrases approximates the rhythm with which the text appears on the screen. Individual dreams are separated from one another as Friedrich has indicated. —S.M.

Wander through   large quiet   rooms
An old friend says   What
are you doing here?

I say   The weavers
worked as slaves   to make   these rugs
Think

She shouts   Why
do you come here
and SPOIL everything?

———

Walk into church
My mother   trembles
                trances
                reciting a prayer about orgasm
I start to weep

———

In the water   near a raft
I see a woman
swimming and diving
in a wet suit

See her pubic hair

———

A woman   sits on a stage
hunched over   in the corner
She calls up a friend from
the audience
asking her   Come and make love to me

She does
I can't watch

———

She mutters   I CAN'T
can't hold you
The last time was too

Two images from one of the dreams in Su Friedrich's *Gently Down the Stream* (1981). Courtesy Su Friedrich.

tense   So many
memories

——

Woman on the bed shivers
I wake her
She is angry
Smears spermicidal jelly
on my lips

NO!

——

Walk into church
A bloody furry arm   is torn
from the body of an animal

Did it rip its own arm off?

——

I make a second vagina
beside my first one

I look in surprise

Which
is the original?

—

Building a model house for
some man
Do it
without getting paid
Do it
wrong

—

I draw a man
take his skin
inflate it
get excited
mount it

It's like being in love with
a straight woman

—

I lie in a gutter
giving birth to myself
two fetuses   dark green
and knotted up
Try to breathe so they don't suffocate
I can pull one out
but it starts to crumble up

——

Five women sing   a cappella
funny harmony
they spell the word truth
in German
I spell   B   L   I   N   D   N   E   S   S
A man says
Their Song Is A Very Clever Pun
I say   I can't agree
I don't know German

——

A leopard
A   LEOPARD   EATS   TWO   BLUE
two blue hummingbirds
humming
I feel the feathers
MY   TONGUE
fl   utter   on my

BONES mutter   HEARTS utter   FEATHERS

humming   on my   tongue

Script of *Sink or Swim*

After the opening credits, each visual word is
followed by narration. In several instances,
the reverse-alphabetized words are not followed by narrated stories. "X chromosome"
and "Y chromosome" are followed by silent
visuals. The sound for "Kinship" is a song by
Franz Schubert that is not translated in the
film but is translated here. And "Ghosts" is
the only synch sound passage in Sink or
Swim; in it Friedrich types a letter, which is
reproduced here (in the film, the image is presented in negative). In "Discovery" an animated graph of "the American Kinship System" is presented before the narrated story is
read. The lyrics of the ABC song sung during
the (untitled) epilogue are included. In the
film the song is sung as a round, six times, in
conjunction with the final sequence: six layers of a home movie shot of Friedrich as a
child, each layer superimposed on the one(s)
before, as a visual round. The closing credits
are included.—S.M.

Opening credits:

SINK OR SWIM

By Su Friedrich

Dedicated to
Maria and Pete

ZYGOTE

The Greek god Zeus had a wife named Hera, but he also had numerous love affairs and many illegitimate children. Furthermore, he had one child who was born without a mother. This was his daughter Athena, the goddess of war and justice, who sprang from his head fully grown and dressed for battle. She became chief of the three virgin goddesses and was known as a fierce and ruthless warrior. Because she was his favorite child, Zeus entrusted her to carry his shield, which was awful to behold, and his weapon, the deadly thunderbolt.

Y CHROMOSOME
(no story with this section)

X CHROMOSOME
(no story with this section)

WITNESS

There was a little girl
Who had a little curl
Right in the middle of her forehead.
When she was good
She was very, very good
And when she was bad
She was horrid.

VIRGIN

When the girl went out to play, the water running in the gutter was the Nile River. Her tree house was a harem filled with beautiful women wrapped in silk and covered in jewels. When she got on her bicycle, the girl rode bareback on a great, black stallion. Whenever she swam near the jetty, she saw mermaids with golden hair darting through underwater caverns. And her father was the smartest and most handsome man she'd ever met.

UTOPIA

The girl and her sister were forbidden to eat sugar, and their father refused to buy a television set, but once a week they were transported into a world of pleasure.

On Friday night at 7:30, they went across the hall to the home of an elderly man. He took them first to the kitchen, where they were allowed to make their own ice cream sundaes. He always gave them several flavors of ice cream and toppings, and assorted fruits and nuts and sprinkles to choose from.

When everything was ready, they carried their sundaes to the living room. The lights were turned off, the TV was turned on, and they sat in the dark for an hour and watched Don Ameche's Flying Circus Show.

TEMPTATION

On her seventh birthday, the girl's father gave her a book about Greek mythology. She would sit in the closet and read the stories long after being sent to bed. One night, her father came home late from work and caught her in the middle of a

Women's bodybuilding contest, from the "Temptation" section of Su Friedrich's *Sink or Swim* (1990). Courtesy Su Friedrich.

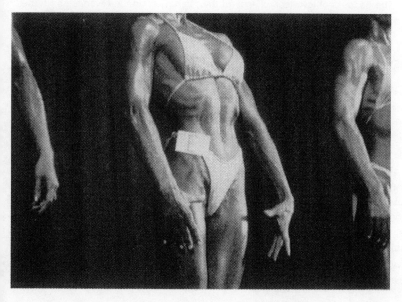

chapter. He lay down on the bed, put his hands behind his head, and asked her to tell her favorite myth.

It was the story of Atalanta, who was abandoned at birth because her father had wanted a son. She was left in the forest to die, but was discovered by a female bear and raised to become a great athlete and hunter. When her father heard the news, he realized that she was as good as a man, and took her back into his home.

Atalanta had vowed never to marry, and would race any man who hoped to win her hand. Although they were punished by death for losing the race, many men tried and failed. But Aphrodite, the goddess of love, thought it was time for Atalanta to lose both the race and her heart, and so she offered to help a young man named Hippomenes.

On the appointed day, he came armed with three apples made of solid gold. The race began, and as soon as Atalanta overtook Hippomenes, he dropped the first apple at her feet. She stopped to retrieve the precious fruit and then soon caught up with him, but he threw the second apple across her path. She decided to stop once again, but now it became more difficult to overtake him. When she did, he threw the last apple far from the track. Atalanta couldn't resist veering from her course, but as a result she lost the race and was forced to accept his hand in marriage.

SEDUCTION

The girl's father had fallen asleep while she told the story of Atalanta, so he didn't get to hear the end of it.

Atalanta was married soon after losing the race, and to her surprise she found happiness in her new life with Hippomenes. Because the power of Aphrodite had brought them together, they were obliged to pay homage to her. But like most newlyweds, they thought only of each other, and neglected to fulfill their sacred duties. The goddess of love took offense at their behavior, and in revenge she turned them both into lions.

REALISM

One day the girl told her father that she wanted to learn to swim. That evening they went to the university pool. He took her to the deep end, explained the principles of kicking and breathing, said she'd have to get back all by herself, and then tossed her in.

She panicked and thrashed around for a while, but finally managed to keep her head above water. From that day on, she was a devoted swimmer.

When they went to New Hampshire the following summer, she spent most of her time at a nearby lake. The water was a strange orange color, but it was sweet and cool, and the banks were lined with birch and pine trees.

Her father could swim all the way across, but sometimes he would stay near the shore with her, or sun himself on the raft while she practiced her dives. One afternoon, as she watched the water dry on her skin, he began to tell her about water moccasins. They live in nests on the bottom of lakes, he said, and if someone happens to come swimming by, they rush to the surface and cover the person with poisonous bites. The girl stared at the water and wondered whether they could even bite through her bathing suit.

That evening, she read the encyclopedia entry and discovered that water moccasins live primarily in the South, and a few midwestern states. Her mother explained that this meant they were thousands of miles away from her, but a geography lesson wasn't enough to comfort the girl.

QUICKSAND

One evening, the girl's father took her to see a movie about a man who invents a machine in which he can travel through time. When he gets to the year 20,000, he discovers a world full of beautiful, happy and passive people. He also finds a library full of rotting, unused books and realizes that the beautiful people no longer understand or care about the principles of Western civilization. As a result, they devote their lives to pleasure, and then let themselves be eaten by green monsters who live in underground caverns.

The relationship between the two groups is simple: Every time the monsters get hungry, they ring a siren, and the beautiful people rise like zombies and march into the caverns to their death.

The girl was terrified by the wail of the siren, and didn't want to see the people get slaughtered like animals. Covering her eyes, she begged to leave the theater. Her father reached over, pulled her hands from her face, and insisted that she watch the rest of the movie.

PEDAGOGY

The girl loved to play games, and also loved to win. It gave her a special thrill whenever she beat a boy in a race or a wrestling match. They always expected her to give in first, but she'd let them break her arm before she cried "Uncle."

Her father didn't like to play games, but he was fond of chess and offered to teach it to her. Unlike the boys, he expected her to be an aggressive opponent. The girl was happy to have a game to play with him, and took his lessons seriously. After many attempts, she beat him for the first time. The victory tasted sweet until she realized that the price of it had been the loss of her favorite partner. From that day on, he never played with her again.

OBLIVION

Because he was an anthropologist and linguist, the girl's father told her many stories about how other people celebrate the rites of childbirth, puberty, marriage, and death. She liked to imagine being an Indian or an African girl, dancing and singing in one of those ceremonies. By comparison, American rituals began to seem dull and superficial. She thought that might be why her father took so little interest in trimming their Christmas tree or going to mass with her on Father's Day.

But one year he suggested that she have an ice skating party for her birthday. When they got to the rink, all her friends lined up for a chance to skate with him. The girl offered to go at the end, and drank some hot chocolate while they circled past. Her friends seemed to be enjoying themselves, but when her turn came she was surprised at how fast he skated. She couldn't keep up with him, and couldn't convince him to slow down. After a while, she just let herself be pulled along over the bumpy ice.

NATURE

One summer, her father went away to teach at a different university in the midwest. A few miles from the campus, there was an abandoned quarry which had been filled by the spring rains. He set out alone one evening, hoping to go for a swim under the full moon. At the quarry, a sign was posted warning people not to enter the water. Her father was hot and tired after the long hike, but decided to wait and ask someone about it. When he did, they told him he was a very lucky man. The previous summer a visiting professor had gone there for a swim and was attacked and killed by a nest of water moccasins.

MEMORY (part one)

The girl's father had a sister whom he loved very much. As children, they lived on a farm in New England, and went swimming during the summer at a neighbor's pool, which was fed by ice cold spring water.

His sister usually waited until he finished his chores, but one day she went alone, knowing that he would come by soon after. She ran quickly down the unpaved road and was covered with dust and sweat by the time she arrived. It was a hot afternoon, but the pool was deserted. She tore off her shoes, dove into the icy water, and died immediately of a heart attack.

When her brother came back from work that day, no one was at home. He expected to find everyone at the pool, and started walking towards the neighbor's house. He heard a scream. He started to run. The screams grew louder. He raced into the front yard, and saw his mother kneeling on the ground beside the lifeless body of his sister.

The wake was held at their home, and throughout the following nights he sat and watched over her. No one blamed him for her death, but he carried the burden of guilt and loss for many years.

MEMORY (part two)

Twenty years later the girl's father wrote a poem about the first week in the life of his first-born child.

He describes walking the streets with her, sitting quietly as she takes a bottle, and staring into her dark eyes. He realizes that no one can predict the course of a child's life, but tries to imagine her as a young girl running off to school, or as a grown woman with a life of her own. He ends the meditation by saying, "All this must come as the questions are answered, but now there is only the quiet face that replaces a drowned sister at last."

LOSS

The girl liked to sleep late, eat between meals, keep her room messy, and fight with her sister. She made her mother miserable, but couldn't stop doing what she wanted to do. Her father didn't seem to care as much, because he spent most of his time at the office. Once in a while, though, he would come home in the middle of a huge fight and the girl's mother would beg him to do something about her crazy children.

Since threats and minor punishments had almost no effect, he decided one evening to try a different approach. While the girls continued to fight, he went into the bathroom and turned on the faucets. A few minutes later he went down the hall, grabbed the girls by their hair, dragged them into the bathroom, and made them kneel beside the tub. After warning them not to disobey their mother anymore, he pushed their faces into the water.

The girl started to scream. The screaming made her start choking. She kicked and punched at his legs and tried to wrench her head away, but his hands were large and strong. No. She would have to keep perfectly still now, because every move she made took away another breath. There was a pain spreading through her chest, a pressure building in her head. Let me go, I never meant to be so bad, I just get like this sometimes, let me go, I would have said I was sorry, please, let me go! Her eyes were wide open, her lungs were going to explode, she was grabbing wildly at the air and screaming into the water when she suddenly felt his grip loosen on her neck.

She dropped to the floor, coughing and shivering. Her sister sat across from her in a puddle of cold water, while her mother stood nearby screaming and crying.

KINSHIP

(Instead of narration, this section uses a song by Franz Schubert, called "Gretchen am Spinnrad," or "Gretchen at the Spinning Wheel." The recording is in German; no translation of the text is given in the film.)

Meine Ruh' ist hin	My peace is gone
Mein Herz ist schwer	My heart is heavy
Ich finde, ich finde sie nimmer	I can never find peace
Und nimmermehr.	And will never again.

Friedrich in Death Valley, from the "Kinship" section of *Sink or Swim*. Courtesy Su Friedrich.

Wo ich ihn nicht hab'	Wherever he leaves
Ist mir das Grab;	Becomes a grave;
Die ganze Welt	The whole wide world
Ist mir vergällt.	Is gall to me.
Mein armer Kopf	My poor head
Ist mir verrückt,	Is coming loose,
Mein armer Sinn	My poor mind
Ist mir zerstückt.	Is shattered.
Meine Ruh' ist hin	My peace is gone
(etc. as above)	(etc.)
Nach ihm nur schau' ich	I look out the window
Zum fenster hinaus,	Just to see him,
Nach ihm nur geh' ich	I leave the house
Aus dem Haus.	Only to find him.
Sein hoher Gang,	His manly stride,
Sein edle' Gestalt,	His noble form,
Seines Mundes Lächeln,	The smile on his lips,
Seiner Augen Gewalt,	The power in his eyes,
Und seiner Rede	The magic flow of his talk,
Zauberfluss,	The clasp of his hand
Seine Händedruck	And oh, his kiss!
Und ach, sein Kuss!	

Meine Ruh' ist hin (etc.)	My peace is gone (etc.)
Mein Busen drängt Sich nach ihm hin; Ach durft ich fassen Und halten ihn!	My bosom aches So much for him; Ah, could I but grasp him And hold him!
Und kussen ihn So wie ich wollt, An seinen Küssen Vergehen sollt'!	And kiss him Just as I want, To melt away Beneath his kisses!
O könnt ich ihn küssen So wie ich wollt, An seinen Küssen Vergehen sollt! An seinen Küssen Vergehen sollt!	Oh could I but kiss him Just as I want, To melt away Beneath his kisses! To melt away Beneath his kisses!
Meine Ruh' ist hin Mein Herz ist schwer	My peace is gone My heart is numb.

JOURNALISM

On her tenth birthday, the girl's sister gave her a diary with a green cloth cover. It came with a lock and a small key, which she carefully hid under the bed. On the first page she scrawled a large note that declared: If anybody reads this diary, they are very mean! It is personal.

For the most part, the girl filled it with stories about doing punishment assignments, fighting with the boys, and playing with her friends. Because she didn't write every day, there were still empty pages left when her parents told her they were getting a divorce.

The girl was too ashamed to tell anyone, and even kept it a secret from her best friend for more than a year, but she did confess it to her diary. It felt as if the act of writing it down would make it really come true, so she used a pencil instead of her favorite cartridge pen.

The next time she looked inside, the entry had been erased. Her mother was the only possible suspect.

From the "Journalism" section of *Sink or Swim*. Courtesy Su Friedrich.

INSANITY

The girls were out of control, the house was falling apart, nothing made sense anymore. In the middle of dinner, their mother would burst into tears and say, "Maybe I should kill myself. Then he'd realize what he's doing to us."

Early one evening, her father came over to pick up a few things. The girl hoped he would stay for a while, but her parents got into a fight and he left a short time later.

Her mother was furious, and called the girl and her sister onto the front porch. She opened one of the casement windows and had the two girls climb onto the sill. As she held her arms around their waists, they stared in fear at the sidewalk far below. Their father was halfway down the block by now, and their mother had to scream to get his attention. He stopped, turned around slowly, and looked up at them. The girl had an urge to wave, but she felt her mother's grip tighten around her waist. Then her mother leaned forward and began to shout down at him, "You think you can just leave us like this—just walk away from your home and your kids. But what if we all jumped out the window now and landed in a pile at your feet? How would you feel then?"

The girl waited for her father to do or say something, but he just stared at them for another long moment and then shook his head and walked away.

HOMEWORK

One of the first things to enter the house after her father left was a black-and-white TV. And because her mother had gone back to work, the girl could come home every afternoon and spend hours watching her favorite shows. She also started getting a small allowance, which she spent entirely on candy.

Letter being typed in the one synch-sound section, "Ghosts," of *Sink or Swim*. Courtesy Su Friedrich.

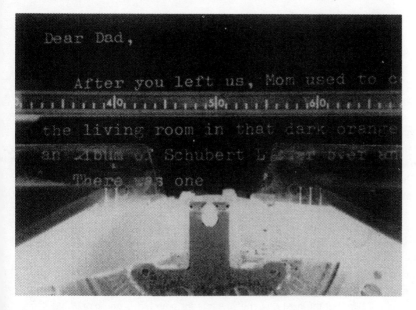

GHOSTS
(This text is shown being typed, rather than heard as a narration.)

Dear Dad,

After you left us, Mom used to come home from work, make us dinner, send us to our rooms, and then sit in the living room in that dark orange armchair and play an album of Schubert Lieder over and over again.

There was one song I particularly loved. I never knew what the lyrics meant, but it was the one that made Mom cry the most. We would come in and tell her we loved her, and we promised to be good so that you would come back again.

I recently got a translation of that song, "Gretchen at the Spinning Wheel." Do you know it already? It's the one about a woman who yearns for her absent lover and feels she cannot live without him.

It's so strange to have such an ecstatic melody accompany those tragic lyrics. But maybe that's what makes it so powerful: It captures perfectly the conflict between memory and the present.

Love,

P.S. I wish that I could mail you this letter.

FLESH

After the divorce papers came through, her parents never spoke to each other, and her father never came to their house. The girl started seeing him again a few years later, but only on rare occasions.

One evening he took her to a Japanese restaurant, introduced her to his second wife, and asked whether she'd like to go with them on a trip to Mexico. She felt nervous at the thought of being around his wife, but agreed to the plan. He called a few weeks later to say that his wife had decided to stay at home, and so they went alone.

The girl was proud to be with her father, and he seemed happy to give her a complete tour of Mexico City. At the end of a hot and tiring week, they headed for Acapulco.

The first day on the beach, the girl was approached by a young boy wearing a pale yellow shirt and a thin gold chain. He didn't speak any English, and she only knew how to say please and thank you. After a few hours with him, she realized that she had forgotten to meet her father for lunch.

He was furious and warned her not to make the same mistake twice. The girl was afraid of him, but the next day she was late for both lunch and dinner. He woke her up early the following morning and told her to pack her bags and meet him in the lobby. When she got there, he said they were leaving for Mexico City so that she could catch the next flight back to Chicago alone.

She sat by herself on the back of the bus and watched the coastline disappear. They didn't speak another word to each other until she left him at the gate and boarded the plane for home.

ENVY

The girl never told her father how it felt to be sent home from Mexico. Ten years later she was surprised to find that he had written a poem about it, entitled, "How You Wept, How Bitterly."

He begins the poem by calling her, "Remote as moonlight since I gutted the family with my exodus."

Later on he asks, "Did you need that Adonis of the beaches?"

And he ends the poem by declaring, "Your eyes at our parting condensed all children orphaned by divorce / A glance through a film of tears at a father dwindling to a speck."

The girl had waited so long to get some kind of apology from him, but this wasn't the one she imagined. He still didn't realize that he had been acting like a scorned and vengeful lover, and that hers had not been the tears of an orphaned child, but those of a frustrated teenage girl who had had to pay for a crime she didn't commit.

A facsimile of the chart that precedes the narration in the "Discovery" section of *Sink or Swim*. Courtesy Su Friedrich.

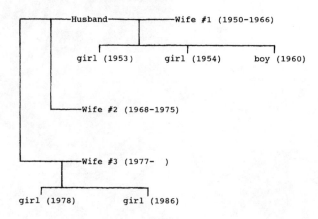

The American Kinship System
ca. 1950-1989

—Husband——————Wife #1 (1950-1966)

girl (1953)   girl (1954)   boy (1960)

—Wife #2 (1968-1975)

—Wife #3 (1977-)

girl (1978)   girl (1986)

DISCOVERY

The girl had always looked forward to the evenings, when she would see her father and tell him about what she had done at school. She had been disappointed whenever he called before dinner to say he wanted to keep working for a few more hours. That meant she wouldn't see him for the rest of the night.

Many years later she went to the library and looked him up in the card catalogue. She wondered what he'd been writing while deciding to get a divorce. The only book available was a collection of articles entitled, *Language, Context and the Imagination*. She discovered that two of the articles written that year involve the study of kinship systems. One is called, "The Linguistic Reflex of Social Change: From Tsarist to Soviet Russian Kinship." The other one is entitled, "Proto-Indo-European Kinship."

In the hopes of learning something about his approach to family life, she carried the book to a nearby table. For an hour she tried to read through the first one, but couldn't understand a word he'd written.

From the "Competition" section of *Sink or Swim*. Courtesy Su Friedrich.

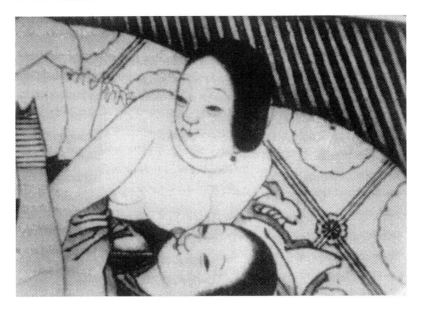

COMPETITION

He did write one book which the girl read from cover to cover. It's a detailed study of Aphrodite, the goddess of sexual love and desire, whom he compares with Demeter, the goddess of maternal love and devotion.

In the final chapter, he analyses the age-old schism between the two kinds of love. He points out that patriarchal cultures have always felt threatened by the coexistence of sexual desire and maternal devotion in a woman. He speculates that there may have been an earlier goddess who embodied the qualities of both Aphrodite and Demeter, and argues for the need to reintegrate those two states of being.

The book is dedicated to his third wife.

BIGAMY

Ever since the girl became a woman, she and her father have tried to remain on friendly terms. They write each other often and see each other rarely. They even exchange birthday and Christmas presents, although the woman doesn't send any to his third wife or their two daughters.

Last summer the woman had a job teaching in a city close to where her father lives. She invited him to come up for a visit, and he offered to bring along his eleven-year-old daughter. The woman hadn't seen the girl for several years, and said she looked forward to meeting her again.

The following Sunday she picked them up at the bus station and took them to her house for lunch. As they ate ham sandwiches in the yard, the woman sat quietly and

Friedrich bathing in the "Bigamy" section of *Sink or Swim*. Courtesy Su Friedrich.

listened to the conversation between her father and the young girl. No matter what
they talked about, it came out sounding like a debate or a lecture.

The woman took another sip of lemonade. She wanted to join them, but felt she
was in the presence of something too familiar. Just then her father stopped the girl in
midsentence to say that her story didn't interest him. The woman became rigid with
fear. This was her childhood, being played out all over again by the young girl. And
then it occurred to her that the girl was the same age she had been when her father
left their home so long ago.

She got up quickly, carried their plates into the kitchen, and opened a bag of
cookies. She was sure that her father would never leave his new family: He was older
now and seemed happily married. She looked out the window and saw that he had
gone to lie down in the shade. At that moment, she didn't know whether to feel pity or
envy for the young girl who sat alone in the sunshine trying to invent a more
interesting story.

ATHENA / ATALANTA / APHRODITE

Every time the woman went back to that orange lake in the country, she would try
to swim all the way across. Her father had done it many times, but whenever she got
half way over she'd start thinking about those water moccasins. No doubt they'd
migrated all the way from Louisiana and were lying in wait for her as she neared the
opposite shore.

On her last visit, she went with friends. For a few hours, the woman read and
played around in the shallow waters, but then decided it was time to start her
journey across the lake. As she swam, she began to worry . . . she fought with

herself . . . the shore got further away . . . her legs began to cramp . . . he loves me in spite of this . . . he loves me not . . . I have to do this . . . I'll never make it . . . I'm halfway there . . . I want to rest.

It frightened her to stare into the deep water, so she turned over and began doing the backstroke. Then she thought, maybe the water moccasins will put me out of my misery. Or maybe I'll drown trying to do this. If that happens, will he realize what I wanted to accomplish? Will he know I was doing it for his sake?

But she remembered her mother, who had held on to him so long after he was gone. Was it any different with her now, stuck in the middle of the lake, and not knowing whether to go further or turn back?

She stopped swimming and began to float under the bright sky. The sun warmed her face, and the water surrounded her like a lover's arms. She thought of her friends lying on the sandy beach, and realized how tired she had become. It was time to start the long swim back to shore.

On the way, she only stopped once, to turn around and watch her father, as he beat a slow and steady path away from her through the dark orange water.

(EPILOGUE—there's no title on this section. This is sung as a round; the song is repeated six times.)

A, B, C, D, E, F, G
H, I, J, K, L, M, N, O, P
Q, R, S, T, U and V
W, X and Y and Z
Now I've said my ABCs
Tell me what you think of me.

Friedrich as a child in the epilogue of *Sink or Swim*. Courtesy Su
Friedrich.

Closing credits:

Script, camera and editing by Su Friedrich

Voiceover by Jessica Lynn

Technical assistance by Peggy Ahwesh, Leslie Thornton,
Pete Zuccarini

"Gretchen am Spinnrad" by Franz Schubert,
sung by Kathleen Ferrier

Special Thanks to Leslie Thornton

Ann Marie Fleming

Ann Marie Fleming is the youngest film-maker included in this volume: indeed, her first films were not completed until the late eighties. But both *You Take Care Now* (1989) and *New Shoes: An Interview in Exactly 5 Minutes* (1990) center on spoken narratives of considerable power. *You Take Care Now* is Fleming's cinematic reminiscence of two events: of being raped in Brindisi, Italy, and of being run down by two cars on a street in Vancouver. The story of these events is spoken on the sound track and is accompanied in the visuals by a montage of motion picture imagery of Vancouver, still photographs, still frames of motion picture images made on an optical printer, enacted (visual and/or vocal) fragments of scenes, animated paintings (the film is framed by hand-painted title and credits), and several visual texts. The film has much in common with Su Friedrich's *Gently Down the Stream* and *The Ties That Bind*: the text of Fleming's narration (like Friedrich's scratched dream texts/ questions) is the foreground and the visual imagery provides emphasis and metaphor; the vocal timing of Fleming's nar-

ration is effective (Fleming's experience as a stand-up comic may have had an effect here); and the film's imagery and narration intersect in both obvious and subtle ways. Most remarkable is the film's density: though only eleven minutes, *You Take Care Now* effectively communicates something of the complexity of a young woman's confrontation with contemporary gender politics as they are dramatized in two painful physical/psychic shocks.

New Shoes: An Interview in Exactly 5 Minutes was the first of two attempts to present a true story about a woman (Gaye Fowler), who in her teens was chased down a Toronto alley way and shot by her ex-fiance who then turned the gun on himself. In this presentation of Fowler's story (in 1990 Fleming completed a dramatic feature, *New Shoes*, that centers on the same events), Fowler tells her story to the camera, with Fleming asking questions or responding to details. Visually, *New Shoes: An Interview in Exactly 5 Minutes* intercuts between the interview and Fleming dressed in a Cinderella outfit and doing a series of actions that (as in *You*

Take Care Now) visually "interpret" the story we see and hear. The Cinderella fantasy sequence is elaborated by superimposed animated material. For Fleming, the short version of the *New Shoes* story was a way of exploring, among other things, the way in which the "text" of a personal memory evolves as the teller explores/exploits her own experience—in this case, to fit the telling of the events into the format of "Five Feminist Minutes," a series of short films sponsored by the National Film Board of Canada's Studio D: during *New Shoes: An Interview in Exactly 5 Minutes*, the sound of a clock ticking can be heard, and at the end of the film, Fleming indicates to Fowler that she has only ten seconds to explain how her ex-fiance's new shoes are relevant to her story.

Included here are the complete transcription of the interview from *New Shoes: An Interview in Exactly 5 Minutes* and the text of Fleming's narrative in *You Take Care Now*, along with the dialogue from a scene dramatized on the sound track (it occurs immediately after she is hit by the two cars), and the four quotations presented visually during the film.

Transcript of *New Shoes: An Interview in Exactly 5 Minutes*

My transcription of the interview between Ann Marie Fleming and Gaye Fowler is nearly verbatim: in a very few instances, I eliminated a "you know" or some other vocal mannerism that, if included in the printed transcript, would distort the reader's sense of the interchange between the two women. I have also used brackets to indicate the film's infrequent use of sound effects.—S.M.

[Opening of song, "My Old Flame, I can't even think of his name . . ."]
Ann Marie Fleming: Go ahead.
Gaye Fowler: OK, I'll tell you how I broke up with him, OK?
AMF: Yeah, yeah.
GF: I once had a boyfriend named Albert. And he was my first great love—two virgins, bad sex—you know the story. And I put the pressure on him to buy me an engagement ring because, you know, everybody else in school who wasn't mustached had an engagement ring and was getting engaged that year so . . . We never really talked about marriage but we knew at some point in the future we were going to go out and buy tacky plaid furniture and go live in an apartment somewhere—that was what engaged meant. And when we broke up, I just kind of cut him off. And I remember he came over that day. He had bought me a stereo for one Christmas. It was like the equivalent of a close-and-play, and he wanted it back. He told me I could keep the ring but could he have the stereo. And I was adamant, no—he could have the ring back. It was a diamond that had a great big black carbon flaw in the middle of it. Anyways, he got the ring and I got the stereo.

And the next time I saw Albert (he phoned me a few times), I just couldn't stand the sight of him. I had no experience in breaking off with people, relationships. I thought: you just stopped seeing them and that's it and that's what I did, and it worked fine for about two months and then he started phoning and I just couldn't stand the sound of his voice or the look of him. So I just was curt on the phone. So then that wasn't getting anywhere so he started coming around a bit [a single bang on the soundtrack], and would come by my work sometimes and try to run me over, and come by my house and start big fights—you know, the average Toronto scene.

Anyways, I was on my way to work this one morning after the long weekend and I came walking out the laneway and I saw him pull up in his car [sound of fluttering birds] with this friend of his and I got scared. I knew something awful was going to happen but I didn't know what. And I thought that if he was going to hit me or beat me up, if we had contact I could reach him and stop him. Anyway, he jumped out of the car and had a rifle with him and he just started cocking the gun and shooting it, holding it at his hip and shooting it, and I just ran back and forth in front of him, not really going anywhere. And then after three shots, I decided I had to get closer to my home [sound of running on gravel] so I turned around and started running back through the laneway over the gravel. And I got to my backyard and I realized that it wasn't going to do me any good. I couldn't get in the house, so I just—it wasn't going to help me any. He ran up behind me. I didn't hear the gun go off and so I turned around to see where he was. And the gun had jammed. And then, as I was turning around, he fired and it hit me in the back and I spun around and I landed on my back, face up. And I looked and he was running towards me and he had the gun aimed down and he cocked it as he was running. And I remember thinking that this wasn't what I wanted to see if I was going to die, so I looked up in the air [sound of fluttering birds], and I saw the tops of these trees and I heard nothing except all these birds fluttering over the tops of trees—like hundreds of them. And when I rolled my eyes back down again to see where he was and what was going to happen, he was right at my feet. And I remember I held my breath and I couldn't say anything and it was silent. And I looked up and he turned the gun around and he blew off the top of his head. [Phrase of "My Old Flame," then sound of something hitting a chain-link fence] And he landed at my feet and the gun landed between us and I could hear a chain-link fence slapping in the background where the brain matter had gone.

AMF: [laughter]

GF: I don't think that's very funny, really. So then we were laying there and it was silent again, so I had to scream to know that I was alive is how I felt . . .

AMF: Oh, what about the new shoes, the new shoes, we have ten seconds.

GF: I looked down, and I remember thinking: why would he kill himself? He had on brand new shoes. Why would he buy new shoes if he was going to kill himself? So the soles of his feet were staring at me, and I was thinking that . . .

[Last phrase of "My Old Flame"]

Transcript and Text from *You Take Care Now*

The script of Fleming's narration is presented as transcribed from the sound track, with occasional (bracketed) interruptions that attempt to clarify particulars of her presentation. From time to time, words are spaced in unusual ways, to give the reader a sense of Fleming's emphasis. The texts of the superimposed quotations from Lewis Carroll and Shakespeare are included in brackets. The text of the dialogue between Fleming and the ambulance man, which is dramatized near the end of the film on the sound track, is also included verbatim, in italics. In three instances, snapshots provided by Fleming (and originally included in the film) are reproduced at the moments in the narrative when they're referred to, and in a few other instances, bracketed comments briefly describe visual imagery seen at a particular moment.

My representation of You Take Care Now does not, by any means, create a clear sense of the film's complex visual montage, which flows back and forth between the illustrative and the mysterious so quickly that, especially during early viewings, one has a sense only of the stream of consciousness that underlies the narrator's interpretation of her past.—S.M.

[Opening credits]
YOU TAKE CARE NOW, a film by Ann Marie Fleming

I'm starting now.

[Printed text: "Whatever it was, Alice fell quickly through it . . . /(Lewis Carroll)"]

Close your eyes and think of a hotel room in Brindisi. You're sitting at a desk, looking out the window onto the street below. It's siesta time and there's not a lot going on out there. You're writing an entry in your journal. If you're having trouble visualizing, it looks like this:

[Motion picture of architectural detail]

You've been traveling on a train for the past three days, from Switzerland on down to the heel of Italy, trying to make it to Greece before your Eurail pass expires. You haven't washed or slept in all that time; it's early in the morning and you have all day to wait for a night boat to the Peloponnesus. The friend you met on the train has gone back to some other town to pick up a machine part he forgot. It's September. Tourist season is over. And you're alone in a city everyone has been telling you is the armpit of the world. The travel agent takes pity on you, and offers you his place to crash, have a shower, store your stuff. He calls a cab to take you there. The driver knows the place.

Oh, I almost forgot. You're female, and you're twenty-two.

So, you're writing, after a lunch of fresh steamed prawns and enough coffee in your body that you feel yourself burning inside. You're in his room. You want to leave, but you just   can't   think. So you stay anyway. Because you don't trust your intuition. And then the locked door turns open, and the first fire starts.

Now the next bit is a little hard to explain. You get the idea don't you? You get raped.

Now, you're lying there waiting for something violent to happen, to be hit or beaten or for yourself to do *something*, like scream or fight or maybe pull out that ever-handy Swiss Army knife. But nothing like that passes. Because you're afraid you might hurt him, or you're afraid he might get angry and hurt you, or he'll call the police and tell them that you stole something, and you don't speak Italian. And you've heard all about the police. And you lie there, passive and violated, feeling like someone told you you were going to win an award, and then you didn't get it. Except the award was your dignity, your sanity, your middle-class inviolability. It was taken away and given to someone else who never made the mistake of going to a hotel room in a strange place with a strange man. And all you were worried about was how to get out of there with your luggage intact, how to avoid upsetting this man who not only had a black belt in Tai Kwon Do but also had your ticket for the boat out of that nightmare land,

and how to get somewhere safe to sleep. God, you wanted to sleep, so   bad. But he'd told you that you look just like the Giaconda, and she hasn't closed her eyes in over four hundred years. So, you take a picture of yourself so that you can remember what the Mona Lisa looks like when she realizes Leonardo is just another letch.

[Two snapshots are presented, one at a time.]

Snapshots filmed in Ann Marie Fleming's *You Take Care Now* (1990). Courtesy Ann Marie Fleming.

Outside again, amidst the shuffling feet of grapepickers waiting for a job by the piazza fountain, you find yourself followed by a midget who tells you you look like Brooke Shields. All tall women probably look like Brooke Shields to a small man. You've already had your life's worth of trauma so you're not expecting it when he locks you in a small room and tries to push his tongue down your face. You don't throw him across the room, but push him gently under the rock where he came from and go out into the street with his tiny, offended ego following you, crying:

[A close-up of a man's lips, mouthing "Slut, bitch, poutaina; slut, bitch, poutaina, hey! Slut, bitch, poutaina, hey!"]

So you go back to your ticket taker, now your port of refuge. After all, what *else* can he do? And he gives you a lecture on how you're too trusting and you have to take better care of yourself, and to remember that men here are assholes.

[A male voice with a heavy accent says:]
"Even I'm a little bit of an asshole. But then, you know that. Heh, heh, heh."

So, he buys you dinner, kisses you on the cheek and tells you to keep in touch, gives you his name and his address. Oh, sure.

[Printed text: "—the innocent sleep. / Sleep that knits up the ravelled sleeve of care."]

You take a taxi to the pier. It's dark out. Your friend from the train is there, and asks you how your day was. You say, "I had a really bad day, a really   bad   day." But then you look down at yourself, and you are all in one piece, and you think, at least I'm still here.

This is the second part. It's January, it's cold out, it's dark, and it's just beginning to rain. You are just a few blocks away from your apartment, in Vancouver. You are with your boyfriend and you are crossing the street. The street looks like this:

[Motion picture of street fades to black.]

He runs across the street before you, but you, being extra cautious, extra careful, wait for a better opportunity to cross. You wait for one side of the traffic to pass by, and then you walk out to the yellow line, to wait. Except you don't   feel   good. You start to panic. You think *some*thing is going to happen. Why didn't Ross wait? You start talking yourself out of it: There are no cars coming that way, they can see you, you're *in* the fucking street, there *are* lights, it's okay . . .

Okay, you know what happens next. You feel this great black force hitting heavy against your hip, and you think, "Omigod, I'm *hit*!" and then you try not to fall. But you know you are falling. And then you hit the ground, on your face, looking up at a curb, which curb? And you think, "Oh, no." And that's all there is time for before a car runs over both your legs, and you're twisted up towards the sky, and you can hear brakes screeching and tires sliding and you think you are dead. And there are no flashbacks and you know there is nothing more after this. And you think your face is going to be run over. And you start to scream.

But then, nothing happens. There are faces above you, and they are all helping. And you get angry, wanting to know where the driver is, and why didn't he stop? And they tell you that he did stop, and that there were two cars, and you think, "Yeah, I guess there must have been."

And when the ambulance attendants come to get you, you   don't   want to be   touched. Something feels very, very wrong, and you're not sure that you can move a thing, but there's this searing pain in your leg, and they put the oxygen mask over your face, and you decide to let it ride.

[Fleming's narration pauses here while we hear one of the ambulance rescue team talk with her as they prepare to take her to the hospital:]

"Hey, we just want you to lie still, all right? We're going to put a collar on your neck to keep your head from moving. Just lie still. That's it. And here's a mask, just want you to breathe normally through this mask, all right? OK, just lie still, we're going to load you into our car. [pause] *First we go down, then up again.* [pause] *Just want you to breathe normally, all right? Can you tell us where you're having your pain?"*
  "It's both my legs."
  "Do you hurt anywhere else besides your legs? How 'bout your head or neck?"
  "Um, yeah, my head."
  "Can you wiggle your toes for us? [pause] *Do you remember what happened in the accident? Were you awake all the time?"*
  "Yes."
  "Do you know what day it is today?"
  "Oh, Sunday."
  "Do you have any past medical problems? Do you take medication from a doctor? Are you taking medications?"

[The voice of the rescue-team man fades out as Fleming's narration continues.]

And finally, Ross is there again, but he didn't see you hit. He thought you merely slipped on the yellow line. But it didn't help to hear him say, "Please don't die, please don't die," because that wasn't really the point.

In the ambulance the attendant keeps repeating, after he threatens to tie you down if you don't stop jerking up with pain, "You know, you look really familiar. Do I know you from someplace?" And you say, "It must be the mask." And they leave you in the hospital and say, "You take care, now." Like, that wasn't what you'd been trying to do all along. And all you wanted to do is sleep, but the pain won't stop, and it won't stop for months now. And you wonder what you ever did to get raped and run over in one lifetime. And you realize there is only one.

[Printed text: "Hush, little baby, don't say a word . . ."]

You go home, and get on your bed, and Ross takes a picture of you. You lie there, small and helpless, black and white. And it looks like this:

Snapshot filmed at conclusion of Fleming's *You Take Care Now.* Courtesy Ann Marie Fleming.

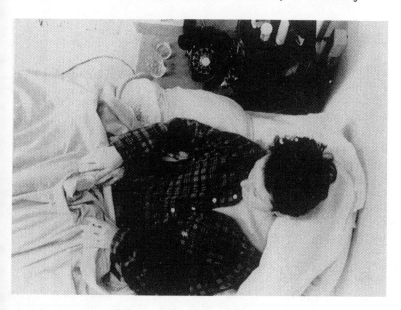

And you think, wow, pictures   don't   tell   you   *any*thing.

[Final credits]

Yvonne Rainer

No filmmaker has explored the two general areas of text represented in this volume more extensively than Yvonne Rainer. Since the beginning of her career as a feature filmmaker in the early seventies, Rainer has combined an interest in developing screenplays that critique conventional industry melodrama and an interest in the potential of printed text. Indeed, these two interests have functioned as central means for achieving essentially the same result: the construction of new, more progressive melodramatic forms.[1]

Early in her career, Rainer discovered that printed text was a way of interrupting both what came to be called the "male gaze" and the conventional assumption that melodramatic narrative needs to proceed clearly and directly to a specific conclusion that provides viewers with a sense of completion (what Laura Mulvey would subsequently term "plenitude").[2] Printed text was a way of developing narrative action while impeding conventional film-narrative thrust, and a way of creating a more complex set of viewer identifications than is common in conventional film: since readers read themselves into texts, the inclusion of complex visual texts from a variety of sources diversifies the nature of viewer identification and response.

Rainer uses many kinds of printed text in her early films, and the result in some instances is the creation of multiple levels of reality experienced simultaneously. One famous shot from *Film About a Woman Who . . .* , for example, confronts the "male gaze" by having the camera track toward a nude woman standing among several onlookers (including

---

1. In 1989, the screenplays for her first five features—*Lives of Performers* (1972), *Film About a Woman Who . . .* (1974), *Kristina Talking Pictures* (1976), *Journeys from Berlin/1971* (1980), and *The Man Who Envied Women* (1985)—were published in *The Films of Yvonne Rainer*, by Yvonne Rainer (Bloomington/Indianapolis: Indiana University Press, 1989).

2. See "Visual Pleasure and Narrative Cinema," in *Visual and Other Pleasures,* by Laura Mulvey (Bloomington/Indianapolis: Indiana University Press, 1989).

Yvonne Rainer's face (and clippings about Angela Davis and George Jackson), from *Film About a Woman Who . . .* (1974). Courtesy Yvonne Rainer.

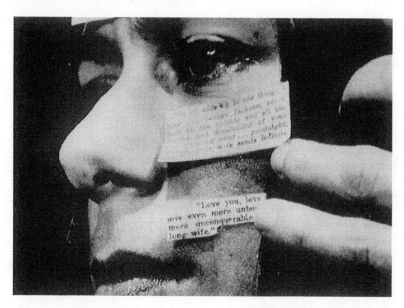

Rainer), while a man (his eyes on the camera, not the woman) pulls her bloomers up, covering her nakedness; finally the camera tracks to the left of the woman and moves in for an extreme close-up of Rainer's face to which are affixed clippings of the press coverage of the relationship of Angela Davis and George Jackson during the latter's imprisonment. Viewers read these texts, superimposing the scenes they describe over the scene photographed by Rainer's camera. The two levels work together to remind us of how the media uses eroticism as a means of deflecting our consciousness from issues of race and class.

Rainer's screenplays, within which her visual texts play integral parts, are constructed so as to confront viewer assumptions developed by years of consuming commercial melodrama. In general, Rainer is at pains to avoid the sorts of events conventional melodramas focus on: even her romantically involved characters are more likely to discuss politics than the state of their erotic relationships, and Rainer never dramatizes violent action or a hair-raising chase. Her characters are engaged—and engage viewers—in a struggle to find a place for themselves in a world of conflict and injustice. And in general, Rainer's screenplays demonstrate her determination to use filmmaking as a way of modeling more progressive interactions between people. Rainer has come to rely increasingly on recycled texts, and the process of composing screenplays has, more and more, become a question of assembling extended quotations from other writers (and filmmakers) within an overall narrative design. This commitment to assemblage is an extension of the spirit of collaboration Rainer developed in her performance work and her earlier features, and it provides a set of external references that implicitly urge viewers to expand their awareness of contemporary life by using filmgoing not as a substitute for reading, but as a means back into a more complete engagement with insightful literary texts.

Privilege (1990), Rainer's most recent feature, takes as its central subject a crucial dimension of human experience that has been relentlessly ignored, not only by commercial cinema and television, but by all forms of independent film and video making: menopause. Menopause has become the quintessentially *unfilmic* topic, signifying the end of a woman's desire and desirability, and thus her capacity to be of interest to a film's protagonists or viewers. The narrative skeleton of *Privilege* is Jenny's (Jenny is played by Alice Spivak) current thoughts about menopause and her memories of her early years as a dancer in New York City (these are loosely based on Rainer's own experiences). It is fleshed out with a set of interviews with menopausal and postmenopausal women, and with a variety of other quotations, spoken by characters or presented as visual texts. Taken together, these sources of information suggest that the current stereotyping of menopause bears a general similarity and relationship to the cultural marginalization of African-Americans, Puerto Rican–Americans, and other "nonmainstream" groups. *Privilege* argues that what conventional American culture has defined as "privilege" is for most people—for all women (since menopause is inevitable), for African-Americans, Puerto Rican–Americans—a constriction of privilege, and paradoxically, that the cultural taboo of menopause has become a way of hiding the fact that life after menopause (and life outside "mainstream" culture in general) brings with it some important advantages, not least of which is a potential freedom from that set of expectations about women's bodies so relentlessly promoted by commercial film and television.

The complete script of *Privilege* follows.

Script of *Privilege*

Rainer's screenplay includes both the dialogue from the film and all visual texts, in this instance filmed off the screen of a word processor. Shifts from one mode of text to another are both textually and graphically indicated. She describes the film's action in italics. Abbreviations are used to indicate camera position ("MS," medium shot; "CU," close-up; "LS," long shot; "WS," wide shot; "MLS," medium long shot; "MCU," medium close up), and other aspects of image and sound ("V-O," voice-over; "MOS," without sound; etc.). "Y.R." always means Yvonne Rainer; "Yvonne W." refers to Rainer's alter ego in the film, "Yvonne Washington" (Novella Nelson).—s.m.

MCU, interview with Faith Ringgold, an African-American woman in her late 50's.

Faith: The attitude is wrong . . . I mean, getting older . . . getting older is a bitch! *(She laughs uproariously.)*

MS, interview with Shirley Triest, a seventy-four-year-old white woman. She is seated at a diningroom table. Yvonne Rainer questions her from off-screen.

Y.R. *(V-O)***:** Did you have any symptoms, like hot flashes?

Shirley: No, nothing at all.

Y.R.: Then we have no story here.

Shirley *(laughing)***:** Yes, we have no story here. I told you . . . the parts of me that work, work *very* well!

MS, interview with Helene Moglen, a white woman in her late 50's. She is seated in front of windows which look out on trees and distant hills.

Helene: Yes, I realize that one of the things that has made it so much of a positive experience for me is that my life is so very comfortable. So I have genuine alternatives now that I can take advantage of. And I think it would be very different if I didn't.

Film clip from TV movie Between Friends. *Elizabeth Taylor and Carol Burnett are drinking white wine in a fire-lit, well-furnished room.*

Taylor: Well, it's no big deal. It's no big deal for him. He doesn't have a uterus. Anyway, I don't want to go around uterusless.

Burnett: Y'know, when you're over forty the whole apparatus seems to reorganize. Wouldn't y'know, after all these years I finally got my head together and my ass falls apart. *(They both laugh.)* Oh god, I'm going to *will* menopause away!

Cut to black velvet drapes. Audience applause is heard as Yvonne Rainer enters and sits down in CU. She is a white woman in her mid-50's. She removes her glasses and earrings, then looks directly at the camera.

[Music begins: Chet Baker playing "My Funny Valentine" on the trumpet.]

Intertitles appear on a word-processor screen:

PRIVILEGE

A FILM BY
YVONNE RAINER
AND MANY OTHERS

WITH

ALICE SPIVAK
BLAIRE BARON
RICO ELIAS
GABRIELLA FARRAR
DAN BERKEY

AND

SPECIAL GUEST APPEARANCE BY

NOVELLA NELSON

Cut to Y.R. in front of black drapes. She picks up a large bottle of moisturizing lotion and holds it next to her face. Camera pulls back to Medium.

Footage from an educational film on menopause: A white, middle-aged male doctor, sitting in a garden, addresses the camera.

Doctor: In our counseling we emphasize the fact that even though the role of motherhood is over, the menopausal patient can now enter a new role as a wife and a woman, a role which needs redirection and reevaluation.

Footage from same film: Another white, middle-aged male doctor addresses the camera, from behind a desk.

Doctor: I think we should not forget that our ultimate objective is to improve the relationship of the couple. Tragic though it may be, this is often the only chance that this couple will have to talk to a sympathetic and understanding third party. And the doctor may have a golden opportunity to improve the well-being of the couple as well as of the wife.

Intertitle: Related materials on menopause are available from Ayerst Laboratories.

A series of titles follows in quick succession, delineating warnings, precautions, and possible adverse reactions as a consequence of undergoing estrogen replacement therapy.

Y.R. reappears in front of black drapes.

[Music fades out.]

She smears flaming red lipstick over her lips without regard for accuracy, then begins to read aloud:

Y.R. *(sync)*: It's sort of appropriate that this is my last major, I think, public address here to talk to women, because I do believe that the future lies with us—in a very deep way. And one of the reasons I'm stopping is that I have to go away and work out how we do it, because *we've done nothing yet.* And, uh,

MS of an African-American woman signing in American Sign Language (ASL). She stands center-frame in front of the black drapes. Y.R. (still speaking in sync) appears in a small oval in the lower right corner.

we talk all this equal rights, and we beg men for equal rights and we've achieved nothing. Like—I could say a rude word, I'm an Australian, but I won't say it. Fifty-two percent of us are women. And where is the proportional representation in the Congress? Like, *nowhere!* And it's not right. And you know whose fault it is? It's ours, because we are pathetic. We haven't got any guts. And I say this advisedly and with deep sorrow, and I'm one of you. And I haven't got any guts either. And do you know why I'm retiring? Because the men did me in . . .

Intertitle:

PRIVILEGE

A FILM BY
YVONNE WASHINGTON
AND MANY OTHERS

Yvonne Washington *(V-O)*: I was bone tired. I had been careening around the country at a break-neck pace

Again cut to signer in front of black velours, signing the V-O.

for too long. Even to *my* ears my lectures were beginning to sound like ranting and raving. I had been threatening to retire, so why didn't I stop beating my head against those would-be benefactors, those smug English-speakers charged by the nation with improving the plight of the deaf, while turning a deaf ear to the history of struggle by the community of signers.

Y.R. reappears in lower right corner. ASL signer continues to interpret center-frame.

Y.R. *(sync)*: OK, nuclear war. Every single town and city in your country is targeted with at least one bomb. All the nuclear power plants are targeted. If you drop a big bomb on a reactor, you can terminate permanently an area the size of West Germany. All military facilities are targeted; all universities participating in nuclear and military research, which is this one; all corporations making weapons, which is almost all the corporations now in the United States of America. So everything's targeted. Nuclear war will take about one hour to complete bilaterally . . .

Intertitle:

HELEN CALDICOTT, 1986

ASL signer reappears, still center-frame. Y.R. is gone.

Yvonne Washington *(V-O)*: The deaf community has historically spurned the pathological model of its situation, favoring instead a social model: deaf signers have seen themselves not as deficient but as different, and what makes the difference is not their hearing loss but their ostracized language of signing, a language that has been actively banished for over a century by the hearing establishment concerned with the deaf. The long and short of *my* part in this story is that recently studies began to emerge showing that American Sign Language shares the complexity of patterning characteristic of spoken languages, and therefore warrants the same kind of scientific examination. This meant that I could begin to relax in my advocacy. Besides, I needed a change. My own change-of-life pointed the way. I had gone into early menopause at the age of 45 because I was so overworked and tired. Why not make a documentary film about menopause? I have medical training, so I was fairly up-to-date on the physiological effects of menopause and female aging. It was the dominant medical attitudes that needed exposure, the attitudes that tell us we are "deficient" and "diseased"—much like the deaf—only *our* "disease" begins when we can no longer make babies. Friends have asked me, whom would I be addressing? Menopause is a well-kept secret, something you don't want to know about unless you're a woman who is past her prime . . . over the hill . . . has seen better days . . .

CU of Y.R.'s face center-frame. Her voice is muted behind that of

Yvonne Washington *(V-O)*: . . . let herself go.

Y.R. *(sync)*: Twenty-two percent of the children in this country live in poverty . . . *Twenty-two percent!* Thirty-four million people live in poverty, and they are almost *all* women and children and black. Right? Fifteen million old women live on an amount of $5,000 a year or less—15 million old women in the richest country in the world! . . . So! what are we going to do, folks?

She is silent and looks at the camera.

Yvonne Washington *(V-O)*: Why do young women respond with such reluctance and dread? What do they fear?

Ten seconds pass.

Daytime. Yvonne Washington's apartment. Jenny, a white woman in her late 50's, is about to be interviewed by Yvonne W. (off-screen).

Jenny *(V-O)*: Where do you want me? Over here?

Yvonne W. *(V-O)*: This is my workroom. Here, let me move this out of your way.

There is a blur of movement as Yvonne W. in extreme CU crosses frame. Jenny sits down so that her face is in CU. The following dialogue is punctuated by three alternating images and two interwoven voices of Jenny, played by both Alice Spivak (Jenny #1 and #2) and Minnette Lehmann (Jenny #3). Jenny #1 has been shot in 16mm; Jennies #2 and #3 are transferred Video 8. Jenny #1 wears white pants and a gray cotton jacket over a black top. Jennies #2 and #3 wear black leather jackets and bright red lipstick. If not otherwise noted, Alice Spivak's Jenny #1 is the speaker.

Jenny: The problem with Caldicott is that she paralyzes us with horror rather than inspiring us to protest . . . **(Jenny #2:)** All that apocalypse and doom . . . *(She looks around.)* So Yvonne, what am I here for?

Yvonne W. *(V-O)*: I thought I told you. I'm making a documentary about menopause.

Jenny: Menopause! Not *that* again. I thought you were going to interview me about my brilliant career *(laughs)*.

Medical footage:

Doctor *(in garden)*: Is her creative life over simply because she's reached the age of forty-five, or fifty, or fifty-five?

MCU, Jenny in Yvonne W.'s apartment.

Yvonne W. *(V-O)*: Whaddya mean "Not that again?" Who's talking about it? Don't you know that menopause takes the prize for being the thing that the least number of people say they want to know anything about?

Jenny #2 *(speaking with Jenny #3's voice)*: Oh, it just seems like everytime

CU Jenny #3.

Jenny #3 *(sync)*: I turn around I see an article on it somewhere.

Yvonne W. *(V-O)*: Mostly in medical journals. In the mass media you don't hear about it that much. How about you? Did you have an easy time?

    MCU Jenny #1.

Jenny: Not really. What kind of film are you making? If it's informational, I've done tons of research on the subject. *My* story's not that interesting. What you should do is start with what the word means. It's derived from the Greek and means "cessation of the month." And then you should go into the distortions that the doctors and shrinks have foisted on us. Like the psychoanalyst Helen Deutsch, **(Y.R.'s voice:)** that traitor to her sex, **(Jenny:)** who described menopause as "women's partial death" or the gynecologists who call it "a living decay" . . .

[She continues to talk (MOS)]

Doctor *(V-O)*: My present thinking is that the menopausal syndrome is a deficiency state analogous to hypothyroidism, in the sense that it can be treated, and treated effectively.

Jenny *(V-O)*: . . . and then turned out to be in the pay of a couple of drug companies.

    MS, Jenny #3, who watches as Yvonne W. (off-screen) paces back and forth.

Jenny *(V-O)*: Let's face it, Yvonne, we live in a sexist culture that considers women old at an earlier age than men. . . .

Jenny #3 *(with Jenny #1's voice)*: Why are you so restless?

Yvonne W. *(V-O)*: I hear you. And all of that will be in there. But what about you, Jenny? Did you have hot flashes?

    MS, Jenny #1.

Jenny: Oh god did I have hot flashes!

Yvonne W.: For how long?

Jenny: Oh, it's been endless. And it's still going on. But we really do live in a culture that is terrified of aging. There's this poem by Eve Merriam:

    During the following recitation, camera dollies to extreme left to reveal Yvonne W.'s back as she stands leaning against the wall of books.

Last night I dreamed of an old lover
I had not seen him in 40 years.
When I awoke
I saw him on the street
his hair was white,
his back stooped.
How could I say hello?
He would have puzzled all day
about who the young girl was
who smiled at him.
So I let him go on his way.

Yvonne W. *(moving out of frame to right)*: That's nice. But Jenny, would you please tell me

Yvonne W. sits down, back to camera, on a red Chesterfield couch in the foreground. Jenny is seated opposite her in the background.

(sync): how long your hot flashes went on. Was it months, years, how long?

Jenny: *Five* years. It's been at least five years of that ridiculous sweating. I'm famous for suddenly throwing off half my clothes. But, Yvonne, really now, why talk about it? We'll just be reducing women to their biological processes all over again. Anatomy is destiny. When you're young they whistle at you, when you're middle-aged they treat you like a bunch of symptoms, and when you're old they ignore you.

Yvonne W. *(V-O)*: They do, huh?

Jenny: Yeh. And besides . . . [She continues to speak *MOS*.]

Woman's voice *(from medical film)*: I don't mind being middle-aged at all. I really don't.

Jenny *(sync)*: But don't let me give you a hard time. . . . Ask me as many silly questions as you want *(laughs)*. We go back a long way, Yvonne . . . and I probably owe you one, right?

Yvonne W.: Jenny, if you think you owe me something, that's fine with me. Frankly, you must know something I don't, or you have an unnecessarily guilty conscience. I have fond memories of dancing with you years ago and maybe we'll get into that later. But for now let's try and keep our personal history out of this, OK? First of all,

She gets up from couch and leaves frame-left. Jenny's gaze follows her movement.

(V-O): when you talk about biology and "them," you're confusing biology with patriarchy. Just because some men invoke *our* biology for their own advantage doesn't mean *we* have to go along with them.

   CU, Jenny #3.

Jenny #3: Keeping one's dignity as you enter menopause is like fighting city hall.

   MCU, Jenny #2.

Jenny #2: Aren't you interested in my reminiscences about being a luscious young starry-eyed dancer in New York?

   MCU, Jenny #1.

Jenny #1: I'm not trying to be funny. Aging has been such an emotional subject for me. No one ever told me how many hours of the day I'd spend mourning for . . . what? Myself? I don't know what . . . some part of me . . .

   Interview with Helene Moglen.

Helene: That awareness of one's body, the sense of all kinds of things connected with one's girlhood and young womanhood. I think at that time it was very concerning for me. It's been quite astonishing to me since, though, how after my menopause was over how liberated I felt, and liberated I feel.

Y.R. *(V-O)***:** Liberated.

Helene: I feel off the hook in all kinds of very surprising ways.

Y.R. *(V-O)***:** Such as?

Helene: All of a sudden I feel like one of those wise women one read about in college in anthropology. I feel as though I've come into a special place, very free from needing to please other people in all kinds of ways.

   MCU Jenny #2.

Jenny #2 *(yelling)***:** Why do you want to interview *me?* What about *black* women? Do you have any black women lined up? White women have been interviewing one another for years.

   Jenny #1 reaches for a low stool and places it beside her chair just in time to receive a tray (in CU) with coffee urn and cups brought in by Yvonne W., whose response increases in volume as she draws closer to Jenny.

Yvonne W. *(V-O)***:** Let me worry about that. Just because I'm African-American doesn't mean I can't deal with anything but so-called "black" problems. Thanks . . . *(CU: Yvonne's hands pouring coffee.)* Tell you what:

> *CU of Yvonne W. holding a cup and saucer. Her face is on left edge of frame. Behind her, prominently centered, is a fancy CD player.*

Yvonne W. *(Sync)***:** Let's do a trade-off. OK? If you tell me about your menopausal symptoms and your life as an aging

> *Very brief Intertitle on word processor screen:*

WHITE

woman, I'll listen to you talk about the period in your life when they whistled at you.

> *MCU, Jenny #2.*

Jenny #2: Well! . . . Yeh, come to think of it. . . . Y'know, there's this incident—I know you'll be interested in—when I first came to New York and that I've never discussed with anybody. (**Jenny #1:**) In fact . . .

> *As she continues to talk, her voice fades out. She tears off her jacket, digs a fan out of her pocket, and briskly fans herself. Camera zooms in to CU, which goes out-of-focus and dissolves to*
>
> *Daytime. A New York street lined with tenements. Jenny, shot from behind, played by Alice Spivak and dressed the same as in the interview—white pants and black V-necked tee shirt—strides across the street past Carlos, a tan Puerto Rican around thirty, and Stew, his African-American friend, both of whom are seated on Carlos's front stoop. A man walking in the opposite direction turns and whistles at Jenny.*

Yvonne W. *(V-O)***:** Hey! What's going on?

> *MCU of Carlos and Stew.*

Carlos: There she goes, the new *blanquita*. I think she's a dancer or something.

Stew: She thinks her shit don't stink.

> *They both laugh and do a "low five." Jenny enters her building, which is next door to Carlos's.*

Hallway of Jenny's building. Brenda, a white woman around thirty, with short hair and dressed in men's pants and shirt, pokes her head out of the doorway of her apartment as Jenny walks by.

[Lotte Lenya's voice, singing "Mack the Knife" from *The Threepenny Opera*, floats from interior of Brenda's apartment.]

Brenda: Hey, ducks.

Jenny *(slowly turning)*: You talking to me?

Brenda: Yeh. Hi. You must be the kid who took over Jack Walton's apartment.

Jenny: Yes, I'm right over you.

Brenda: Great. I'm . . .

[Silence. They continue to talk *MOS.*]

Yvonne W. *(V-O)*: So what's her name?

Jenny *(V-O)*: I can't remember.

Yvonne W. *(V-O)*: Really! Why not?

Jenny *(V-O)*: I don't know. I seem to have blotted it out somehow.

Yvonne W. *(V-O)*: But we've got to call her something.

Jenny *(V-O)*: OK, let's call her . . .

Jump-cut to a second take.

Brenda: Great. I'm Brenda.

Jenny: I'm Jenny.

Brenda: You want to stop by for a drink later?

[Again the sound drops out though they continue to speak.]

Brenda takes a few steps toward Jenny, who steps away. This is repeated, through the use of different takes, four times during the following V-O.

Yvonne W.: What year did you say this was?

Jenny: '61, '62, somewhere around there.

Yvonne W.: But something's wrong here. It's *your* flashback . . .

Jenny: *Hot* flashback.

Yvonne W.: Whatever, and you look exactly the way you look now in 1989. You're even wearing the same clothes.

Jenny: So what? I can't be bothered trying to look the way I did then. And besides, I don't remember. Are you going to hold up this show for some expensive illusionism? Let's get on with it.

Yvonne W.: No one's going to believe this.

> *Brenda has by now entered her apartment and closed the door. Jenny walks down the hall away from the camera.*
>
> *Brenda's livingroom later that same day. Jenny sits down in MCU on a black couch against overstuffed, tapestry-covered cushions. As the scene pro-gresses other furniture can be seen: a wooden Eames chair, a beige canvas-covered butterfly chair, a kidney-shaped coffee table on top of which are a Life Magazine and large turquoise bowl, a somewhat massive buffet/cabinet against a wall papered with a black-and-white photomural of bookshelves and books that covers most of the wall. Over the couch are three photos: a large print of the famous Andre Kertesz photo of a woman in black halter dress lying with limbs akimbo on a couch, and two small framed photos of Djuna Barnes and Virginia Woolf. During her opening lines Brenda ner-vously changes chairs, finally settling in the wooden Eames opposite the couch.*

["Pirate Jenny," sung in German by Lotte Lenya, is heard in the background during most of the scene.]

Brenda: Have you met any of your neighbors yet? Lila is the great old dyke down the hall. She's a retired scenic designer and lives alone with her Yorkshire terrier. When I asked her, "Who's the sexy kid in the white ducks?" she told me you had moved into Jack's apartment. Yeh, Jack and George split up, so Jack decided to move out to Hollywood to paint portraits of the stars . . .

Jenny: Yeh, he left this mural on the w . . .

Brenda: They had a lot of nice things. Did they leave anything else?

Jenny: A 1910 toaster and a couple of lamps.

Brenda: George will probably come sniffing around, just to get some salt rubbed in his wounds. I moved here two years ago to be near work. I'm a lab technician at Bellevue. The first decent job I've had. I'm only just beginning to get on my feet. I had huge debts. I don't have the apartment quite where I want it yet, but it's coming along. Do you like Lotte Lenya? What do you want to drink?

> *She jumps up and moves toward the buffet.*

Jenny *(V-O)***:** Yes . . . uh . . .

> *CU tracking along top of buffet, revealing stack of records and miniature furniture, ending in Brenda's hands putting ice and pouring vodka into glasses.*

I asked her about the Saturday night commotions that tore through the airshaft from the next building every weekend. In fact, the whole block sometimes had a carnivalesque air which I tried not to notice.

> *MS, Jenny on couch.*

Jenny *(sync, sipping her drink)***:** Y'know, I don't own a pair of white ducks. Those were frontier pants.

["Deserie," a hit song from the late '50s, sung by The Charts, begins, and continues through the following two shots.]

> *Daytime. WS of exterior of Jenny's and Carlos's buildings, followed by left-to-right tracking past exteriors of a tenement block. People saunter past and lounge on front stoops.*

["Deserie" ends.]

> *Nightime tracking—in opposite direction—of building facades. The street is now deserted.*

[A melange of sounds can be heard: sirens, laughter, screams, voices speaking a mixture of Spanish and English. When we are halfway down the block, "Deserie" fades up, continues until:]

> *Four Hispanic male adolescents come into view, sitting on steps and mournfully monotoning:*

I'm satisfied
You're satisfied
We're satisfied
They're satisfied
She's satisfied . . .

As camera zooms slowly toward them

[their singing fades out and "Deserie" fades up. "Deserie" continues at lower volume as the following shot begins.]

> *Night. Bedroom of Jenny's apartment. Jenny, dressed in pale pink nightgown and blue-and-white striped bathrobe, is sitting up on a mattress that is on the floor. She is reading "The White Negro" and eating an apple. On the floor beside the bed are an alarm clock, lamp, phone, and small framed photo of Martha Graham performing in "Letter to the World."*

[Digna's voice, yelling in a mixture of Spanish and English from a neighboring apartment, begins to intrude on her consciousness.]

Digna *(V-O)*: Help! Police! You mother fucker. Carlos! Don't touch me, man. Don't touch me . . .

[Digna's voice fades down.]

> *Jenny returns to her reading.*

[Digna's voice becomes more strident.]

Digna *(V-O)*: Police! Please help me. Help! He's killing me! . . .

> *Jenny puts down her book and dials phone.*

Jenny: Brenda? Sorry to wake you. It's Jenny.

Brenda *(V-O)*: I'm awake. It's Carlos and Digna brawling again.

Jenny: Should we call the police?

Brenda: Yeh, I guess it *is* more horrendous than usual.

[Sounds of sirens, slamming cardoors, muffled voices.]

Brenda *(V-O)*: There's the cops. Jesus, what a circus.

CU of Jenny looking through Venetian blinds. Voices speaking in Spanish can be heard.

Digna *(V-O)*: He tried to kill me, that *cula Dios mio*, where are you taking me? Help, save me, *ayudame*!

Digna in Bellevue. A Puerto Rican woman in her late 20's, she is wearing a blue-and-white seersucker hospital robe. She sits in front of a peeling, yellowed wall and addresses the camera in Spanish, which is translated in English subtitles.

Digna: Victorian doctors used to say, "Religion and moral principles alone give strength to the female mind. When these are weakened or removed by disease, the subterranean fires become active, and the crater gives forth smoke and flame." *(She laughs)* Today religion and moral principles have been replaced by thorazine for the control of the female mind, especially the Latina female mind. Tell me, why are Puerto Rican women in this country more vulnerable to mental illness than the general population? Why do we not flourish here? Psychiatrists have different names for our condition. Most of you would be labeled manic-depressive. Me they call schizophrenic. The head honcho here asked me to name the presidents of the U.S., beginning with the current one and working backwards. Of course, he refused to speak Spanish. So I named a few presidents: Kennedy, Eisenhower, Truman, Roosevelt. Then I got stuck. And guess what: He finished the job. He went all the way back to Lincoln. He was very proud of himself. Imagine! A history lesson from the head shrink of Bellevue Hospital.

Daytime. Carlos and Stew seated on steps as before. Stew's body is bisected by the right edge of frame. Carlos addresses the camera mainly in English. When he speaks in Spanish, English subtitles appear.

Carlos: I was born in Fajardo, Puerto Rico, *un cariduro.*

Stew *(leaning into center)*: Yeh, a hick!

Carlos *(in Spanish)*: None of us choose the situation we are born into, not the time, the place, or the color we come in. *(in English)*: I happen to be what my countrymen call *trigueño*, meaning that I was born with the same permanent tan the beautiful people spend millions to maintain. You know, racially speaking, being a Puerto Rican in New York City is totally different from the way we look at ourselves in Puerto Rico. Here we're caught between white and black. Here your skin color determines who you are. Not only are there no gradations, but if you look white but have a black Mama, you're still considered black. In Puerto Rico you'd be white. Here skin color precedes other kinds of identification. In Puerto Rico there are a lot more classifications than white or black skin. Besides color, there's class, facial features, and texture of hair.

There are the *blancos*, for instance. My two brothers, my sister, and my mother are all blancos. Then there are the *indios*, or the Indians; the *morenos*, who are dark skinned with a variety of features, both Negroid and Caucasian; *negros*, who are like U.S. blacks. And there's the term *trigueño*. In Puerto Rico a black can become a *trigueño* by achieving economic status or becoming a friend. And he hasn't physically changed and isn't seeking escape from identification as a *negro*. *Hola!* Brenda, *que tal?*

> *Carlos gets up and leaves frame. Cut to Brenda's back as she strides toward Jenny's building. Carlos darts in front of her, blocking her way.*

Carlos: Do you know the cops took Digna away last night?

Brenda: So that's what happened. Where is she now?

Carlos: They took her to Bellevue.

Brenda: Why her? It sounded like you were killing her.

Carlos: Oh no no. I didn't touch her. She was real drunk and jealous. We had a fight and she went *loca*. You work at Bellevue, don't you? Maybe you can get her out.

Brenda: She's probably in the psychiatric ward. I don't know anyone there. I work in the laboratory. I don't think I can help you, but I'll think about it.

> *She goes into her building. Carlos shakes his head in a bemused way. Cut to MS of Stew still seated next door. Carlos enters frame and sits down. He again addresses the camera. His Spanish is rendered in English subtitles.*

Carlos *(in Spanish)*: Like an angel of love, yes? She is my freedom and my bondage. Forbidden to me. Also her building—forbidden to me. Right next door, but I can't live there. It might as well be Sutton Place . . . *(in English):* The intermingled white, black, and tan world of Puerto Rico is foreign to people in the U.S. Puerto Rico is inhabited by people of many colors, and these colors are not associated with different ranks. My friend Stew was always riding me:

Stew: "You fuckin' yeller-faced bastard! Yuh goddamned Negro with a white man's itch! Y'all think that bein' Porto Rican lets you off the hook? Tha's the trouble. Too damn many you black Porto Ricans got yer eyes closed. Too many goddamned Negroes all over this goddamned world feels like you does. Jus' 'cause you kin rattle off some different kinda language don' change your skin one bit. Whatta y'all think? That the only niggers in the world are in this fucked-up country? They is all over this whole damn world. Man, if they's any black people up on the moon talkin' that moon talk, they is still Negroes. Git it? Negroes!"

Intertitle on word processor screen:

Piri Thomas, 1967

Yvonne Washington's apartment as before. Jenny is still in the "hot seat."

Yvonne W. *(V-O)***:** What are you doing now, Jenny?

Jenny: "What am I doing now?" What're *you* doing now? Why are you interrupting my flashback? *You* know what I do. I drift.

Yvonne W.: Well, I mean, how do you support yourself?

CU: Jenny #2 heaves a deep sigh.

Jenny #1: I live on the remains of my parents' failed farming venture in the '30s. They sold off everything but a tiny wedge of land that—lucky for me—turned into a corner of a major intersection in southern California. So now it's leased to a Burger King. And me, a vegetarian . . . Y'know, it's funny. I had everything. Affordable housing; recognition in my profession; more than adequate income; the most unpressured teaching job you could imagine. I was so much better off on the whole than most of my artist friends. And I gave it all up. Or almost all of it. It was as though I wanted to do more than just retire; I wanted to throw it all away.

Yvonne W.: Everything but the Burger King. You say you drift . . . what do you mean? You're obviously not a bag lady.

Jenny: Well, in a manner of speaking I *am* a bag lady.

MS of desk with word processor. On the wall hang two large framed photos, each one a portrait of a young black girl. During the following monologue the camera scans the space around and under the desk. A cat licks itself. A suitcase, then a trash bag with blanket sticking out, can be seen under the table. When Jenny herself finally comes into view again, her speech is way out of sync.

(V-O): About a year ago I gave up the idea of a permanent address and decided to live a little dangerously. You have to sniff the wind more carefully, know when you've used up your welcome, especially when you're staying with family members. Not everybody is intrigued with my silences and obscure pieces of information. Do *you* want to know that in the lifespan of the average white American there are twenty-three different sexual partners?

Yvonne W.: No kidding!

Jenny *(on camera, but out-of-sync)*: Yeh. How many have you had? I've had thirty-two. Ha! I've had more colds than that. And who wants to know that Natalie Herzen spent the greater part of the year of revolution 1848 in a dangerous paroxysm of erotic excitement? *(sync)*: And *this* ought to interest you: After menopause women don't have REM sleep anymore. What d'you think of that?

Yvonne W.: REM. You mean "rapid eye movement"?

B&W footage of Jenny "fleeing" as she looks behind her with a terrified expression on her face. Camera tracks left to right, following her movement. In back of her is Brenda's living room. Jenny and Yvonne are now both speaking in V-O.

Jenny: Yeh, what happens in the first couple of hours after going to bed when you dream and have the most restful and deepest sleep. We don't get that kind of repose anymore. And we no longer dream. No wonder we're all so cranky.

Yvonne W.: I don't believe it.

Jenny: What?

Yvonne W.: That older people don't dream. *I* still dream.

B&W footage: Two young black men are perusing the front page of the New York Times *"Help Wanted" section, which is pinned to the wall. As the camera tilts down and dollies back, we see first a sign:*

LOST:

MEMORY
MUSCLE
FRIENDS
HUSBANDS
LOVERS
DREAMING

then two young black women in bed. They are sleeping, entwined in each others' arms.

Why, just last night I had the weirdest dream.

Jenny: I've always known you're an exceptional woman. I'll bet men dream till the day they die. *I* sure as hell don't. And while I'm on the subject of loss, I could talk about lots more of that, like memory . . . but where were we?

The woman on the left suddenly sits up, a startled look on her face.

Reverse angle, her point of view reveals Jenny, standing as though on the foot of the bed, returning the younger woman's gaze.

Yvonne W.: Menopause,

Another reverse to the younger woman, still looking intently up at Jenny.

menopause.

Jenny: Ah yes: A week after Brenda had spoken to Carlos on the street . . .

Digna as before, in "Bellevue," in front of the peeling wall. She addresses the camera in English.

Digna: Yeh. Why me and not Carlos? Why me beat up and why me in here? Victorian doctors used to make fine distinctions of complexion, spinal curve, and personality between those women who were merely assaulted and those who were actually murdered. Just like they distinguished between criminals and normal people. Would you ever dream that criminals and prostitutes have darker hair than you? How about my eyebrows? Does the way I tweeze my eyebrows make men unable to resist hitting me? And are my rages at Carlos more irrational than his violence toward me? I was no more out of control that night than he was. I just *acted* like a crazy woman. *(She pauses.)* "Peter Piker picked a pep of pickled peckers, how many pecks . . ." *(She breaks up, laughing.)* The latest development in proving women are biologically more prone to nuttiness than men is this test: They have you say this tongue-twister when you have your period and also when you don't have your period:
> "Peter Pecker picked a pack of pickled . . ."
Ha, ha, ha . . . I'm not menstruating and I still can't do it!

Nighttime. Jenny's bedroom. She is sleeping. A woman's screams propel her upright. She freezes. In the following sequence, all of the shots of Jenny's bedroom are in color while those of Brenda's bedroom are in B&W.

Nighttime. Brenda's bedroom. Brenda rolls over, turns on her bedside lamp and recoils in horror as she sees Carlos standing stark naked beside the bed.

Brenda: *Jesus K. Christ!* What are *you* doing here?!

MS, Carlos. He moves toward her.

(V-O): Oh no,

Brenda scrambles to the foot of the bed and throws him a bathrobe that is lying there.

(sync): no you don't. Back off. Hold it right there. Here, put this on.

Reverse angle: Carlos receiving the tossed bathrobe.

Carlos: You're so beautiful.

MS, Brenda with Carlos's shoulder in the foreground.

Brenda: Oh sure. And you're so naked. Who the fuck asked you, anyway?!

[She continues speaking *MOS*. Screams are heard, obviously not emanating from the on-screen Brenda. They continue into next shot.]

Jenny's bedroom. CU of her bare feet pacing back and forth beside her bed. Camera follows her as she sits on bed and dials phone.

Brenda's bedroom. MCU of Brenda as before.

Brenda: Oh sure. And you're so naked. Who the fuck asked you anyway?!

She goes to closet and takes a robe off of hook, glaring at Carlos as she puts it on. We see his back and also his reflection in a full-length mirror.

Look, I'm going to make some coffee and we're going to talk this thing through. Just who do you think you are? You've got absolutely no right barging in here like this.

Jenny *(V-O)***:** Operator, could you get the police?

Jenny's bedroom. MCU of Jenny on the phone.

(sync): My neighbor's in trouble. I think someone's broken in downstairs . . .

[Energetic violins from the educational film lead into:]

A succession of five white middle-aged male doctors from the medical film, all of whom address the camera. Each is identified by name in a subtitle. The first shot begins with a CU of an impressionist-like painting of a field of flowers. Camera zooms back to reveal doctor in his white coat behind a desk.

Charles F. Flowers, Jr.: It's not an easy matter to treat the menopausal patient, because she's undergoing certain physical changes.

> *Same doctor, different scene.*

Women who are in their middle years and are premenopausal or menopausal, have certain problems.

Charles W. Lloyd: And in the woman in the climacteric the relationship between endocrine changes and emotional stress is often quite obvious.

Judd Marmor: The way she faces up to these problems has an important bearing on what her menopause will be like.

Robert N. Rutherford: The man's understanding and sympathy are particularly crucial at this time in a woman's life.

> *MS, interview with Minnette Lehmann, a white woman in her late 50's. She is seated at her kitchen table.*

Minnette: There's an assumption, there's a real assumption that what you're going to get is real.

Yvonne Rainer *(V-O)*: What I get on here may not be the real, but your experience will be real.

Minnette: That's true.

Y.R. *(V-O)*: Yeh, there is something real I'm after. For instance, how old are you?

Minnette: Oh, that's terribly real . . . Oh . . . forty-nine.

Y.R. *(V-O)*: Alright . . . uh, you're lying!

Minnette *(laughing)*: Well that's possible, isn't it?

Y.R. *(V-O)*: OK, this is not going to be a real interview.

Minnette: But I'm menopaused, I am definitely menopaused. Not even menopausal. I'm menopaused.

> *Yvonne W.'s apartment. CU of Jenny, who is smoking a cigarette.*

Jenny: The hot flashes began in my early 50's. They were really bad. Every ten minutes I would be drenched in sweat and then I'd be horribly cold. It was worse at night.

Yvonne W. *(V-O)*: Did you try Vitamin E?

Jenny *(V-O)*: Aah, Vitamin E didn't help a bit. I went to the doctor and he wanted to do a hysterectomy. He said he would take out everything but my playground.

Yvonne W.: Playground! What a hip gynecologist!

Jenny: Oh sure. *I* was horrified. Anyway, it was an offer I could and did refuse.

Intertitles on word processor:

> No one knows exactly what causes
> hot flashes. One reason is that
> scientists have been unable to
> detect hot flashes in animals. No
> middle-aged monkey is reveal-
> ing her secrets.
>
> The intervals lengthen on my
> menstrual calendar: "28 days, 27
> days, 30 days" is now giving way
> to "54, 76, 92, . . ." The
> dependability of seasons is
> replaced by . . .

Footage from medical film: A middle-aged woman in sheath dress and beehive hairdo sits at desk in an office. She speaks—MOS—to the camera.

Jenny *(V-O)*: About a year later my periods stopped. The hot flashes continued, but now I had pains in my vagina and pulling sensations there. The doctor said I had atrophic vaginitis and wanted to prescribe Estrogen Replacement Therapy. I didn't like his attitude. He was barely civil,

Woman in office gets up and moves to the left. Camera tracks with her as she goes to a coffee machine and pours a cup of coffee, all the while addressing the camera MOS. The following intertitle is superimposed over her image during this maneuver:

> The most remarkable thing was
> the silence that emanated from
> friends and family regarding the

The most re[...] thing was the silence [...] emanated from friends an[...] family regarding the details of my single middleage. When I was younger, my sex life had been the object of all kinds of questioning, from prurient curiosity to solicitous concern. Now that I did not appear to be looking for a man, the state of my desires seemed of no interest to anyone.

    details of my single middleage.
    When I was younger, my sex life
    had been the object of all kinds
    of questioning, from prurient
    curiosity to solicitous concern.
    Now that I did not appear to be
    looking for a man, the state of my
    desires seemed of no interest to
    anyone.

Intertitle fades out. Woman continues addressing the camera MOS.

Jenny *(V-O)*: . . . very offhanded and unsympathetic. I went to another doctor,

Dissolve to doctor in garden.

Dr. Judd Marmor *(sync)*: Under these emotional stresses she is likely to show emotional changes.

Jenny *(V-O)*: who got annoyed at my questions.

Marmor *(sync)*: She tends to withdraw from her husband . . .

Jenny *(V-O)*: By that time I was taking a very small dose of estrogen . . .

Marmor *(sync)*: . . . irritability . . .

Jenny *(V-O)*: . . . and synthetic progesterone.

Marmor *(sync)*: . . . fretfulness . . .

Jenny *(V-O)*: But the pains continued.

Dr. Marmor *(out-of-sync)*: . . . crying spells . . .

Jenny *(V-O)*: I couldn't have sex . . .

Marmor *(out-of-sync)*: . . . insomnia . . .

Jenny *(V-O)*: . . . and I was conscious of that area all the time.

    Interview with Minnette in her kitchen.

Marmor *(V-O)*: . . . and so forth.

Minnette: . . . and it would be anger, or I'd have to say, "Now you're getting just a little excited, more than usual. What is this?" And it was physiologic.

Y.R. *(V-O)*: That's probably what's happening to me. I was always kind of irritable. Now I'm even more irritable.

Minnette: I've always been irritable too. I'm now much less irritable.

Y.R.: Now that you're out of it.

Minnette: I mean, but less irritable than ever. And that is a delight. Not that I can't *get* irritable, but I was on edge a lot.

    Interview with Jenny in Yvonne W.'s apartment. She is seen over Yvonne W.'s shoulder in the foreground.

Jenny: I'm off hormones now. I got scared off because they couldn't tell me about the future. One doctor told me, "You're too emotional. If you weren't so emotional, you'd be better off."

    MCU. Interview with Catherine English Robinson in her living room. She is an African-American in her late 50's.

Catherine: Male gynecologists don't give you too much information. They would refer you to a book, but they're not able to sit and talk to you. And you have a lot of questions. You don't know what to expect; you hear a lot of stories. So you want someone to kind of talk to you, tell you what to look forward to and what is a symptom of menopause and what is not. And I guess maybe they can't give you the information because they don't know. They know medical theory. But none of them have been through it or have it to look forward to. So I feel there's a gap there.

MCU, interview with Jenny in Yvonne W.'s apartment.

[Her voice is slowed down and deep.]

Jenny: Yvonne, do you realize what you've unleashed? I hate going on about my goddamned body

Jump cut to panning movement from her body to the word processor on the table beside her chair. The titles on the screen scroll simultaneously with Jenny's V-O.

like this. The good feminist in me wags a finger at my belly-aching: "Jenny, all you're doing is confirming what men already think, that our bodies are, by definition, defective and need fixing."

Intertitles on word processor:

```
All  of  a  sudden  she  didn't  know  how
to  dress.  The  body  had  filled  out  in
this  funny  way.  Her  weight  was  the
same  but  her  shape  had  changed.
Exercise  didn't  make  the  same  dents
anymore.  And  when  she  wore  lipstick
she  looked  like  a  transvestite.  Then
the  veins  and  the  swollen  ankles . . . and
the  breast  biopsies.  And  she  couldn't
even  stand  in  anything  but  flat  heels
anymore,  let  alone  walk.  Raging
hormones?  What  about  those  raging
floods  when  your  periods  are  phasing
out?  You  bloody  up  everything.
```

Jenny *(in normal V-O)*: So the medics try to "fix" us with hysterectomies and Hormone Replacement Therapy so we'll stay feminine forever.

Hallway of Jenny's building. Jenny comes down stairs at far end and walks toward camera and Brenda's door. She is wearing her bathrobe.

[A woman's screams are heard.]

Intertitles on word processor:

By age 50, 31% of U.S. women will have had a hysterec-tomy.

Hysterectomy is the most frequently performed opera-tion in the U.S., double the rate of frequency in the U.K.

Hysterectomies are performed most frequently in the south-east U.S. and least often in the northeast, and garner $800 million a year in gynecologi-cal fees.

There is a popular saying among gynecologists that there is no ovary so healthy that it is not better removed, and no testes so diseased that they should not be left intact.

[Screams are heard while the last intertitle is still up.]

Hallway as before, Jenny again walks down stairs and this time reaches Brenda's door, where she pauses, then retreats and pauses at another door halfway down the hall.

Jenny *(V-O)*: Has anyone ever suggested putting men on lifelong doses of testosterone in order to make them stay "masculine"? Why is the aging process perceived as so much more threatening to *women's* sexuality than to men's,

MCU of Jenny inclining her ear to door.

Man's voice: What we don't know won't hurt us.

Footage from medical film: A man enters Dr. Rutherford's office, shakes hands with him across desk. Both sit down.

Jenny *(V-O)*: . . . when in actuality it's the men who have more difficulties in bed later in life.

Rutherford *(V-O)*: We find out that his wife's emotional problems may be related to this particularly trying period.

MS of Dr. Rutherford over shoulder of husband. He speaks MOS.

Jenny *(V-O)*: Yet they retain for themselves the myth and masquerade of virile masculinity long after women are seen as having shut down.

CU of husband.

[Medical film: energetic orchestral strings accompany the following V-O.]

Dr. Marmor *(V-O)*: The glow from estrogen may no longer be apparent. Moreover, her libido

MCU Minnette Lehmann in her kitchen as before. She speaks MOS.

may begin to decline at this time.

Minnette *(sync)*: Once sexuality isn't so physical, it doesn't mean it isn't. It's weird, I know, but I like to be in a room full of testosterone, no doubt about it.

Y.R. *(V-O)*: You know, women produce testosterone.

Minnette: I know, the whole crowd does. And I like that. I can feel it. And I can feel when I'm in situations that are lalibidiness, or without sexuality, and they're just as repressive as they ever were.

Intertitles on word processor:

> What happens to the libido? Her be-
> loved GYN answered some questions:
> "Yes, testosterone, the male sex
> hormone, is produced by women, and—
> yes—testosterone production in-
> creases somewhat after menopause.
> However, since the libido is in the
> head as much as in the hormones, the
> exact role testosterone plays in
> female sexuality is unclear."
>
> . . . . But, if not testosterone,
> something besides her head was mak-
> ing her think about sex all the
> time.

Yvonne W.'s apartment. MCU of Jenny.

Jenny: Y'know, I hate to admit it, but I just can't get used to our screwed up

Found color footage from a 1950s Hollywood movie: a group of adolescents is partying. A girl in very tight pants and top is "boogying" by herself.

morality that denies middle-aged women the right to be beautiful, loving, and idealized by men.

Yvonne W. *(V-O):* Idealized! You mean, like young women? That's what got us into this mess in the first place!

Hallway outside of Brenda's apartment. Jenny stands outside of Brenda's door as the screaming continues.

Brenda *(V-O):* Help! Police! He-e-lp!

Nighttime. Very wide B&W overhead shot of Brenda's livingroom, now revealed as a set in a very large space. Crew members stand around, while production assistants work in the hall area. Brenda leans against the wall next to the buffet. Stew is seated on sofa next to "White Man X," who speaks what Stew, "the ventriloquist," mouths. In the course of the speech, the camera cranes in to CU of Stew. The two men gradually switch roles, so that by the end, it is Stew who is speaking, and "X" is silent. (For the remainder of the film, all of the scenes in Brenda's apartment are in B&W.)

"White Man X": Yes, I became a rapist. To refine my technique and modus operandi, I started out by practicing on black girls in the ghetto—in the black ghetto where dark and vicious deeds appear not as aberrations or deviations from the norm—and when I considered myself smooth enough I crossed the tracks and sought out white prey.

"X" and Stew: Rape was an insurrectionary act. It delighted me that I was defying and trampling upon the white man's law, upon his system of values,

Stew: and that I was defiling his women, and this point, I believe, was the most satisfying to me because I was very resentful over the historical fact of how the white man has used the black woman. I felt I was getting revenge. And I wanted to send waves of consternation *(CU of Stew)* through the white race. After I returned to prison I took a long look at myself and, for the first time in my life, admitted . . .

[His words fade down behind those of Yvonne W.]

Yvonne W. *(V-O):* Jenny, why are you telling me all this? I don't need to hear how Eldridge Cleaver raped to save the black race! He made a much bigger contribution than inflaming white paranoia.

MS of Brenda leaning against the wall, her arms folded across her chest.

Brenda: The problem with men is their dignity is located in their balls.

MCU of Carlos seated on the couch.

Carlos: [guffaws].

MS of Brenda. She moves toward the camera, turns away, then turns back, passing through "noirish" shadows along the way.

Brenda: You think I'm dying for it, don't you? Next you'll be telling me I want to be raped. But you don't know a damn thing about me. Can you even conceive that I might have *liked* you if . . .

CU of Brenda's back as she sits down in the foreground in the Eames chair. It faces the couch on which Carlos is seated in MCU. He stares intently at her, not speaking, as camera zooms slowly in to extreme CU of his face during the following V-O.

Carlos *(V-O)***:** She has an avid curiosity about my sexual endowments. She enjoys imagining the fucking that goes on among blacks and Latinos on this block. She thinks we are "looser" and less inhibited because we come from the steaming tropics. What's weird is *she's* the one who kept her shades up and walked around with no clothes on.

Carlos *(sync)***:** When you look at me you see a dark continent, something unknown, exciting, frightening, exotic, different.

MS of Brenda rocking back and forth in a child's rocking chair.

Brenda: Hey, I'm supposed to be the dark continent. Freud called women a dark continent. And when you look at me the word lesbian might never have been invented. Now you listen, you doctor

Series of right-to-left swish-pans that ends in MCU of "White Man X" seated on the couch.

Brenda *(V-O)***:** lawyer Indian chief, you engineer ayatollah shudder in the loins, you landlord Lenny Bruce chairman of the board, you . . .

[Her voice fades down.]

Yvonne W. *(V-O)***:** So who is this dude? This is all very confusing.

Jenny *(V-O)***:** I'm just trying to point out that rapists come in all colors.

Yvonne W. *(V-O)***:** *Thank you, ma'am. Thank you!*

[Brenda's voice fades up.]

Brenda *(V-O)***:** . . . *you engineer ayatollah shudder in the loins, you landlord Lenny Bruce chairman of the board, you party chairman, chief justice, raving queen, you . . . you gang of chancellors,*

> *CU of Brenda in the rocking chair, rocking furiously.*

(sync): you head of sanitation.

> *Reverse-angle two-shot of Brenda and "White Man X." He is seated on the right, holding a miniature coffee cup and saucer. At the beginning of the scene she pours coffee from an urn. A large projection of an aerial view of mid-Manhattan fills half the background. In the dimly lit recesses beyond the set, people move about performing tasks of some kind.*

Brenda: As man conquers the world so too he conquers the female. You're no different from Genghis Khan, one of the first guys to make a direct connection between manhood, achievement, conquest, and rape.

> *Extreme CU of Brenda in profile.*

Brenda: Man equals human, hero, the active principle of culture, the establisher of distinction, the social being, the mythical subject.

> *Extreme CU of "X" in profile.*

Brenda *(V-O)***:** Woman equals immutable matter, procreative earth, landscape, monster, Sphinx, Medusa, Sleeping Beauty, inert obstacle to his transformative striving.

> *Brief, sequential shots of Faith, Shirley, Jenny, Vivian Bonnano (a Hispanic woman in her mid-40's), Claudia, another woman from the medical film, Audrey Goodfriend (a white woman in her late 60's), and Gloria Sparrow (a white woman in her mid-50's). All of the women speak MOS.*

Brenda *(V-O)***:** As women we are trained to be rape victims. At an early age we hear the whispers: *girls get raped.* Not boys. Every three minutes a woman is beaten. Every five minutes a woman is raped. Every ten minutes a little girl is molested. Half of all rape victims are total strangers to their attackers.

> *MS, Gloria Sparrow sitting in a backyard.*

Another 30 percent are slightly acquainted. The statistics are silent on rape by husbands.

Woman's voice: I can't believe that, Gloria!

Gloria *(sync)*: Why? What do you mean?

Woman's voice: You were your father's darling!

Intertitle on word processor, simultaneous with its utterance in V-O by Brenda:

> **One out of every four
> women in the U.S. is
> introduced to sex
> through rape.**

Brenda *(V-O)*: Most rapists don't have as political a motive for their acts as you have. Most rapists are of the same race as their victims.

Intertitle:

> **95% of rapes are
> black-on-black or
> white-on-white.**

MCU, overhead. Stew and Brenda lie on the floor with their heads toward the camera. Brenda rests on one elbow.

Brenda: Do you think it matters to the victim what the motive is? Sadism or politics? And anyway, I don't think you're as special as you make out. Your politics smacks of sadism like all the rest.

[Screams are heard.]

Color. Corridor as before. A man and woman in bathrobes now stand with Jenny outside of Brenda's door.

B&W MCU of Carlos seated on couch in Brenda's livingroom.

Carlos: The black man among his own in the twentieth century does not know at what moment his inferiority comes into being through the other. In talking about this problem with black friends, together we protested, we asserted the equality of all men in the world. And then the occasion arose when I had to look into the white man's eyes. An unfamiliar weight burdened me.

Daytime panorama. (This and the following shots in the park are in color.) On the far side of a pond a white man in Bermuda shorts stands watching his three dogs cavort at the water's edge.

Carlos *(V-O)***:** The real world challenged my claims. In the white world the man of color encounters difficulties in the development of his bodily schema. Consciousness of the body is solely a negating activity. It is a third-person consciousness . . .

MLS, Carlos sitting and smoking on a park bench. A white man in a suit and carrying a briefcase walks by. Carlos continues to speak in V-O.

provided for me by the other, the white man, who had woven me out of a thousand details, anecdotes, stories.

LS, edge of pond. A pregnant white woman in a white summer dress is throwing breadcrumbs to off-screen ducks while a five-year-old girl beside her blows bubbles with a bottle and wire loop. The businessman from the previous shot walks down the path behind them and out of the frame. Carlos's V-O continues. At the beginning of the shot the woman points to something off-screen.

"Look, a Negro!" It was an external stimulus that flicked over me as I passed by. I made a tight smile.

Cut to another white man, walking his dog down a path. Camera follows them as they pass the mother and child by the lake, stays on mother and child as man and dog leave the frame.

"Look, a Negro!" It was true. It amused me. "Look, a Negro!" The circle was drawing a bit tighter. I made no secret of my amusement . . .

CU of child blowing bubbles.

"Mama, see the Negro. I'm frightened."

MLS, Carlos on bench.

Carlos *(sync)***:** Frightened! Frightened! Now they were beginning to be afraid of me. I made up my mind to laugh myself to tears, but laughter had become impossible. I could no longer laugh, because I already knew that there were legends, stories, history.

B&W MCU of Carlos on Brenda's sofa. Camera zooms in to CU during following V-O.

Carlos *(V-O)*: I moved toward the other . . . and the evanescent other, hostile but not opaque, transparent, not there, disappeared.

Black (no) image.

Nausea . . .

Carlos on park bench as before.

(sync): I was responsible at the same time for my body, for my race, for my ancestors. I subjected myself to an objective examination, I discovered my blackness, my ethnic characteristics; and I was battered down by tom-toms,

A 1940s cartoon of Florida alligator menacing a black infant.

(V-O): slave-ships, cannibalism, intellectual deficiency, fetishism, racial defects, and above all else, above all: "Sho' good eatin'." On that day,

MCU, Carlos on park bench, smoking.

(V-O): completely dislocated, unable to be abroad with the other, the white man, who unmercifully imprisoned me, I took myself far off from my own presence, far indeed, and made myself an object. But I did not want this revision, this . . . this thematization. All I wanted was to be a man among other men. I wanted to come lithe and young into a world that was ours and to help to build it together.

Intertitle on word processor (simultaneous with its uttered V-O):

> **I wanted to come**
> **lithe and young into a**
> **world that was ours**
> **and to help to build it**
> **together.**
> Frantz Fanon, 1940

Daytime, street, CU of Digna. She is wearing a summer dress and addresses the camera in English. The neighborhood ambience is extremely noisy.

Digna: Many people back home tell you how wonderful life is here. There's television and the movies; they give another impression. Anyway, I never been glamorous or anything like that, and when Carlos proposed, I couldn't believe it. I saw a chance to get away, to see what was going on in other places, to live in New York, another kind of life. At home it was always so easy; with the sound of the first rooster crowing, I would open my eyes and start the day. I see the morning mist settling like puffs of

Digna (Gabriella Farrar) leans against convertible. Courtesy Yvonne Rainer.

smoke over the range of mountains that surrounds the entire countryside. Sharp mountainous peaks covered with many shades of green foliage that change constantly from light to dark, intense or soft tones, depending on the time of day and the direction of the rays of the brilliant tropical sun.

As camera begins to zoom back, we see that she is leaning against a blue 1960s convertible.

I take the path following the road that leads to my village. I inhale the sweet and spicy fragrance of the flower gardens that sprinkle the countryside. The country folk in every mountain village on the island of Puerto Rico pride themselves on their flower gardens.

[A new voice is heard: It is Digna's off-screen voice, which slowly begins to override her on-screen voice. The street sounds—children voices, traffic, horns—that had previously all but drowned her out, slowly recede, replaced by the "idyllic" quiet of her new voice.]

Oh, Papi's flower garden! There were bright yellows, scarlet and crimson hues, brilliant blues, wild purples; every color imaginable flourished on the plants and shrubbery that blossomed in my father's flower garden. I feel the soft, cool, gentle morning breeze as I stand by the road and dig my bare feet into the dark moist earth.

Intertitle on word processor:

MS, B&W, Brenda on her couch. She is silent for about ten seconds.

Brenda: *Damn!* Why'd you have to say I'm beautiful? I don't need that kind of stuff from the likes of you.

The face of Yvonne Rainer enters the frame, in CU, her mouth smeared with lipstick as at beginning of film. She addresses the camera and then leaves frame.

Y.R.: She is the kind of woman who was never desired by men.

Stew: Hasn't anyone ever told you that before?

Brenda: No *man* has told me that.

Reverse angle, MCU of Stew in wing chair. Behind him is the studio space cluttered with lights and equipment.

Stew: They should have.

Brenda *(V-O)*: It just doesn't matter to me what men think of my looks.

Stew: Then why'd you bring it up?

MS Brenda.

Brenda: *Women* find me beautiful. That's what matters to me. But why am I even talking to you about this? *(She leans forward and speaks in an intense whisper.)* Your desire has always been the death of us.

Stew *(V-O)*: Eldridge Cleaver said:

Reverse angle, MCU Stew.

(sync): "If a lesbian is anything she is a frigid woman, a frozen cunt, with a warp and a crack in the sky-high wall of her ice. She is allured and tortured by the secret intuitive knowledge that the walking phallus, symbol of the Supermasculine Menial, can blaze through the wall of her ice, plumb her psychic depths, melt the iceberg in her brain, detonate the bomb of her orgasm, and bring her sweet release. (In case you're wondering, that phallus is me.)"

MS, Brenda, laughing hysterically.

Reverse, Stew, also laughing.

Brenda *(V-O)*: You're putting me on.

Stew: Maybe, maybe not.

Yvonne W. *(V-O)*: Jenny, you are not going to let him get away with that, are you?

MCU of Brenda.

Brenda: Venus, ever since they knocked
                    your block off
                    your face is so vacant
                    waiting to be moved in on
                    by men's imaginations.
                    How could anybody love you?
                    having the ugliest mug in the world,

Corridor as before (color). Jenny stands with outstretched arms as though holding up the walls of the narrow passage. There are now five (white) people in bathrobes behind her.

                    the one that's missing.

Almost immediately camera tracks left-to-right into apartment (image changes from color to B&W), rhyming its movement with Carlos's as—left-to-right—he backs Brenda "up against the wall," pushing her swiftly and somewhat roughly across the thirty-foot width of the space. This happens repeatedly, sometimes in MCU, sometimes in CU, alternating slow motion and normal speed.

Brenda *(V-O)*: Is it time to invoke the mothers who held us—or refused to hold us? Or is it time to name the common enemy? Our blackness, femaleness, shit, and blood dictate the moves of white men.

(sync): By the age of four the white man knows what the score is.

(V-O): By then the universe is radically split along lines of goodness and badness. In both, what is good is pure, clean, and white and what is bad is

(sync): impure, dirty, smelly, and black.

(V-O): What is good in the world comes from the mind and what is bad comes from the body. In the culture of the West, the necessity for the white male infant to repudiate both his magical preoccupation with shit and his fantasized oneness with the mother create

(sync): the duel aversion to blacks and women.

(V-O): In contrast with the light color of the body of the Caucasian, the dark color of feces reinforces the connotation of blackness with badness. And since this dark brown color is derived from blood pigments, since in fact blood is the only internal bodily substance which is dark,

(sync): you the black, and I, the female,

(V-O): share the stigma imbedded in ideas of shit and blood, with their

> *MS. Jenny in Yvonne W.'s apartment.*

Jenny *(speaking with Brenda's voice)***:** association of blackness, evil, danger,

> *Carlos slams Brenda into the wall in slow-motion with a resounding crash. Her lip movements mime the final words.*

(V-O): and worthlessness.

> *MS. Jenny in Yvonne's apartment.*

Yvonne W. *(V-O)***:** What an obnoxious idea!

Jenny: What's obnoxious?

> *Yvonne enters frame and sits down on couch in the foreground, her back to the camera.*

Yvonne W. *(sync)***:** How shit gets connected up with blackness-as-badness. What happens between black people and *their* shit?

Jenny: But she's clearly talking about the racist conditioning of *white* people in the West.

Yvonne W.: I didn't hear anything about *people* in there. It was white *men* she was dishing the shit to. And even so, your shit theory doesn't tell us when and how this particular alienation took hold.

> *She lies down, disappearing into the couch, only her Converse-clad feet visible frame-right. Immediately the camera begins to track left, arcing around the end of the couch to bring Yvonne's head into view toward the end of the following monologue.*

Did you know that racism didn't exist before Columbus stumbled upon North America?

Before Europeans began to think about expanding their empire they didn't have notions of racial—or genetic—superiority. Religious superiority, maybe, like what propelled the Crusades, but not genetic. They had fantasies of wealthy black kingdoms somewhere in the East Indies, and, in their minds, these kingdoms were culturally superior to their own. It wasn't until they needed cheap labor to extract wealth from their colonies that they had to justify economic exploitation in terms of racial superiority. Before the era of European empire there was always a fluid assimilation between conqueror and conquered. Alexander the Great and Genghis Khan may have been sexists, but they weren't racists. It's capitalism, pure and simple, that's given us racism. So much for shit.

> *She pauses, then suddenly sits up, framed in CU.*

But what's *your* investment in this psychoanalytic stuff? I won't go so far as to say it's total rubbish, but I do think it occupies much too big a place in your story.

> *MCU, Jenny.*

Jenny: I guess I'm attracted to it because it's so elemental. Alimentary. *(laughs)* It holds out the promise of an ultimate explanation for racism, its earliest formation in the human psyche. I dunno, it gives me a much greater feeling of power and understanding than your historical, economic explanations.

> *Camera tilts down and tracks toward couch, revealing along the way an inert form lying on the floor under crumpled newspapers, finally settling in MCU on Yvonne by the time she's saying "You've put the egg . . ."*

Yvonne W. *(V-O)*: But the psyche itself is the product of external forces, like history and economics. Economics is the greatest single factor that *produces* the psyche, like homelessness pushes people over the edge into madness. Economic relations *reproduce* the family interactions that in turn incubate the psyche. *(sync)*: You've put the egg before the chicken. And another thing: You've let Brenda off the hook.

Jenny: What d'you mean?

Yvonne W.: You've let her make this dubious alliance with Carlos against white men through the common stigma of their dark bodily secretions, and she does this without once implicating *herself* in the racist system. White women always manage to use their own victim status as a way of pleading innocent to the charge of racism. But *she's* enjoying life in that exclusive white building right along with you. So please, get your ass back in that apartment. You have more work to do!

> *MCU, Jenny.*

Jenny: No-o-o! I can't, I just can't. I'll only fall deeper into the soup.

Yvonne W. *(V-O)*: Hey, that's a new note: self-pity.

Jenny: Don't expect me to get it right. Just telling you this story in its barest form took all of my gumption. I'm scared of you now in ways I never was before.

MCU Yvonne.

Yvonne W.: I don't expect you to "get it right." I guess I'd just like you to put yourself in my shoes so I don't have to explain everything. *I'd* like to forget about racism just as much as you. The difference is, you can . . . and I can't.

Series of intertitles on word processor screen begins:

WHO SPEAKS?

QUOTIDIAN
FRAGMENTS:
RACE

[Music begins: Amelia's aria, Scene 1, Act 1, from Verdi's *Simon Boccanegra*. It is a very scratchy recording.]

1

During my 1940's childhood my mother hired a series of black cleaning women who came once a week to clean the house. Mary Ellen would carefully cut the crusts from the sandwiches that my mother prepared for her lunch and leave them on the plate. Mama, who never allowed us to leave food on our plates, thought Mary Ellen was "putting on airs." Submerged in feelings of social inferiority, my mother knew the state of things all too well. If her own position of white, lower-middleclass housewife was implacably fixed, what right had the black cleaning-woman to mime the upper crust?

2

One day during my first year in high school I was taking the bus home from school. A black woman who had sat down beside me watched as I leafed through the pages of a *National Geographic*. As I paused at a color photograph of an African man dressed in traditional warrior garb, the woman remarked, "What a handsome man." Her simple utterance was a revelation to me. This was my first encounter with self-hood from a black perspective, with a black person's sense of being-in-the-world. Here was no strange, alien creature. Here was a handsome man.

3

In my early 30's I was in an intensive care unit after passing the critical stage of a serious illness. Theresa, the Puerto Rican day nurse, was trying to haul me out of bed and into a chair for the first time. I was so weak my legs wouldn't support me. As she struggled, I felt an inexplicable contempt for her. Some days later, after I had been transferred to a ward, my neighbor in the adjacent bed spoke admiringly of Theresa. When she too had been in intensive care, Theresa had cared for her "like an angel."

4

Roy Wilkins said somewhere that the most he could ever hope to be was a permanent recovering sexist. Is "permanent recovering racists" the most *we* can ever be?

5

A woman who is just entering menopause meets a man at a conference at the University of El Paso. They hit it off. Later, after hearing his lascivious remarks about a much younger woman, she is shocked at having misinterpreted what she had thought was mutual sexual attraction. Toward evening, from the hilltop heights of the university, a Mexican-American student points out to her the sprawling shanties of Juarez across the Rio Grande. In the gathering dusk she realizes she is on two different sides of two frontiers: Economically, she is on the advantaged side overlooking a third-world country. And sexually, having passed the frontier of attractiveness to men, she is now on the *other side* of privilege.

Night. Robert's bedroom (color). Robert sits on the edge of the bed, his bare back to the camera. He is wearing only his pants and, as the scene begins, we hear the thud of his shoes hitting the floor.

Yvonne W. *(V-O)*: Who the hell is that?

Camera keeps him in frame as he bends over Jenny, who is under the covers. They embrace passionately.

Jenny *(V-O)*: That's me, silly. Don't you recognize me?

Yvonne W.: Oh for Chrissake, not you—*him!*

Jenny: Oh! That's Robert, the assistant D.A. who handled the case.

Yvonne W.: What case?

Jenny: Brenda pressed charges against Carlos for attempted rape.

Hallway outside of Brenda's apartment. Jenny pounds on Brenda's door.

Jenny [in her best *basso profundo*]: OK. Open up in there. This is the cops!

The door opens and Jenny pulls a terrified Brenda out of the apartment.

Daytime. Robert's office (color). Robert and Brenda sit on either side of his well-appointed desk. He is in his early 30's, tall and imposing though not conventionally handsome, impeccably suited, very self-assured. At the beginning of the scene he lights a cigarette with an elegant lighter. He is very much in command, but not overtly patronizing. Brenda too is self-possessed, not at all nervous, even when describing her frightening experience. In the establishing shot of the scene the camera dollies from wide to MCU of Robert.

Robert *(after a long, leisurely exhalation)*: And then what happened?

MS of Brenda over Robert's right shoulder. As she speaks, camera dollies right-to-left behind him, ending with Brenda seen over his left shoulder. An American flag can be glimpsed in the background, in the space between them.

Brenda: Something woke me up. I didn't know what, I was half asleep and reached over and turned on the light. And there you were, standing beside the bed, bare-assed naked. I started to scream. Maybe I yelled "Get out of here." I'm not sure. And you said—and I'm not sure of the sequence—"You're very beautiful. I want to talk to you. Don't be afraid." It all went very fast. I kept yelling. My bed is wedged in a corner of the room, so I couldn't get out. You were blocking my way. Then you hit me very hard on my left breast. It must have been then that Jenny rang the bell. You immediately ran into the kitchen and must have crawled back across the airshaft into your apartment. All I could think of was getting out of there.

[The phone rings.]

MCU Robert. He sits dumbfounded, staring at her for a few moments before answering the phone.

Robert: Excuse me. Yes? . . . Yes . . . Great. That's all we need to know. Let's throw the book at him. He'll never do his filthy act in this town again. *(He hangs up.)* Now, you've said that you had spoken to him previously in the street. How many days or weeks before the assault had this taken place?

MCU of Brenda over Robert's left shoulder. Camera begins to track clockwise in a half circle, panning, in the process, from Brenda to members of the crew, who sit immobile in the shadows off-set, finally settling on Robert. He is listening intently, his cigarette burning down to a butt.

Brenda: Wearing my voluminous flannel nightgown, I knelt before the small wood-burning stove, trying to see why the fire was so fragile. I felt huge and awkward in that position, aware of my rump and falling breasts, but the cold night air demanded that the fire be encouraged to burn at a brisker pace. My younger lover, small and tight in her body, sat on the couch watching me. I did not like what I thought she saw. I did not like the bigness of my ass, the weight of my body on my knees, and then just as I worked very hard to accept my lack of appeal, she said in a low firm voice, "You look so fuckable that way."

I froze, caught in that moment of self-hatred by the clarity of her desire. I stopped all movement, awed once again by the possibilities of life. I knew she was walking toward me. I felt her stand behind me, felt her hands shape my nightgown to my curves. I heard her breath come quicker, and still I did not move. She grew impatient and reached under the gown, piling up its lengths on her arm like a fisherman pulling in his nets, and then against all my fear, she entered me. The fire blazed up, and so did my hope as I finally left the burden behind me and rode her hand with all the grace love had ever given me.

Robert is transfixed, showing no reaction until his cigarette burns his fingers, at which point he hastily stubs it out in the ashtray.

Intertitle on word processor:

JOAN NESTLE, 1987

CU of Robert's hand stubbing out cigarette.

Jenny *(V-O)***:** He called me in as a witness for the prosecution. The defense attorney was a real schmuck.

> *Courtroom (color). Jenny is on the witness stand, being cross-examined by the defense. The mise-en-scene is indicated only by an encircling spotlight on Jenny and the direction of her gaze as she addresses the defense attorney (downward, frame left) and the judge (upward, frame right). On the wall behind her is a large photo of W.C. Fields before a judge.*

Defense *(V-O)***:** Miss Doe, do you live in an apartment?

Jenny *(sync)***:** Yes, I do.

Defense: What floor is your apartment on, Miss Doe?

Jenny: The second floor.

Defense: Do your windows face the street, Miss Doe?

Jenny: Yes.

Defense: Can people on the street see you when you are at your windows, Miss Doe?

Jenny: I suppose so.

Defense: Yes or no, Miss Doe.

Jenny: Yes, I suppose so.

Defense: Miss Doe, did you at anytime prior to the incident you have described ever have occasion to appear at your windows?

Jenny: What do you mean?

Defense: I mean just what I said, Miss Doe.

Jenny: Well, what does that have to do with anything?

Judge: Please answer the question.

Jenny: Sometimes I look out of my windows and sometimes I wash my windows.

Defense: And what did you wear when you washed your windows, Miss Doe?

Jenny: For heaven's sake, what difference does it make?

Judge: The witness will kindly answer the questions as asked, without commentary.

Jenny: I wore clothes.

Defense: What I am asking, Miss Doe, is, were you ever in a state of incomplete attire when you washed your windows? In other words, were you indecently dressed?

Jenny: No, I was not indecently dressed.

Defense: What were you wearing, Miss Doe?

Jenny: I was wearing . . .

> *Yvonne's apartment. MCU, Jenny. She is seated in the "interviewee's chair," wearing a shocking-pink, off-the-shoulder, see-thru dress. The lighting is hot and garish.*

Jenny *(V-O)***:** a dress!

(sync): There's this Lenny Bruce schtick: After his performance at a club in a small Midwestern city, a middle-aged couple invited him to have a drink with them at their table. As Bruce put it, "The woman was wearing one of them see-through dresses, only ya don' wanna."

> *Robert's bedroom as before. Robert and Jenny are fucking, "spoon-fashion," on their sides. At the beginning of the shot Robert is having an orgasm. It is hard to tell what Jenny is doing or experiencing.*

Jenny *(V-O)***:** So what do I do now that the men have stopped looking at me? I'm like a fish thrown back into the sea, still longing to be hooked. Women like me never get used to it. It's hard to admit that I still want them to look. Don't think I'm proud of having been a woman that men look at. It's a chronic disease that you never get over.

Jenny (Alice Spivak) addresses camera. Courtesy Yvonne Rainer.

Robert rolls over on his back. Clutching the blanket around herself, Jenny rears up and addresses the camera. The effect is slightly ludicrous, but also touching.

Jenny *(sync)***:** My biggest shock in reaching middle age was the realization that men's desire for me was the linchpin of my identity.

Interview with Jenny as before. She is dressed as at the beginning of the film.

Jenny: Suddenly the things you used to do and didn't even know you were doing don't seem to work anymore. Is my smile so different now? Maybe my smile has been dampened by my sweaty palms. Did you ever shake someone's hand when you were in the middle of a hot flash?

Yvonne W. *(V-O)***:** Are you going to finish the story?

Jenny: Which story—the race story or the change-of-life story? And now we have yet another possibility: the class story. Yvonne, don't tell me you're getting fed up with menopause already?

Yvonne W.: No, of course not. But now that you've got me

Clip from the climax of Tiger Shark *(Howard Hawks, 1932), printed backwards: the thirty seconds or so in which Edward G. Robinson has fallen into the water and is rescued from a shark's attack.*

hooked, I'd like to know how your flashback turned out.

Jenny *(V-O)*: Well, there's not much more to tell. I was so pissed at the defense attorney that I perjured myself and said I saw Carlos in Brenda's apartment. The truth was that I couldn't possibly have seen him from the hallway, and we didn't go back into the apartment until the police showed up a few minutes later, so by that time, if he had been in there, he would've had plenty of time to escape. Carlos was sentenced to three or four months in jail and disappeared from the neighborhood. The assistant D.A. asked me out on a date, and we embarked on a six-month love affair. It was great while it lasted. The upper middle class was a total turn-on for me. I wouldn't have admitted it then, but

> *Daytime. WS, Digna, now dressed as Carmen Miranda, in a red, white, and black tiered, ruffled dress and a turban full of fruit, still leans against the blue convertible. Jenny and Robert enter frame-left. Jenny is wearing her "interview clothes." Robert wears a navy blazer, white shirt, and paisley silk ascot. He opens the car door for Jenny, then goes around to the driver's side and gets in. In this and the following scenes, they are totally oblivious to Digna's presence. Digna continues to address the camera, in English.*

Digna: She never saw Carlos again and she never saw me at all. Not like her mother, who was an intuitive expert on class, Jenny took her own social status for granted. Which meant pretty much ignoring it. Social distinctions were invisible to her, as I was invisible to her. Jenny was such a dummy when it came to class, a *tabula rasa* unable to recognize, much less examine, her own blind spots.

> *Robert starts the car. Digna hoists herself into the back seat and continues to speak as the car pulls out of the frame.*

Like the limits of social mobility. Her father was a house painter and she didn't go to college.

> *MCU of Jenny and Robert in the front seat of the convertible. They are having a gay old time as she stuffs blueberries into his mouth as he drives and he tries to bite her fingers. Their hilarity is all MOS. Digna addresses the camera over their shoulders from the back seat.*

Digna: But why should I concern myself with *her*? Ordinarily I'm not an envious person, but here is this big fine car right in front of my house. What was I to think? Should I want to take her place in the rich man's car? Jenny thought she was free and unencumbered by such things. She wouldn't have admitted to being impressed by Robert's Harvard education, elegant manners, and professional status. How could she predict that not recognizing her own social disadvantage would be her undoing? Jenny was no Emma Bovary. Oh yes, so much fun, all this *(she gestures)*. There is more that distinguishes the upper from the lower classes than bread crusts left on a plate. The number of heart attacks, for instance. *(pointing to Robert) He* is much less likely to die from a heart attack after making love than Carlos. A coca-colonial diet doesn't lead to long life expectancy . . .

[Robert and Jenny break up in *(sync)* laughter.]

> *Reverse angle. The camera is now located behind the car. We can see that the car is being towed by a truck, in the back of which sit the director, assistant director, sound recordist, script supervisor, and assistant cameraman. Digna twists around in the back seat and again addresses the camera.*

Digna: . . . This country has the highest infant mortality rate in the industrialized world. Some people's stories have premature endings. Jenny's tale is no exception. Her disappearance from Robert's story will happen almost as quickly as Carlos's exit from hers. You'll see: Robert will get tired of her drunken displays of affection at social gatherings and six months from now he'll dump her. But don't worry. I won't allow myself to be disappeared from Jenny's story like Carlos and Brenda. I'm going to hang around.

[Music begins: Chet Baker singing "My Funny Valentine."]

> *Succession of shots: Robert and Jenny in a restaurant; J modeling a ball gown in front of R and then running to sit on his lap, R and J dancing, R and J in bed. Digna—in her summer dress—"hangs around" in every shot, watching.*

Jenny *(V-O)***:** To Robert I must have represented some kind of kooky Bohemian plaything. He was still sowing his wild oats and fancying himself an occasional artiste. He had an easel set up in his duplex with a permanently unfinished oil painting on it.

[Chet Baker's voice surges up: "You are my favorite work of art," then subsides to background.]

We did things I've never done before or since. He took me to a charity ball at the Waldorf Astoria in his mother's mink stole after picking out a ball gown for me. Such *haute bourgeoisie* shenanigans made me ignore things that have since come back to haunt me.

> *Digna is now sitting with her legs propped on Robert's bed, smoking and looking off-screen (toward the head of the bed) in a contemplative mood. Camera pans along bed and comes to rest on Jenny and Robert, who is nuzzling her neck affectionately.*

Yvonne W. *(V-O)***:** "Oat bourgeoisie?" Is there something called "Wild Oat bourgeoisie"?

Jenny *(V-O)***:** [laughing] No, no, no. "h-a-u-t-e," *high* bourgeoisie. You know what I mean.

> *Daytime. Jenny and Robert walk down a street in the Village toward the camera. Digna accompanies them. Robert's gaze follows a young woman who has crossed their path.*

Robert: You know something?

> *CU of Robert.*

You can always tell how a woman feels about herself just by looking at her legs.

> *Camera pans in CU to Jenny and Digna. Jenny looks blankly at the camera; Digna looks from the off-screen woman to Jenny's face.*

Lenny Bruce's voice: Really weird . . .

> *Interior of a nightclub. CU of Robert's hands playing with keys on a red-and-white checked tablecloth.*

. . . OK, "an accident victim who lost a foot in an accident, who made sexual advances to a nurse while in an ambulance taking him to the hospital."

[His voice fades to background.]

> *Camera zooms out to reveal Jenny and Robert laughing while watching the off-screen Lenny Bruce. Digna is sitting at their table, dressed as in preceding scene. It is dark and smoky. Digna addresses the camera, in English.*

Digna: Jenny shut up like a clam.

Bruce's voice: There's a big difference between men and ladies.

[His voice fades to background.]

Digna: Isn't it amazing? All the ways in which we agree to inferior status in our daily lives. She made no objection, *not even to herself.* She didn't even ask herself the question: Must a woman's feelings about her *self* depend on a man's assessment of her *body*? The doors of her thought-storage tanks clanged shut. In total abjection, she handed over the keys.

Lenny Bruce's voice: Guys can detach and ladies can't.

> *MS, clip of Lenny Bruce performing.*

Bruce *(sync)*: A lady can't go thru a plate glass window and go to bed with you ten seconds later. When they don't feel good they don't feel good. But *guys* can have head-on collisions with Greyhound buses, disaster areas, fifty people lying dead on the highway. On the way to the hospital in the ambulance the guy makes a play for the nurse.

> *MS, Robert, Jenny, Digna as before. R and J explode in laughter, along with general audience laughter. Digna looks "meaningfully" at the camera.*

Bruce *(V-O)*: She goes, "How could you do a thing like that?" "I got hot." "You got hot!" How could he get hot, his foot was cut off? "I got horny, I dunno."

> *Bruce performing, as before.*

(sync): You don't understand where they're going. The appellate court's going to look at this: "Can you make any sense of this?" "Shit, no." And there's a difference, you know, between

> *He turns to the wall and pantomimes drawing on a black board.*

a big piece of art with a little shit in the middle, a big piece of art, a little shit in the middle, a big piece of art. Then a big piece of shit with a little art in the middle . . .

[His voice fades to background.]

Jenny *(V-O)*: Robert's office would subsequently mount a legal vendetta against Bruce after we broke up. I could hardly believe it when I read about it in the *New York Post*. They became Lenny Bruce's East Coast scourge.

Yvonne W. *(V-O)*: What did you talk about when you were together?

Jenny *(V-O)*: Art, movies, the usual New York cultural things. The *New York Times* art reviews of John Canaday. I took him to far-out music and dance events. All I remember of our conversations are some remarks about blacks and lesbians.

Yvonne W. *(V-O)*: What kinds of remarks?

> *Yvonne W.'s apartment, MCU Jenny in the "hot seat."*

Jenny *(sync)*: Remember that '50s sociologist . . . what's 'is name? . . .

Yvonne W. *(V-O)*: Reisman?

Jenny: No . . . Shockley! William Shockley.

322

Yvonne W.: Oh no, not that nutty physicist!

Jenny: Yeh, his theories about race and congenitally inferior intelligence were going around. I remember Robert arguing that Negroes *are* different; they have longer arms than whites.

[They both laugh.]

Jenny: Another time he said he had figured out that Brenda was a lesbian because she didn't lower her eyes when she uttered the word "breast."

CU of her face. She demonstrates lowering her eyes as she says:

"He hit me across the breast." A straight woman would have been more modest.

Yvonne W. *(V-O)***:** How could you put up with him? Didn't you protest?

Jenny: Oh god, let's get back to menopause, shall we? I've told this whole story hoping to find an answer to that very question. Who was that woman who put up with such vicious twaddle? If I argued, I didn't argue very hard. Being loved by him was more important than anything else. I was ready to sell my soul for a mess of pottage . . . a mass of penis. Yvonne, really, this is too painful. Why don't *you* try it? Y'know, I think it's about time we changed places. You've been behind that camera too long, gloating at my discomfort.

Yvonne W.: I haven't been gloating.

Jenny: You've been lurking. I'm tired of being your whipping boy. C'mon, get your ass out from behind that camera. It's your turn to be in the hot seat.

Camera zooms out as she gets up and leaves frame. We see only the empty chair and bookshelves as sounds of a tussle are heard, along with giggles, squeals, and shrieks from both of them.

Yvonne W.: No! No! No! No!

CU and MCU, hand-held camera. They fight it out over and around the leather couch. It is a kind of good-humored charade, not too serious, but very physical. During the tussle a few words can be heard:

Yvonne W.: What do you want from me? Absolution?!

Jenny: Who has the Macintosh and the CD . . . VCR? . . . CAPITAL!

Yvonne W.: CAPITAL?! And who has the Burger King?!

CU of Catherine Robinson.

Catherine: Well, we're traveling, which is something that we both like to do. What gives me pleasure? Going out to eat and not having to cook. Truthfully and selfishly, my youngest son has just finished his first year in college, so he was away all winter, and I just enjoy having the house to my husband and I after cooking for a big family. To shop for two, to cook for two, to have to wash dishes for two: *That's* an enjoyment to me. I'm enjoying—you know—this period of just he and I. You know, you love your children, you enjoy them, but then, now the rest of this life is for *me.*

MCU of Yvonne W. sitting in the chair vacated by Jenny.

Yvonne W.: Jenny, there's one thing I'm curious about. Did you ever make it with Brenda?

Jenny *(V-O)*: Hell no. I was terrified of women.

Numerous shots of the "wrap party." All of the actors and crew, and some of the interviewees are present in shifting combinations and groupings.

[Undifferentiated cacophony of voices is heard, which lasts throughout the credit sequence that follows.]

Credits rise from bottom of frame:

Jenny	ALICE SPIVAK
Yvonne Washington	NOVELLA NELSON
Brenda	BLAIRE BARON
Carlos	RICO ELIAS
Digna	GABRIELLA FARRAR
Stew	TYRONE WILSON
Robert	DAN BERKEY
Signer	CLAUDIA GREGORY
"Helen Caldicott"	YVONNE RAINER
White Man in	
Brenda's apartment	MARK NIEBUHR
Jenny's double	MIHNETTE LEHMANN

Interviewees
(in order of appearance)

FAITH RINGGOLD
SHIRLEY TRIEST
HELENE MOGLEN
MINNETTE LEHMANN

CATHERINE ENGLISH ROBINSON
EVELYN CUNNINGHAM
GLORIA SPARROW
AUDREY GOODFRIEND
VIVIAN BONNANO

Doctors
(in order of appearance)

JUDD MARMOR
CHARLES W. LLOYD
CHARLES F. FLOWERS, JR.
ROBERT N. RUTHERFORD
JUDITH WEISZ

Two-shot from medical film: Dr. Lloyd and a woman who is identified in a subtitle as Dr. Judith Weisz. They are seated at a conference table.

Lloyd: Judith, it looks as though we're making a lot of progress. It looks as though the rights of women to be first-class citizens are coming along pretty fast. What's this going to mean to us?

CU of Dr. Weisz.

Weisz: There is a danger that while abandoning the old stereotype, we replace it with a new one. That is, the woman who may be perhaps married, without children, not married who devoted a great deal of her energies to developing a career and fulfilling herself outside her home, who comes to you at menopause and then, the stereotype would be trying to attribute her problems to, say, her regrets about not fulfilling her basic biological role,

MS, interview with Evelyn Cunningham, a seventy-year-old African-American woman, in her apartment.

whatever that may be.

Evelyn: Children? No, never had children. Never particularly wanted children, I'm very happy to report. I say that because for so many years, you know, one could not say "I don't want children." That was a no-no. I feel so good now to freely say I never wanted children. I never wanted the responsibility.

Y.R. *(V-O)***:** Yeh, when you're young it's embarrassing to say that. You have to be careful who you say it to.

Evelyn: Are you telling me?! You get in deep trouble. "What kind of woman is she?"

You know, oh, wow, it's really awful. It was years before I could say that. But no children.

MCU Gloria Sparrow, a white woman in her late 50's, seated at a dining table.

Y.R. *(V-O)***:** How has your anarchist background informed your feminism?

Gloria: I can remember that my mother's hero was Emma Goldman. And I can remember that my father's comrades laughed at her, laughed about Emma Goldman and made fun of her in exactly the same way that I remember, decades later when I was here at Cal in the anthropology department in U.C., all these male anthropologists laughed at Margaret Mead.

MCU of Audrey Goodfriend, a white woman around seventy years of age, sitting in a wildly overgrown yard.

Y.R.: But your own relation to change . . . Did they think that it would happen in their lifetime?

Audrey: I don't think they really did. I think that people who remain anarchists generally can't expect change in their lifetime. And I think that one of the reasons that some of the more libertarian aspects of the SDS and those times went down so rapidly is because people had to see change right away, and if you didn't see change right away, you might as well look out for yourself. The notion that anarchism is a philosophy and it's a way of life and a way of interpreting what happens around you stays with you forever whether you're actively involved in something or not. I'm certainly not very actively involved . . .

Y.R.: But it has sustained you.

Audrey: It has sustained me.

Another sequence of credits crawls upward, this time in silence.

Director, Writer, Editor	YVONNE RAINER
Director of Photography	MARK DANIELS
Assistant Director	CHRISTINE LE GOFF
Production Manager	KATHRYN COLBERT
Art Directors	ANNE STUHLER
	MICHAEL SELDITCH
Sound Recordist	ANTONIO ARROYO
Second Assistant Director	ROBIN GUARINO
People in dream	SYBIL SIMONE
	WANDA PHIPPS

	Rick Perry
	Maurice Stewart
People in hallway	Shirley Soffer
	Christopher Hoover
	Leann Brown
	Kevin Duffy
	David Schulman
Boys on stoop	Wilson Leon Gamboa
	Dino Guglietta
	J. Jeffrey Ortiz
	George Vallejo
Whistling Man	Daniel Lopez
Woman and	Katy Martin
Child in park	Sally Jo Brand
Man with briefcase	Michael Selditch
Man with dog	Stanley Crawford
Young Woman on street	Jennifer Rohn
Defense Attorney's voice	William Raymon
Judge's voice	Michael Taylor
Production Coordinator	Carol Noblitt
Design Coordinator	Nancy Swartz
Casting Consultants	Natalie Hart
	Daniel Swee
First Assistant Camera	Tony Hardmon
Key Grip	Luis R. Perez
Gaffer	Tom McGrath
Script Supervisor	Michael Taylor
Second Grip	Frank Dellario
Videography	Ellen Spiro
	Yvonne Rainer
	John Canalli
Second Assistant Camera	Adrian Misol
Extra Electrics	Luke Eder
	Ethan Mass
	Rex D. West

	PETER WALTS
	LIZ FRIERS
Sound Boom	JULIE WILD
Props	CYNTHIA SMITH
Location Manager	DAVID WELCH
Costume Designer	ALEXANDRA WELKER
Hair/Makeup	PATRICIA SCHENKER REGAN
Assistant to the Art Directors	SIMON LEUNG
Assistant Makeup/Costumes	EVE-LAURE MOROS
Photo Mural/Production Stills	VIVIAN SELBO
Photos on Yvonne Washington's wall	CARRIE WEEMS
American Sign Language Consultant	PEARL JOHNSON
Sound Editor	LISA PRAH
Editing Assistance	SUSAN CONLEY
	RODDY BOGAWA
Video Editing/ Additional Sound Recording	MARY PATIERNO
Carpentry	JOHN FIGLEY
	JOHN F. JONES
	JOEL N. NICHOLAS
Translation	PEDRO COSME-PRADO

MCU Faith Ringgold.

Faith: So I think, somehow or other, that women as they get older have to not take on the look, the manifestations, whatever it is . . . don't take that role on. I just don't know all the ways to do it, because the whole idea of thinking about it is new to me. But you don't have to do certain things just because you're older. Do what you want to do. Dress anyway you want to dress, go anywhere you want to go . . .

Another sequence of "wrap party" shots, lasting about two minutes, followed by

Intertitle on Macintosh screen:

UTOPIA
The more impossible
it seems, the more
necessary it becomes.

More shots of wrap party.

MS, Vivian Bonnano in "Yvonne's apartment." She is a Cuban woman in her late 40's.

Vivian: And now I think I can deal with it a bit better. It's a very uncomfortable thing, it's not at all pleasant. It's embarrassing. You suddenly break out in a horrible sweat and you wake up in the middle of the night and your sheets are soaked. It's not nice, but I hope it will be over soon. It's much better, I think, than when my mother went through it. She was convinced that she was going to go mad. That's what happens when you have the change, you go crazy. So my mother was convinced that she was going to go crazy. But now, talking to friends and seeing that they're going through the same thing that I'm going through, it's a lot easier to take. And I imagine soon they'll have TV commercials about menopause. They have them about everything else. So, it's fine. I can deal with it a bit better, but I don't like it.

MS. Yvonne Washington herself is now in front of the camera, in the "hot seat."

Yvonne W.: I try to monitor when my hot flashes occur. I'm watching a video cassette of *Sweet Sweetback's Baadaass Song.* "Why does an embodiment of black protest have to be a stud?" flashes through my mind, and along comes a hot flash. I'm on the subway thinking about a friend. "Forget that family crap," I think. *Flash . . .* Ready to leave, I put on my coat in an overheated room. Instantly I am so hot, I must tear it off . . . Reading about the Supreme Court's latest setback to civil rights. One of the Justices is quoted as saying: "The fact that low-paying, unskilled jobs are overwhelmingly held by blacks is no proof of racism. *Flash . . .* Thinking about what I could have said, should have said: *Flash . . .*

The body manifests itself in new ways. In the Montreal airport en route to New York, I approach U.S. immigration. Suddenly I am burning. Sure that my sweat shows, I remember what the agents look for: signs of nervousness, sweating. My heart skips a beat. The agent asks for more than usual. I must recite my date of birth as she checks it against my driver's license. I falter, almost reverse the 24 and 34. She hands me back the license, and says, "Have a good trip."

Remaining credits rise.

[Party voices can be heard in background.]

Production Assistants

MARION APPEL	RACHEL BARRETT
HILARY BROUGHER	LENORA CHAMPAGNE
SUSAN CONLEY	THEO DORIAN
ROB FRITZ	CHRISTOPHER HOOVER

TAKAHIRO KATAISHI	RACHEL KRANTZ
CRAIG MARSDEN	MARTHA NALBAND
LISA PINO	CATHERINE SAALFIELD
REBECCA SCHREIBER	LINDA YEE

Opticals	Cynosure
	B.B. OPTICS
Negative Cutting	ONE WHITE GLOVE / TIM BRENNAN
Lab	DU ART
Sound Mix	SOUND ONE / REILLY STEELE
Camera	FILM FRIENDS
Grip and Electric Equipment	ELECTRIC FEAT
Dollies	BLAKE PRODUCTION SYSTEMS
Caterer	UPSTAIRS / DOWNSTAIRS

Quotations and Literary Sources

LEFTY BARRETTO

SUSAN BROWNMILLER

LENNY BRUCE

DR. HELEN CALDICOTT

ELDRIDGE CLEAVER

OLIVER C. COX

FRANTZ FANON

PIRI THOMAS

JUDY GRAHN

HERESIES COLLECTIVE #6

CALVIN C. HERNTON

JOEL KOVEL

HARLAN LANE

TERESA DE LAURETIS

NICHOLASA MOHR

JOAN NESTLE

CLARA E. RODRIGUEZ

NTOZAKE SHANGE

ELAINE SHOWALTER

FILM CLIP FROM
"LENNY BRUCE"
COURTESY OF
JOHN MAGNUSON ASSOCIATES,
SAN FRANCISCO

"MY FUNNY VALENTINE"
(LORENZ HART / RICHARD RODGERS)

COURTESY OF
WARNER/CHAPPELL MUSIC, INC.

"SEERAEUBERJENNY"
USED BY PERMISSION OF
STEFAN BRECHT AND
EUROPEAN AMERICAN MUSIC
CORP., AGENT FOR THE KURT WEILL
FOUNDATION FOR MUSIC, INC.

"DESERIE"
(LESLIE COOPER/CLARENCE JOHNSON)
COURTESY OF
LONGITUDE MUSIC CO.

CHOCOLATE BOX LABEL
COURTESY OF
JANETTE FAULKNER'S COLLECTION
"ETHNIC NOTIONS"

Special Thanks to

THE KITCHEN
LAUREN AMAZEEN
JOHN FIGLEY
THE LESBIAN HERSTORY ARCHIVES
NEW YORK CITY MAYOR'S OFFICE
OF FILM, THEATRE AND BROADCASTING

Additional Thanks

JOANNE AKALAITIS   MAURICE BERGER
DONNA BINDER   VIVIAN BROWN
MAUREEN BURNLEY   RUDEEN DASH
LILLY DIAZ   JUNE EKMAN
LYNN ELTON   MARTIN ELTON
CLAIRE GLOVER   TAMI GOLD
THYRZA GOODEVE   DAVID KAUFMAN
ALEXANDER KLUGE   KATE LAMBERT
BENI MATIAS   NANCY MEEHAN
LELAND MOSS   SHEILA McLAUGHLIN

NELLI PEREZ AND THE CENTER
FOR PUERTO RICAN STUDIES

MARK RAPPAPORT B. RUBY RICH
FAITH RINGGOLD LAPACAZO SANDOVAL
JUDY SIMMONS DR. NELLY SZLACHTER
POLLY THISTLETHWAITE EVA WEISS

Special gratitude to the following
for their support and criticism:

JOAN BRADERMAN
TRISHA BROWN
MARTHA GEVER
ERNEST LARSEN
SHERRY MILLNER
BELLE RAINER
IVAN RAINER
BÉRÉNICE REYNAUD
MARTHA ROSLER
MICHELE WALLACE
CARRIE WEEMS

This film has been made possible
by funding and awards from

New York State Council on the Arts
National Endowment for the Arts
Rockefeller Foundation
John Simon Guggenheim Foundation
New York Foundation for the Arts
American Film Institute
Brandeis University

IN MEMORIAM

RONALD BLADEN
LYN BLUMENTHAL
CLAUDIA GREGORY
MICHAEL GRIEG
LELAND MOSS
" LOUIE "

Distribution Sources

This listing is divided into two parts. The first part alphabetically lists the filmmakers whose work is included in this book: relevant films are listed alphabetically. The second part lists other films mentioned: here, the listing is alphabetical by title (the filmmaker's last name follows the title in parentheses). In some cases, films are available from the filmmakers. In those instances, I include the filmmaker's address only once, with the first listing of such films.

In both parts of the listing, film titles are followed by primary rental sources. In many instances, particular distributors handle films by several filmmakers discussed here. Those distributors are indicated by single words or by abbreviations:

AFA (American Federation of Arts, 41 East 65th St., New York, NY 10021)

BFI (British Film Institute, 21 Stephen St., London W1P 1PL, U.K.)

CC (Canyon Cinema, 2325 Third St., Suite 338, San Francisco, CA 94107)

CFDC (Canadian Filmmakers Distribution Centre, 67A Portland St., Toronto, Ontario M5V 2M9)

Circles (113 Roman Rd., London E2, U.K.)

Drift (219 East Second St. #5E, New York, NY 10009)

FACETS (video only: 1517 W. Fullerton Ave., Chicago, IL 60614)

FMC (Film-makers' Cooperative, 175 Lexington Ave., New York, NY 10016)

FR (First Run, 153 Waverly Place, New York, NY 10014)

LC (Light Cone, 27 rue Louis-Braille, 75012 Paris)

LFC (London Filmmakers' Co-operative, 42 Gloucester Ave., London NW1, U.K.)

MoMA (Museum of Modern Art, Circulating Film Program, 11 W. 53rd St., New York, NY 10019)

WMM (Women Make Movies, 225 Lafayette St., Suite 207, New York, NY 10012)

Major distributors of commercial features (New Yorker, Films Incorporated . . .) are indicated by name only.

James Benning
American Dreams: CFDC, FR
8 1/2 × 11: FMC
11 × 14: CFDC, FR
Grand Opera: CFDC, FR, LFC
Him and Me: CFDC, FR
Landscape Suicide: FR
Used Innocence: FR

Morgan Fisher
Documentary Footage: CC, FMC, LFC
Phi Phenomenon: FMC
Projection Instructions: Fisher (1306C Princeton St., Santa Monica, CA 90404)
Standard Gauge: Fisher, MoMA

Ann Marie Fleming
New Shoes: CFDC
New Shoes: An Interview in Exactly 5 Minutes: CFDC, Picture Start (221 E. Cullerton, 6th Floor, Chicago, IL 60616)
You Take Care Now: CFDC, Picture Start

Hollis Frampton
Gloria!: FMC, MoMA
Lemon: FMC, LFC, MoMA
nostalgia: FMC, MoMA
Poetic Justice: FMC, MoMA
Surface Tension: FMC, MoMA
Zorns Lemma: FMC, LFC, MoMA

Su Friedrich
But No One: CC, FMC
Damned If You Don't: CC, CFDC, FMC, LFC, MoMA, WMM
First Comes Love: CC, CFDC, Drift, LC
Gently Down the Stream: CC, CFDC, Circles, Drift, FMC, LC, LFC, MoMa, WMM
Sink or Swim: CC, CFDC, Drift, LC, LFC, MoMA, WMM
The Ties That Bind: CC, CFDC, Circles, Drift, MoMA, WMM

William Greaves
All Greaves films mentioned are available from Greaves (230 West 55th St., New York, NY 10019)

Laura Mulvey/Peter Wollen
Riddles of the Sphinx: BFI, New Cinema (75
Horner Ave. #1, Toronto, Ont. M8Z 4X5
Canada), MoMA

Yoko Ono
All Ono films mentioned are available from
AFA.

Yvonne Rainer
Film About a Woman Who . . . : BFI, CFDC,
Zeitgeist (247 Centre St., 2nd Floor, New
York, NY 10013)
Journeys from Berlin/1971: BFI, CFDC,
FACETS, MoMA, Zeitgeist
Kristina Talking Pictures: BFI, CFDC, MoMA,
Zeitgeist
Lives of Performers: BFI, CFDC, Zeitgeist
The Man Who Envied Women: CFDC, MoMA,
Zeitgeist

Peter Rose
Babel: CC
Digital Speech: CC, CFDC
Genesis: CC
The Man Who Could Not See Far Enough: CC,
CFDC, FMC, LC
Secondary Currents: CC, CFDC, FMC, LC
SpiritMatters: CC, LC

Michael Snow
So Is This: CC, CFDC, FMC, LFC
*Rameau's Nephew by Diderot (Thanx to
Dennis Young) by Wilma Schoen:* CFDC,
FMC
Wavelength: CC, CFDC, FACETS, FMC, LFC,
MoMA

Trinh T. Minh-ha
Naked Spaces—Living Is Round: Circles, Idera
(2524 Cypress St., Vancouver, BC V6J 3N2,
Canada), WMM
Reassemblage: Circles, Idera, LC, MoMA,
WMM
Shoot for the Contents: WMM
Surname Viet Given Name Nam: Circles,
Idera, MoMA, WMM

Other Films

Note: When films are distributed by the film-maker or when a distributor handles the films of only one filmmaker, the relevant address is included with the first listing of a film by that filmmaker.

23rd Psalm Branch (Brakhage): CC
1857: Fool's Gold (Elder): CC, CFDC, FMC
1933 (Wieland): CC, CFDC, FMC, LFC
Anemic Cinema (Duchamp): MoMA
Argument (McCall/Tyndall): McCall (11 Jay St., New York, NY 10013)
Bang! (Breer): FMC, LC, MoMA
The Big "O" (D'Avino): D'Avino (Route 2, Box 350, Hammond, NY 13646)
The Big Red Awk (Irwin): CC
Bleu Shut (Nelson): CC
Blood Story (Snider): Drift
College Chums (Porter): MoMA
Cortex (Burford): LC
Cosmic Ray (Conner): One Way (1035 Guererro, San Francisco, CA 94110)
Film in Which There Appear to Be Sprocketholes, Edge Lettering, Dirt Particles, Etc. (Landow): CFDC, FMC, LFC
The Fall of the House of Usher (Watson/Webber): MoMA
Le film est deja commence! (Lemaitre): LC
Films imaginaires (Lemaitre): LC
The General (Keaton): MoMA
Geography of the Body (Willard Maas): FMC
Home of the Brave (Robson): KP (P.O. Box 16022, Monterey, CA 93942-6022)
Illuminated Texts (Elder): CFDC, FMC, LFC
Intruder in the Dust (Brown): Films Inc. (5547 N. Ravenswood Ave., Chicago, IL 60640-1199)
The Is/Land (Goldberg/Oblowitz): Unknown
Jazz of Lights (Hugo): MoMA
The Journey (Watkins): CC, FACETS
The Last Laugh (Murnau): MoMA
The Lead Shoes (Peterson): BFI, CC, FMC, MoMA
Let's Be Pals (Irwin): CC
The Life and Death of 9413—A Hollywood Extra (Florey/Vorkapich): MoMA
Light Reading (Rhodes): LFC
The Living or Dead Test (Barrie): Cecile Starr (50 West 96th St., New York, NY 10025)
Lost Boundaries (Werker): Twyman

Love (*Ai,* Taka Iimura): CC, FMC, LC, LFC
Manhatta (Sheeler/Strand): LC, MoMA
A Movie (Conner): MoMA, One Way
Musical Poster No. 1 (Lye): BFI, LC, MoMA
Notebook (Menken): FMC, LFC
Peliculas (Clancy): Clancy (63 East 62nd Terrace, Kansas City, MO 64113)
Permian Strata (Conner): One Way
Pinky (Kazan): Films Inc.
Private Property (Public Domain) (Fleming): Fleming (Dept. of Filmmaking, School of Art Institute of Chicago, Columbus Dr. at Jackson Blvd., Chicago, IL 60603)
La Raison Avant le passion (Wieland): CC, CFDC, FMC, LFC
Rat Life and Diet in North America (Wieland): CC, CFDC, FMC, LFC
Razor Blades (Sharits): FMC, LFC
Remedial Reading Comprehension (Landow): CC, CFDC, FMC
Sailboat (Wieland): CC, CFDC, FMC, LFC
Tom, Tom, the Piper's Son (Jacobs): FMC, LFC
Trade Tattoo (Lye): LC, MoMA
Treatise on Drivel and Eternity (Isou): Unknown
Tung (Baillie): CC, FMC, MoMA
Un Chien Andalou (Buñuel/Dali): EmGee (6924 Canby Ave., Suite 103, Reseda, CA 91335), MoMA
Vo/Id (Beauvais): CC, LC
Walden (Mekas): FMC
The War Game (Watkins): EmGee, FACETS
White Calligraphy (Iimura): CC, FMC, LFC
Word Movie/Fluxfilm (Sharits): CC, FMC

Selected Bibliography

In instances where collections of writings have a particular relationship to this collection, I have listed specific works.

Baldwin, Craig. *Tribulation 99: Alien Anomalies under America.* New York: Ediciones La Calavera, 1991.

Barthes, Roland. *Image Music Text.* Essays selected and translated by Stephen Heath. New York: Hill and Wang, 1977.

Beauvais, Yann, ed. *Mot: dites, image.* A catalogue for a show of films at Musée National d'Art Moderne, Centre National d'Art et de Culture Georges Pompidou, October 19–November 13, 1989. Includes Jean-Michel Bouhours, "Musique de l'image"; Gil Wolman, "L'image-mot"; Yann Beauvais, "Des mots encore des mots"; Alain-Alcide Sudre, "L'écriture comme materiau filmique"; Scott MacDonald, "Le texte comme image."

Berlandt, Hermann. *Poetry Film Festival Catalogue 1978–79.* San Francisco: Poetry-Film Workshop, 1980.

Bory, Jean-Francois. *Once Again.* New York: New Directions, 1968.

Carson, L. M. Kit. *David Holzman's Diary,* a screenplay from a film by Jim McBride. New York: Farrar, Straus and Giroux, 1970.

Curtay, Jean-Paul. *Letterism and Hypergraphics: The Unknown Avant-Garde 1945–1985.* Catalogue for a show at Franklin Furnace, 1985.

Curtis, David. *Experimental Cinema.* New York: Dell Publishing, 1971.

Dorland, Michael, and William C. Wees, eds. *Words and Moving Images: Essays on Verbal and Visual Expression in Film and Television.* Canadian Film Studies/Etudes canadiennes du cinéma 1. Montreal: Mediatexte Publications, 1984. Includes William C. Wees, "Words and Moving Images: An Introduction"; Michael Snow,

"Present Tense Situation: Michael Snow, Comments on *So Is This*"; Bruce Elder, "On the Concepts of Presence and Absence in Michael Snow's *Presents*"; Michel Larouche, "De l'expression verbale dans le jeune cinéma expérimental"; Kay Armatage, "About to Speak: The Woman's Voice in Patricia Gruben's *Sifted Evidence*"; Brenda Longfellow, "Feminist Language in *Journal inachevé* and *Strass Café*"; Richard Hancox, "Engaging Poetry with Film: A Personal Statement"; William C. Wees, "Words and Images in the Poetry-Film"; Wendy L. Rolph, "Voice-Over Narration in Carlos Saura's *Elisa, Vida Mia*"; Bart Testa, "François Truffaut and the Language of Romanticism"; Paul Tiessen, "A New Year One: Film as Metaphor in the Writings of Wyndham Lewis"; J. Yamaguchi, "Pornography Is Perception"; Maurice Yacowar, "*Ronnie Hawkins—The Hawk and Friends*: Implicit and Explicit Structures in a Canadian TV Documentary"; Denyse Therrien, "Evolution du language dans le cinéma québécois des années 60 à 80"; and Seth Feldman, "The Silent Subject in English Canadian Film."

Foster, Stephen, ed. *Lettrisme: Into the Present.* Special issue of *Visible Language,* vol. 17, no. 3 (Summer 1983).

Frampton, Hollis. *Circles of Confusion.* Rochester, N.Y.: Visual Studies Workshop Press, 1983.

Gallagher, Steve, ed. *Picture This: Films Chosen by Artists.* Buffalo: Hallwalls, 1987. Diverse writings and photographic pieces about and from film, including John Baldessari, "Two Men (One with Vertical Lines; One with Radiating Lines)"; Barbara Bloom, "*Alphaville*"; John Maggiotto, "*American Gigolo*"; Barbara Broughel, "*The Blob*"; Ericka Beckman, "A Treatment for an Untitled Film (After the Brig)"; Tim Maul, "In Search of . . . *Casino Royale*"; John Carson, "*Darby O'Gill and the Little People*"; Barbara Bloom, "Object as Subject/*Les Favoris de la Lune*"; David

Robbins, "Hollywood Out-Takes and Rare Footage"; James Casebere, "House of Horrors"; Daniel Levine, "It's a Gift"; Robert Longo, "La Jetée"; Dan Graham, "Commentary/The Lickerish Quartet"; Louise Lawler, "A Movie Will Be Shown without the Picture"; Peter Nagy, "Mondo Cane"; Vito Acconci, "Some Notes on Phantom of the Paradise"; Jennifer Bolande, "• • • 1/2 . . ."; Chris Hill, "Skin Angles/Pumping Iron II: The Women"; Barbara Kruger, "The Rose Tattoo"; Lynne Tillman, "Call It Local/Specter of the Rose"; Silvia Kolbowski, "Thriller"; Andrea Fraser, "The Will Rogers Foundation Audience Collection Trailer."

Gidal, Peter. Materialist Film. New York, London: Routledge and Kegan Paul, 1989.

————, ed. Structural Film Anthology. London: British Film Institute, 1978.

Heath, Stephen. Questions of Cinema. Bloomington, Ill.: Indiana University Press, 1981.

Horak, Jan-Christopher. "Modernist Perspectives and Romantic Desire: Manhatta." Afterimage, vol. 15, no. 4 (November 1987): 8–15.

James, David. Allegories of Cinema. Princeton, N.J.: Princeton University Press, 1989.

Klotman, Phyllis Rauch. Screenplays of the African American Experience. Bloomington and Indianapolis: Indiana University Press, 1992. Includes scenarios and screenplays for Ganja and Hess, by Bill Gunn; Killer of Sheep, by Charles Burnett; Losing Ground, by Kathleen Collins; Illusions, by Julie Dash; A Different Image, by Alile Sharon Larkin; and Sidewalk Stories, by Charles Lane.

Kostelanetz, Richard. Visual Lit Crit/Precisely: Three Four Five. West Coast Poetry Review, vol. 5, no. 3 (1979).

————, ed. Breakthrough Fictioneers. Barton, Vt.; Brownington, Vt.; Berlin, Germany: Something Else, 1973.

Kruger, Barbara. Love for Sale: The Words and Pictures of Barbara Kruger. New York: Harry N Abrams, 1990.

Le Grice, Malcolm. Abstract Film and Beyond. Cambridge, Mass., and London: MIT Press, 1977.

Loughney, Patrick G. "In the Beginning Was the Word: Six Pre-Griffith Motion Picture Scenarios." In Early Cinema: Space, Frame, Narrative, ed. Thomas Elsaesser. London: British Film Institute, 1990, 211–219.

MacDonald, Scott. "Text As Image (in Some Recent North American Avant-Garde Films)." Afterimage, vol. 13, no. 8 (March 1986): 9–20.

————. A Critical Cinema. Berkeley, Los Angeles, London: University of California Press, 1988.

————. A Critical Cinema 2. Berkeley, Los Angeles, Oxford: University of California Press, 1992.

————. "College Course File: Film and Literature." Journal of Film and Video, vol. 39, no. 3 (Summer 1987): 56–66.

Martin, Katrina. "Marcel Duchamp's Anemic Cinema." Studio International, vol. 189 (January 1975): 53–60.

Mellencamp, Patricia. "Academia Unbound: The Adventures of the Red-Hot Texts of Land, Nelson, and Snow." Cinematograph. no. 1 (1985): 113–127.

Meyer, Ursula. Conceptual Art. New York: E. P. Dutton, 1972.

Mulvey, Laura. Visual and Other Pleasures. Bloomington and Indianapolis: Indiana University Press, 1989.

Ono, Yoko. *Grapefruit*. New York: Simon and Schuster/Touchstone, 1971.

Pipolo, Tony, and Graham Weinbren, eds. *The Script Issue* (a special issue of *Millennium Film Journal* devoted to "artist's pages," that is, reproductions of pages from filmmakers' working drafts of scripts and texts for films), no. 25 (Summer 1991). Includes Ann Marie Fleming, "*You Take Care Now*"; Gary Goldberg, "*Plates*"; Christoph Janetzko and Dorothee Wenner, "*Hollywood Killed Me*"; Jon Jost, "*Slow Moves*"; Ken Kobland, "*Frame*" and "*Flaubert Dreams of Travel*"; Jon Moritsugu, "*Der Elvis*"; Pat O'Neill, "*Water and Power*"; Yvonne Rainer, "*Privilege*"; Ondrej Rudavsky, "*The Wall*" or "*The Bridge*"; Lynne Sachs, "*The House of Science*"; Barbara Sternberg, "*A Trilogy*" and "*The Waters Are the Beginnings and Ends of All Things*"; Jerry Tartaglia, "*Fin de Siecle*"; Sokhi Wagner, "*Film Photographs*."

Rainer, Yvonne. *The Films of Yvonne Rainer*. Bloomington and Indianapolis: Indiana University Press, 1989. Includes screenplays of *Lives of Performers, Film About a Woman Who . . . , Kristina Talking Pictures, Journeys from Berlin/1971,* and *The Man Who Envied Women.*

Schneemann, Carolee. *ABC—We Print Anything—In the Cards*. Benningen, Holland: Brummense Uitgeverij Van Luxe Werkjes, 1977.

Schneider, Ira, and Beryl Korot. *Video Art: An Anthology*. New York, London: Harcourt Brace Jovanovich, 1976.

Silverman, Kaja. *The Acoustic Mirror: The Female Voice in Psychoanalysis and Cinema*. Bloomington and Indianapolis: Indiana University Press, 1988.

Sitney, P. Adams. "Image and Title in Avant-Garde Cinema." *October*, no. 11 (Winter 1979): 97–112.

——, ed. *The Avant-Garde Film: A Reader of Theory and Criticism*. New York: NYU Press, 1975.

——, ed. *The Essential Cinema: Essays on the Films in the Collection of Anthology Film Archives*. New York: NYU Press, 1975.

Solt, Mary Ellen. *Concrete Poetry: A World View*. Bloomington, Ill.: Indiana University Press, 1970.

Spector, Buzz, and Reagan and Roberta Upshaw. *Words As Images* (a special issue of *White Walls*), no. 5 (Winter 1981).

Trinh T. Minh-ha. *Women, Native, Other: Writing Postcoloniality and Feminism*. Bloomington and Indianapolis: Indiana University Press, 1989.

Turim, Maureen. *Abstraction in Avant-Garde Films*. Ann Arbor, Mich.: UMI Research Press, 1985.

Visible Language (first called *The Journal of Typographic Research*), a journal focusing on visual dimensions of language, beginning in 1967. At first it was published by MIT Press, later at the Cleveland Museum of Art. Merald E. Wrolstad was editor and publisher.

Wees, William. "Words and Images in Stan Brakhage's *23rd Psalm Branch*." *Cinema Journal*, vol. 27, no. 2 (Winter 1988): 40–49.

Williams, Emmett. *Collected Shorter Poems 1950–1970*. New York: New Directions, 1975.

——. *Schemes and Variations*. Stuttgart: Hansjorg Mayer, 1981.

——. *THE VOY AGE*. Stuttgart: Hansjorg Mayer, 1975.

——, ed. *Anthology of Concrete Poetry*. New York; Villefranche, France; Frankfurt, Germany: Something Else, 1967.

CPSIA information can be obtained
at www.ICGtesting.com
Printed in the USA
FSHW011231211218
54624FS

9 780520 080256